The
Lost
Villages
of
Britain

THE
LOST
VILLAGES
OF
BRITAIN

RICHARD MUIR

The History Press

First published 2009

The History Press
The Mill, Brimscombe Port
Stroud, Gloucestershire, GL5 2QG
www.thehistorypress.co.uk

British Library Cataloguing in Publication Data.
A catalogue record for this book is available from the British Library.

ISBN 978 0 7509 5039 8

Typesetting and origination by The History Press
Printed in Great Britain

Contents

INTRODUCTION

In an age when building developments seem to be advancing on every small plot of unspoilt countryside, it seems hard to imagine a time when well-established settlements were declining and dying. Such times certainly did exist, and thousands of English and Welsh villages and hamlets, as well as thousands of Scottish *clachans* (large hamlets) and fermtouns (agricultural settlements) have perished. Perhaps we would be more receptive to the evidence of all these deserted places had we not become fixated on the idea that villages are enduring, 'olde worlde' places, and had we not imagined them as being durable rather than vulnerable.

In this account of deserted villages I have focussed attention on the reasons why these places were abandoned. In popular mythology, the prime cause was the dreadful Black Death that arrived in 1348. In reality, this was one of the lesser causes of village mortality. The forced removal of feudal communities by Tudor landlords, who were keen to replace the villagers with more profitable and less fractious flocks, and the Medieval decay of the climate were much more important. It is a great historical irony that the introduction of sheep, which devastated 'Village England' in the later Medieval centuries would have a yet more devastating impact on the communities of the Scottish Highlands and Islands in the late eighteenth and nineteenth centuries. The story of village, *clachan* and fermtoun desertions is one that resonates with injustice and one that serves as a potent reminder of the need to defend and safeguard hard-won democratic rights and freedoms. This lesson is as relevant now as ever it has been.

Deserted settlement sites are all around us and all British people will live within a very few miles of one or more examples. The landscapes of desertion are not as some may imagine. They do not resemble the North American ghost towns of the decades around 1900; rows of dilapidated timber dwellings with doors creaking in the wind and tumbleweed rolling down the old main street. Most of the settlements described here perished in the Medieval period, when the dwellings of the bondsmen and husbandmen were rather flimsy and prone to decay. Empty houses only stand at the relatively recently deserted settlements, like failed quarry villages. In several of the more evocative cases, a ruined church presides over the deserted site. Such churches are usually of flint or cheap rubble, for churches of good quality stone were nearly always robbed for their materials by the landlord. At the typical deserted site, the old High Street, plot boundaries and house sites are marked on the ground by earthworks, while fragments of Medieval pottery may be brought to the surface by moles and rabbits. Some of the settings are extremely beautiful, like that of the famous Wharram Percy or of Holm, at the head of a gorge-like dry valley, both in the Yorkshire Wolds.

Villages existed to play special roles – most were dormitories for bondsmen who toiled in the surrounding fields. When its role vanished, a village had to discover a new one or perish. In the penultimate chapter, I present some unsettling evidence suggesting that the long era of the deserted village may not yet be over.

The study of the historic landscape is amazingly rewarding, and in the final chapter I describe ways in which those who have found the research and commentary in this book stimulating can go on and research a home patch or chosen locality. During the last twenty years or so, I have discovered six hitherto unrecorded deserted villages in England and one village that had migrated from its original site and an unrecorded 'milltoun' (village with a mill) in Scotland. Only in two cases was I actually hunting lost villages and the other discoveries resulted from recognising the signs evident from sources like old maps and earthworks. Four of the settlements discovered lay within a very confined area of a few square miles, showing that there is a great deal still remaining to be discovered. In a land where change and development are everywhere, there may be little time left in which to discover and record these sites.

Chapter One

The Village

Village origins

What were the old villages like before they became lost? Few, if any, facets of the British scene have caused more ink to be spilled than villages. Yet it is because popular writing on villages has generally been so misleading that an introductory chapter such as this is needed. Villages are places; they are communities and they are accumulations of buildings. However, they have also become very powerful symbols of lost causes and of aspirations; like rustic decency, harmonious community, and grassroots steadfastness. All these are harboured and nurtured in cottages of golden thatch. Indeed, the symbolism is more extravagant than this, for the vision of the home-spun and wholesome village has become the core of national identity, although more so for the English than the Scots, Welsh or Irish. Only a small percentage of the population live in villages and most real villages are fraught with social tensions and resentments. But for more than a century, British warriors have gone to their deaths with imprinted mental images of the mythical village helping to lead them on.

All this may not be good for national culture and it is certainly bad for villages. It has given them a celebrity for things that they are not – stable, timeless, resilient – and this can undermine the formation of suitable communal policies for the countryside.

So deeply are villages embedded in the national psyche that it will never occur to most people to ask the basic question: 'Why have villages?' It is certainly possible for farming communities to flourish with few, if any, villages. The homesteaders of the American West largely managed to exist with just isolated farmsteads, small towns and very little in-between. In old Hungary and parts of rural China there were huge villages, more populous than many small British market towns, but in the British uplands, hamlets and farmsteads have always been favoured and such villages as do exist tend to be small. The more examples that we look at, the more we find that farming communities can be found in a wide variety of settlements. Villages do not have to exist, but if they do exist, it is to serve a particular purpose. It follows that if this purpose is extinguished or becomes obsolete, the village must either find a new reason for being or die. This takes us to the lost villages.

When I walk around a deserted village site (and I am sure I am not alone in this), I invariably use the clues from scatters of stone, earthworks, holloways, ponds and so on to attempt to compose a mental picture of how the place looked when it was alive and there were people trudging its lanes. The archaeology that is scattered around is inherently as dull as ditchwater – but when harnessed to informed imagination, it can mentally revitalise a clutch of households. The archaeological relics tell of a settlement of people who struggled and failed – people who were seldom regarded by their 'betters' as any more than free labour, income from rents or sources of tithes. Living in a village does not seem to have done these downtrodden people very much good, so why were they living there?

This is a rather complicated question and the answer requires a brief flight through history. If we could go back to prehistory – the New Stone Age, the Bronze Age or the Iron Age – we would find countrysides that were most usually worked from scattered farmsteads and from little knots of, say, two to six or so dwellings that we might think of as hamlets. Many of these hamlets must surely have accommodated the members of extended families, with the uncles, aunts, cousins and grandparents probably deferring to a relation who was the local patriarch. Scouting around the ancient countrysides, we would come across a few villages in most regions. They would tend to be smallish examples and look quite unlike any Medieval or later settlements. These villages would either be 'open' and undefended by ditches, ramparts or thorny hedges; or else their dwellings might stand within such a compound. Rather than being square, the ancient dwellings were normally circular, with very low walls and a towering conical roof of thatch in which the smoke from the central hearth would hang before seeping away. Such places differed from the later villages in having no distinct structure and form in the way that churches, greens, lanes, high streets and house plots (long 'tofts' or compact 'closes') imparted distinct forms to later villages.

The prehistoric settlements were different in another important way. Whereas the later Saxon, Viking and Medieval villages were permanent unless something specific and unpleasant happened to them, the prehistoric villages were never intended to be permanent. They might be built and occupied for a couple of decades, a couple of generations or even a few centuries, but then they were abandoned. The reasons why this was so are uncertain. It could be argued that after a few decades of occupation the sites of the settlements became foul and contaminated. However, with their polluted wells and lack of drains, Medieval villages were certainly at least as unsanitary and this did not cause their abandonment. Where clues survive, it seems that the communities from the deserted prehistoric settlements did not forsake their precious lands and travel far. Rather, they would move a short distance, erect a new settlement within the home territory and continue to work the same lands. Had they abandoned their lands as well as their homes, then they would have been unwelcome refugees in countrysides that, in the Bronze and Iron Ages, were very well peopled. This footloose attitude to settlements may have persisted among the more 'backwoodsy' indigenous people of Roman Britain, and it was still a characteristic of pagan, and even early Christian Anglo-Saxon, communities.

Some prehistoric villages did exist and there are a few examples with sufficient relics remaining to interest visitors unskilled in archaeology. Where houses were built with walls of moorstone and stone rubble rather than poles, wattle and daub, then clear outlines of 'hut circles' may be found, including the gap in the low, windowless, circular wall that was once the entrance. Occasionally, these hut circles can be seen to form clusters that might be likened to villages. They are a feature of the uplands rather than the vales and plains and a high percentage of them will result from

The double circle of stones in the foreground were the walls of the Iron Age chieftain's house at Din Lligwy on Anglesey. The remains of the dwellings of some of his subjects lie nearby.

an abandonment of the higher ground, which had become cloudy, rain-lashed and incapable of supporting farming communities. This was due to sudden changes in the climate occasioned by massive eruptions of Mount Hekla in Iceland in the Middle Bronze Age, which vented innumerable fine volcanic particles into the atmosphere. Many uplands, like Dartmoor, were never so intensely or effectively populated again (see Ch. 6). In the lowlands, however, layer upon layer of agricultural settlement built up. As a result of rescue excavations associated with the motorway building bonanza of the second half of the twentieth century, and the simultaneous growth of aerial photography, it came to be realised that the British lowlands had sup-ported dense and continuous patterns of prehistoric settlement. There can have been few farmers who could not have seen the roof cones or smoke plumes of several other farming households from their thresholds.

Villages enduring and lost

In seeking an understanding of villages, we need to discover what it was that broke the footloose settlement habits that had existed for eternity and produced villages that were regarded as permanent. Revolutions often occur in times of trouble and the birth of the village does not seem to be a product of slow, stable evolution. Villages seem to have crystallised in a historical flask that had been seared and blasted by the turbulence of the rivalries between English dynasties, and scorched by the desperate wars between the Christian kingdom(s) of England and the pagan Danish and Norse invaders. Somehow, within this maelstrom, a new means of organis-ing estate production was invented and spread to many places, although by no means all. Also, the old manner of dispensing religion through key minster churches, many of them on royal estates, was yielding to an organisation of worship by churches established by local landowners on their estates. These estate churches would become parish churches and many would form an early association with a village – though whether the church attracted the village or vice versa will nearly always be a hard question to answer.

The innovatory way of organising estate farming was the open field system. Nobody knows where it came from – but it was certainly not from the Saxons' continental homelands. Without going into all the details, this was an effective, yet extremely complicated, method of farm-ing and organising the manpower and womanpower of a (proto) feudal community. It involved the sharing of commons, which had surely existed since ancient times; the intricate division of ploughland and meadows; the respect for a labyrinth of boundaries and rights; and required complex arrangements for co-operation to pool beasts to form plough teams and recruit labour gangs to work the lord's demesne. It also required that all the activities of the community were synchronised within one great estate-wide programme of work. Clearly, all this communal integration and fine-tuning would have been impossible had the labour force been scattered across the countryside in farmsteads and hamlets. Also, it is now known to have been the case that when at least some villages were initially set out, this was done in such a way that the man ploughing his strips/selions in a great field or scything his share ('dale' or 'dole') in the meadow had the same people as neighbours on either side as he had at home on the village street – a planning exercise that must have taken some doing!

Not every estate or parish had its own fully-fledged open field system. Parts of Essex, the Welsh Marches, the South West and North may have had property patterns that were too fragmented to accommodate the new methods. It is certainly the case that where there were no big systems of open fields, then villages tend to be fewer, further between and smaller, with hamlets and farmsteads being more numerous and filling the gaps. It is surely a sign of the profound worth of our countrysides that we can look across landscapes that had their defining characters produced by events occurring around AD 800. Thus, 1,200 years of history can last embedded in a scene – until the developers and bulldozers come along. It is doubtless true that the new estate farming techniques spawned new villages to house the labour forces, but villages were not born in an instant. If the first true or intentionally permanent villages arose around AD 800, new villages continued to be founded through the remainder of the Saxon era, through the time of the Norman kings and into the Plantagenet era. Even in the years around 1300, hopeful communities were still being budded-off to work the margins of an increasingly overpopulated realm.

Popular ideas about the growth and appearance of early villages are likely to be wrong. One can warm to the notion that the lanes and trackways of Britain were created by drunkards as they lurched and swayed along their ways. Villages, however, were not created in such informal and haphazard ways. Where there are sufficient clues to allow one to peal back the layers of time's onion, one may discover order rather than spontaneity. The confection of cottages may have buildings of different ages, roofs of different heights and colourful jumbles of stone, brick, pantile, thatch and daub. Yet these seemingly anarchic collections of buildings may well stand on an original village ground-plan that reveals the traces of straight lines and right-angles, measured frontages and back lanes that terminate all the plots together in a line. In a word, villages were very frequently *planned.* This planning could have been there from the outset and have been decreed by a Saxon thegn and village-founder, or else have been demanded by the steward of some Norman magnate. It might have been imposed on an existing community. It could be partial, as when a market green or market square was bashed into an existing village layout, or when an unplanned village gained a planned extension.

From time to time I answer the telephone and find myself in conversation with a television programme-maker or researcher. Invariably, this means that they want some consulting, but do not want to pay for it. Of late, I have learned to say 'no'; this negativity may have been sparked by a prolonged conversation with a researcher about what is a village and what is a hamlet? There really is no easy answer. A settlement with a church, a green and half a dozen dwellings might appear to be a village, though a larger one with eight or nine dwellings might have the 'feel' of a hamlet. A loose rule of thumb seems to be that villages tend to have structured layouts, with greens, side lanes, public amenities (though now, only sometimes) and rather organised house plots, while hamlets tend to consist of an informal straggle of farmsteads strung along a through-road. Having given an expanded version of this, and feeling quite erudite, I then faced the riposte: 'But *how many* houses are there in a hamlet?' In future I may settle for the glib, if not entirely misleading, answer that it is all in the mind.

Had the researcher demanded to know 'What is a village?' I would have had a ready answer; it is easy to say what a village was, though not what it may have become. A village, almost invariably, was a dormitory for a subservient, feudal, agricultural labour force. I am very happy with this explanation, but first the qualifications. I say 'almost invariably' because there were a few villages where agriculture was not paramount. There were fishing villages, though these were few and far between until effective ways of preserving and distributing the catch were found. Some villages had a small industrial component, like potters or wood turners, and a few villages beside castles and palaces housed numbers of retainers as well as agricultural tenants. Next, the use of the word 'feudal' is frowned upon by some when used for pre-Norman societies, but Saxon or Anglo-Danish magnates, whether they were feudal or not, were not short of the means to coerce their tenants. Finally, I say that the village was a dormitory for a feudal agricultural labour force, but even when we substitute 'down-trodden' for feudal, this state of affairs has not existed for well over a century. Villages shed their old roles and adopted new ones. Modern villages give us very little idea indeed of what the lost villages of the eleventh to eighteenth centuries were like.

The deserted Medieval villages that we may discover in the corners of pastures or overrun by woods, and in several other settings, were not remotely like the villages that have survived into the twenty-first century, even though the lost and the surviving villages may have looked much the same some centuries ago. Throughout most of the Medieval period, families occupied dwellings that were cheap, shabby, liable to catch fire or even to blow away. These houses were made from bits and pieces of tat that the paupers could collect under their commoners' rights. The marvellously robust sixteenth-century timber-framed buildings which we see flaunting a façade of costly timber studs in East Anglia or displaying elaborately arching braces in the West Midlands, or the stone-walled and flag-roofed farmsteads of the seventeenth and eighteenth centuries in the northern Dales, are the products of the 'Great Rebuilding'. This movement, which asserted a new confidence in a better future, rolled north-eastwards across the kingdom from late-Tudor to Georgian times. But by then, the Medieval village failures were dead and mouldering. These failed settlements had few, if any, yeomen and no yeoman housing of the quality that still gladdens the eye in hundreds of English villages. In its day, the typical village that was destined for Medieval desertion did not flaunt the jettied-out upper stories, massive curved bracing timbers and lofty zig-zagging gables that we see on pictorial evocations of the 'olde worlde' village. Rather, it was a dingy and dirty place composed of single-storied thatched dwellings looking more like old potato clamps or scenes from Amazonian tribal life than anything appearing on a Christmas card. Most, however, had one building that embodied much communal wealth: the church. Often, these buildings were robbed away for their valuable stone but at a good proportion of deserted villages a church, or its ruins, presides over the empty scene.

Sometimes, the layout of dwellings can be deciphered from the relics of lost villages. A particularly widespread plan for housing poorer folk was that of the long-house. Here, the dwelling was built with its long axis parallel to the roadside or the edge of a green and the house was divided into two chambers by a passage running from front door to back door. In one room lived the household, while the other was a byre for a milk cow, a calf or two, or maybe a sheep. I have found examples where nettles, demanding of nutrients, still form a square block growing exactly where the byre component of a house had been. Various other forms of houses were employed, according to time and status. The raising of the rot-prone beam that carried the wall posts above the damp on rubble footings paved the way for generations of peasant housing that were more durable and sophisticated. From uncertain origins through until the times of the Highland Clearances, low status homes were commonly built using a tent-like or 'cruck-framing' method, rather than the box-framing alternative. 'A'-frames of timber formed the gables and bays of these little houses, which were often interspersed with others that employed the 'box' technique.

Medieval villages were dormitories for feudal agricultural populations. Often, the traces of former cultivation can be found around a village, like this corduroy-like ridge and furrow highlighted by the melting snow at Appletreewick in Wharfedale.

The doomed villages were a mixed collection. Just a few may have somehow battled through the centuries since Roman times. Many were the deliberate creations of lordly schemes to develop and organise estates, and such villages often grew from neatly planned layouts and were furnished with markets. Others had grown in more organic manners as separate knots of buildings standing around adjacent growth poles, like churches, manors, priories or greens. Very often, these original nuclei gradually swelled until they merged in a single, seemingly unified village. Only a very careful examination may reveal that the seemingly homogenous village is really a cluster of merged hamlets. There were also settlements that housed the new communities that pressed into the empty corners of estates during the centuries of population growth leading up to the fourteenth century, and such places were vulnerable when the climate began to decay. For some villages, downfall was caused by the accidents of history, when healthy and hopeful communities suddenly found themselves to be living in the wrong place at the wrong time. However, many places that died had already been diminished and weakened by earlier misfortunes such as war, plague or famine. In their reduced states they were less able to resist the onslaught that would prove fatal.

And so they perished. Sometimes, a single dwelling would endure at the village site to serve as a farmstead that worked the evacuated lands. Dwellings that were not immediately torn down by the destroyers would have their thatch blown away or their turf roofs would sag and collapse.

Walls of daub and wattle (although more so for the English than the Scots, Welsh or Irish) would slump and wall posts would rot, though stone-built walls would topple and yet hang on as piles of rubble. Unless it was still required by a congregation from a neighbouring township, the church would fall into disuse. The bishop might bicker about the loss of tithes, but quite soon the landowner might cart away its valuable dressed stones, even digging up the foundation trenches to recover some of the biggest ones. Then the village would sink down into the countryside that gave it birth, in eternal slumber. After a few centuries, just the shallow troughs worn by the feet, hoofs and wheels that had travelled its lanes, the slightly embanked trapezoidal enclosures that were fishponds, the moat of the manor and faint banks or ditches marking old property boundaries would be all that remained of the village. Today, the uninitiated may walk across most Medieval village sites without realising what they were.

In the next chapter we meet the human community that had made their home out of the local earth, rushes, sheaves and boughs. Their resilience and fortitude must have been amazing – amazing, too, to think that their genetic imprint must still be with us. In the chapters that follow, the different ways in which villages perished are explored. Fate had an armoury stocked with a daunting and potent variety of ways in which villages could be done away with. All those villages that survived were places and communities that had run the gauntlet of change and braved at least some of the challenges. Today, the greatest challenge that a villager may face could be the severance of the bus service or the ominous green planning notice nailed on the telegraph post outside the house next door. The people of the deserted Medieval villages seem so very distant. Could we meet them, we would be repelled by their dirty clothes and stench, we could scarcely follow a word that they said and we would be threatened by several of their parasites and infections. And yet, they could tell us so very much that we are now in danger of forgetting – messages about what it is like to be devoid of rights and to be powerless in the face of corruption and outside forces. They endured privations that we would be too weak to resist, and for this alone they merit our attention.

CHAPTER TWO

THE BLOOD OF THE VILLAGE

The local scene

The Medieval village impinged on all the senses, but the first intimation of
its presence was likely to arrive via the nose. On closer acquaintanceship,
the ears not only heard the shouts and chatter, bleats, clucking and rooting
of its occupants but also, during most of summer, the hiss and buzz from
the swarms of flies hanging over the dwellings like a fog of white noise.
On a still, humid day, the villagers' world is glimpsed through a haze of
dithering, metallic dots. Their lifelong familiarity with the middens, dung
heaps, cess pits, gutters, ditches and field spreads of human and animal
waste has left the villagers largely unaware of the stench, while the flies
are as much a part of summer as the birdsong and thunderstorms – and no
more amenable to change.

There are no signs at the roadside to announce the village. Only local
people and tax collectors have any real interest in it – and they already
know where it is and what it is called. Those best equipped to describe
the landscape of a Medieval village were the Medieval people themselves.
Oppressed and illiterate, they have not told us very much, but we learn that
in the areas of open field farming (in contrast to the situation in the surviving ancient or woodland countrysides), landscape is perceived in terms
of 'town and field', the 'towns', as they were known, being the villages and
the fields being their associated communal ploughlands. The town and its
fields combined to form a township or vill ('village' was a later importation from France). In his description of Elizabethan England written in
1577, a few decades after the end of the Middle Ages, the churchman,
William Harrison (1534-1593), contrasted the settlements of the open
field and the woodland countrysides, 'The houses of the first lie uniforme-
lie builded in euerie town togither, with streets and lanes; whereas in the
woodland countries (except here and there in great market townes) they

stand scattered abroad, each one dwelling in the midst of his owne occupi-eng'. Thus, much of old village England was characterised by quite tightly clustered dwellings that stood in their own plots ('tofts' or 'closes') and they were divided into groups by roads and lanes.

Mentally reconstructing such a village from the evidence of archives and earthworks, it is hard to distinguish the point at which the rutted, wheel-juddering road ceases to be a rural highway and becomes the village High Street. The existence, on its flanks, of what the British would today call a 'pavement' and Americans a 'sidewalk' is debatable. True, outside the rutted area there is a rather uneven ribbon of public ground with a narrow strip of earth and muddy hollows tracing a bare, trampled course across the less-trodden grass. Between this pathway and the house plots runs a ditch – though to be more accurate, in summer it is foetid and foul and scarcely runs at all, while in winter, it gushes, deep and swift. More lethal than any mad bull or armed invader, it harbours the bacteria that have sent scores of villagers to the graveyard. It is a task of the village to keep this ditch clear and flowing freely. This is something that one would imagine they would want to do, though a few glances at the rolls of the manor court reveals that, like most other public works, it is done patchily, with much reluctance and only after threats from the exasperated authorities.

Villagers making the transition from their abodes to the public highway must negotiate the ditch. This might not seem so very great a problem – until one has experienced the suffocating blackness of an un-illuminated village in an unlit countryside in a realm where the towns are minute and their people almost as early to bed as the villagers. To assist the transit, small plank constructions known as 'bridge trees' are set across the ditch at convenient places, offering assistance to most, except for those with their vision impaired by a spell in an alehouse. Meanwhile, the dire condition of the High Street reflects the difficulties of recruiting villagers for tasks of which they would, themselves, be the main beneficiaries. Among the ruts and potholes are hollows where cobbles have been dumped as token gestures of road mending. On the outer limits of the village, the cess pit belonging to one of the households intrudes into the road, presenting a special challenge to those who are strangers to the locality. Somewhere deep in the village psyche is lodged a revulsion at the notion that some nameless traveller, a foreigner from outside the township, might benefit from the collective efforts. This imagined unfairness is more potent than the idea that the community would be doing itself a favour if it made a decent, all-weather village street.

Perched on the outskirts of the village, one can survey its landscape. It does not look very much like those places that simper at one from the large, shiny pages of today's 'olde worlde' village books. If anything, our village looks, sounds, and certainly smells like a collection of shambling, rambling old farms. Hedges packed with useful trees for fruit and browse outline the house-plots, so that the leafy, compartmentalised landscape of the countryside is carried through into the village. The place certainly does not seem alien or threatening in the way that the cliff-sided houses of brick, fake-stone and tiles on our new housing estates do. Rather, one might imagine that the settlement somehow rose quietly from the ground overnight, like a set of molehills. This is not so far from the truth. The thatched roofs, slowly rotting and pulled apart by sparrows, came from the wheat fields and from the reed beds beside the meadow. The wall timbers, slight though they are, recall the customary right to take timbers for house building and they came from the common wood and from the roadside hedge trees. The wattle between the wall timbers came from a hazel coppice and the mud, dung and fibre in the daub plastered over it came from a nearby clay pit, from the hair on cow skins destined for the tanning yard and from cow pats in the pasture. And so it is not surprising that the village seems at one with its setting, for there is nothing in its fabric that came from more than a mile or so away.

The village seems old, even ageless. Its occupants, to the extent that they have given any thought to the matter, consider that it has been there forever. For them, 'forever' is a concept that comes into play for all periods preceding one's great grandparents. In fact, there is nothing in the scene that is much more than thirty years old, for most of the houses have experienced thoroughgoing rebuildings every generation or so. If the village is 'homely' it is so in the American rather than the British sense of the word. The village itself is a dormitory for land-workers and the houses are perhaps as much shelters as they are homes. This is to say that they do not constitute inviting venues for domestic life. Viewing them from outside, we see smoke wafting from holes in the upper gables and seeping out from under the thatch, like steam escaping from under a pie crust. The smoke – to the extent that it can be smelled amongst the headier village odours – often has a rather oily odour of peat. Could we step inside one of the village dwellings, we would step into a veil of this peaty smoke that hangs in the open roof space beneath the rafters – the taller the visitor, the more smoke that will be inhaled. The exit of smoke through the smoke hole is leisurely and spasmodic but its source is easily traced to a hearth smouldering in the centre of the rectangular floor space. Stone slabs floor the hearth, a few stones define it and there are sheets of locally-quarried 'bakestones' to hand to serve as hotplates. As our watering eyes clear, we see that the internal space is surprisingly tidy. Besom marks trace faint lines of sweeping through the dusty soil of the floor, though in some houses the blood of cattle has been poured to give the floors a hard, dark crust. Not all the squalor of the village is avoidable but the house interior is one place where cleanliness can, to some small degree, triumph.

Even visitors blinded by smoke would find little inside the house to trip over. In an average village dwelling of the twelfth or thirteenth century there might be a low stool, suitable for milking, and consisting of a section cut from the trunk of a youngish tree that was then augured to take three stubby legs. An un-worked section of tree trunk could form another low stool and there might be a plank bench or form against a wall. If the sitting provision is modest, the flattened bags of straw on the ground, optimistically including some fleabane and other insecticidal herbs, are so infested with lice and other vermin as to be deterrents to sleep for all but the most exhausted or hard-bitten cases. Their presence in the house does not exemplify the filthy nature of the Medieval village family, but rather their inability to do much more about the lice in the seams of their garments or the typhoid in the well than they can about the tapeworms and other parasites infesting their bowels. For storage, a few stacked planks form a frame in which oddments can be stored. These are not the sort of smooth and even planks that come neatly formed from a sawpit or a band saw. Like other planks, they had been split in sheets from a trunk by hammering in a line of wedges. Thus, they are rather wavy and uneven and were coated in splinters until usage wore them smooth. In general, the floor is the main storage area and it supports a variety of kiln-fired clay storage pots and turned timber

The Hangleton house at the remarkable Weald and Downland Museum at Singleton, West Sussex, is actually based on two similar examples, deserted in the perilous fourteenth century, that were excavated at Hangleton, near Hove. It is more robust than many dwellings of its day, with walls of flint and a window barred with slats. There is no upper storey or chimney stack.

vessels, a functioning wooden milk pail and a worn-out one that contains the sand used to clean the knives and food vessels, as well as the costly bits of ironwork used when cooking over the fire. One day, our household may acquire a table consisting of a board supported on tressles. For the moment, they simply balance their platters and bowls on their knees.

Forks are unknown, while food is contained in vessels turned from green wood. Liquids – fermented drinks rather than the lethal water straight from the wells and watercourses – are drunk from wooden beakers. All these vessels are turned locally on simple 'pole lathes' set-up in coppices and employing the energy stored in a bow-like contraption of pole and twine. The wood is worked 'green' and the turner's products will twist, bulge and split long before the scouring in sand at the end of each meal can wear holes in them. Above the hearth, the gruesome subjects for future meals dangle to smoke in the fug. The energetic steward might find examples of his lord's fish or hares suspended up there among the portions of the family hog – perhaps even a haunch of venison, though probably not.

The house is not a particularly inviting venue for family affairs, and so it is the habit that, whenever the weather allows, meals are taken on the worn ground by the front door, or perhaps among the vegetables, herbs and small livestock in the toft behind. (Even when living in modern homes packed with comforts, true country people seem ever-drawn by invisible green magnets to the spaces around. There is so much more to see and do: growing plants to prune, weeds to tug out, nests, butterflies and seed trays, all needing to be observed and noted). The Medieval village house was not a cosy place and was anything but quaint. It was as close to the period cottages in the glossy village books as a warthog is to a Pekinese. However, if domestic comfort was something that one had never known, something never enjoyed by a single forbear, then one could not miss it. The family who had seen no piece of furniture more grand than the crudely-formed aumbry glimpsed through the door of the hall would hardly miss the sofa that they had never known. If given one, they might use it as a gate.

Surveying the landscape of a fairly typical Medieval village once more, we note that the landmarks, facilities and items of quaintness or patronage that are associated with the modern and the Victorian village landscapes are largely lacking. Most obviously and attractively, there are no parked motor vehicles or intrusive items of street furniture and no vehicle parks, also no bus shelters and no telephone boxes. Disharmonious clutter is not there. In fact, apart from the church, the only public structure to be found is the pinfold, a small fenced and gated enclosure whence animals that have caused a nuisance by straying into private holdings are led by the appointed pinder, and impounded. They will stay in the pinfold until their owners pay a fine or break open the gate, and so become liable for a larger one. The pinfold occupies a corner of the green and is bracketed by houses that have encroached upon the common space.

The market in our recreated village has commandeered another corner of the green, having drifted down here from the churchyard at some forgotten time. A stubby cross, a shack to house the gear and stalls and a couple of parallel walkways worn in the turf are its only expressions in the village landscape between market days. The lord formalised his ancient market by purchasing the necessary royal charter allowing a weekly market and a fair on the day of the saint to whom the church is dedicated. Every week, a few traders drift in, but never so many as to raise the dust on the approach roads. Even so, the presence of an old man leading a lamb, a widow with a crate of ducklings and a pinioned goose, somebody from the next township with a bag of dried beans, someone else with a collection of elm, oak and maple saplings for hedging and a few other similarly prosaic traders causes considerable excitement in the village. Excitement must depend on one's expectations, for it is certainly the case that a favoured form of punishment in these simple times was to oblige the offender to pass market day inside, alone and in repentance. Perhaps the social interactions would have been missed more than the commerce? Even so, to Medieval eyes one of today's smaller car boot sales must have seemed like a virtual World's Fair. Evocative in a different way is the trampled circle of grass on the green that recalls the location of the maypole. The young people of the village can seldom glance on it without thinking of the foray they made into the nearby woods to gather may blossom on the eve of May Day — and the nights that some of them spent there before this great festival of youth and courtship.

In considerable contrast to the Victorian village, with its numerous specialised craftsmen and artisans, the lack of distinctive workshops in our reconstructed village may seem surprising. There are various reasons for this, of which the general shortage of purchasing power is but one. Many of the most important industries tended to be outside settlements. Smelting and forging were most likely to be found in relatively remote places with good resources of woodland for charcoal and with water power to drive mill wheels and forge hammers. As we have seen, turning was carried out among the coppices where the timber grew, while fulling was often practised in out-of-the-way places, not because of the stench of the urine and chemicals employed but for access to rivers and streams. The milling of grain could be a village industry where the settlement and chosen millstream coincided, though the windmills that became more numerous as the Medieval period progressed tended, like many smelters, to be located on windy hilltops. All communities needed iron tools and knives, but village smithies must have been preceded by workshops of lesser size and refinement where a villein worked periodically to provide forged goods for the manor. The Victorian blacksmith earned the greater part of his income from shoeing the numerous horses and ponies of the locality, but for most of the Medieval period, oxen were the main draught animals and horses were far fewer. Some crafts, like that of the wheelwright, were still to be refined, and while some industries, like those of the spurrier and fletcher, were practised in rural settings, the most highly-paid of craftsmen, the armourers, tended to be found in towns. And so, in rambling around the Medieval village, one might find corners of barns or parts of dwellings or small covered spaces that served as workplaces for crafts, but workshops with painted signs, racks of specialised tools, apprentices, framed certificates and all the trappings of Victorian or Edwardian technological expertise would not be seen.

The Church

In this encounter with an imaginary Medieval village, the church will be the least unfamiliar building, though it has many features that seem unusual. Let us reconstruct the world of the Medieval parish church. As with the village itself, its smell, or rather that from its churchyard, goes before it. The building stands among a sea of hummocks, some of newly-dug earth and some sunken and grassed-over. People of note have been buried inside the church, under the nave and, sometimes, in stone coffins. In the side aisles, the tomb sculptures show a succession of lords who no longer survey the hunting field or the village maids but stare at the rafters in fixed contemplation. Padding past the succession of old masters one can see the slow progression in fashions for armour. Each strap, plate, buckle and length of interlocking chain represents the value of hours of servitude spent ankle deep in flooded meadows or scorching amongst the lord's barley. Less privileged villagers were laid to rest in shrouds rather than coffins and in graves not always deep enough to trap the stench of decay. The absence of proper maps of burials in the churchyard results in the bones, some relatively fresh, which lie unearthed in various places. A solitary cross presides over the churchyard. There are no headstones and all that one may readily deduce about the community from its dead is that suicides and the more disadvantaged or disreputable villagers probably lie on the shady, north side of the building. The lack of obstacles in the form of headstones facilitates the use of the churchyard as a place for games – a group of boys might be seen bouncing an inflated pig's bladder. The hours after Mass on Sundays are the favoured time for games and relaxation, even if the church establishment rather frowns on such things. It also frowns on the trading, bargaining and the amorous entanglements that go on here, but to little effect.

The church is certainly at the centre of the villagers' perceptions of home. On the day of its saint, the village holds a great fair or feast which is preceded by a wake or vigil in which the people are allowed to stay awake all night – another seemingly tedious event that produces great excitement in the Medieval village. Those who have married into the village or arrived here by other means seek to return to their native communities on the days of their wakes. These church feasts provide special opportunities for mixing with outsiders in a way that is usually, but not always, amicable. In the Medieval kingdoms of Britain there were numerous churches that were budded-off from older foundations, perhaps from ancient minsters or early estate churches. On wake days, the congregations of the daughter churches would generally process to the parish of the mother to respect the old ties. Sometimes, however, these friendly reunions become scenes of brawling and even rioting. Perhaps the banners of the approaching retinue are seen as provocative – or perhaps the occasion simply provides an outlet for the militant parochialism that is so deeply rooted in Medieval rural life? Given that the villagers' dwellings cluster around the church tower, whence the tolling of the bells signals the order of services, the approach of danger, and sometimes, the times for entering and leaving fields, it is scarcely surprising that the church is a pillar of local identity. Let us not forget that, with the occasional exception of the manor house or castle, the church is the only stone building in the township and its tower or spire stands over all like a mighty beacon.

In the Medieval village of our vision, the church is plainly a church, though rather different from its descendents. Rather than being mellowed with lichen, the building, rendered and lime-washed, erupts from its setting like a great iceberg. What we see is just the current phase in a long story of growth, retrenchment and renewal that will span more than ten centuries. The new extension to the churchyard tells of a buoyant congregation and as we watch, a trio of peripatetic masons, the only real professional craftsmen present in the village, are appraising a plan to create space for more worshippers in the nave by breaking through its side walls and expanding it sideways with the addition of nave arcades. A fourth mason is elsewhere in the churchyard with one of the several village girls who are captivated by the presence of outsiders. Inside the church, the contrast with the whitened exterior is profound. A few guttering candles reveal an interior that is devoid of pews or seats of any kind, while glowering in the shadows is a hideously uncompromising painting of the Last Judgement that details the damnation of sinners across the breadth of the building. This church deals in terror.

Any theological questions that congregants may have must remain unanswered. The rector has preferred gathering tithes to shouldering a vocation and has appointed a curate to look after his parish. Were there any even half-educated people in the congregation, the curate's grasp of Latin and his understanding of the most elementary doctrinal principles would be ridiculed. However, he might preach in Estonian or Ukrainian and nobody would notice the difference. So long as he attempts the right ceremony on the right day, and so long as the church is believed to be doing its bit to intervene to safeguard the harvest, the people are content. At other times, he can be seen toiling away like any villein on his little church plot or 'glebe', where his talents bring forth greater rewards. Though seldom seen, the rector is responsible, in a general sort of way, for maintaining the chancel, while the village takes care of the nave, struggles to fund the bells, pays for candlesticks and banners and provides a font fitted with a locked cover to prevent the theft of holy water by any practising pagans in the vicinity. The fact that there are none makes the loss of the key a less pressing matter. Some of the contents and fittings of the church were provided by the proceeds from the renting of pieces of land that were left as bequests to the church: the lamps are financed in this way.

The relationship between the villagers and their church is both profound and complex. They do not revere it – rather, they hold it in awe. The relationship is different from that experienced by modern Christian congregations. The church does not really nurture a code of ethics or a sense of social justice. It provides no comfort to those oppressed by feudalism. It punishes sins and it threatens sinners, though punishment of a relatively mild kind is more frequently imposed by the manor court for crimes against the peace and the established order of things. The church legitimises marriages and it provides the emotional support so valued by the bereaved. It takes confessions and it absolves. In these ways, it provides valuable psychological services. However, the religious aspects are just parts of the story. If some gale should invade the church and carry away the altar and all the vestments, crosses and other pegs for liturgy, the church would still have a crucial psychological importance. It was, occasionally, a bastion where threatened folk might hope to sit-out some threat. It could be a storage place, sometimes apparently harbouring the trade goods of a local merchant. More importantly, the yard outside is the first port of call for the bearers and receivers of gossip and it is also a place for games and for dalliance. The Medieval church and its yard offer functions resembling those of today's shelter, social centre, market house, sports centre – and it gave much more besides. To believers it gives some form of insurance against disasters when alive and then, against death itself. At a more practical level, its social guilds operate as the equivalents of the later friendly societies. Above all, for people who seldom venture very far, the church is the hub of their lives and an immense symbol of identity. Given the

The medieval village church was painted with striking religious images. This fourteenth-century wall painting from Little Kimble, Bucks, shows St George and the lady he saved.

uninviting nature of most dwellings, it is more an icon of 'home' than any other place. Attendance at Sunday Mass is not optional and what is offered there is mystifying and often threatening. The church is locked into feudalism and uses its immense powers to support and legitimise it. Its clergy enjoy the fruits of feudal inequality; its bishops wallow in them and the whole edifice of religion is built by extracting produce and income from village paupers already impoverished by the rents and services taken by their lay lords. Even so, church and community are bound tightly together. The church is there, towering at the heart of the village, visible long before the clustered hovels come into view. The fact that, usually, it is still there testifies to the dominion of the bond of local church and local people over the vagaries of doctrine.

The villagers

Moving around our village, we gain an impression of a community of people who are affable, familiar and at ease in the company of each other. This is scarcely surprising, for every villager knows every other villager and most can number more acquaintances within the settlement than outside it. The sense of this fellowship is underlined when we realise that virtually all the men, most of the single girls and several of the widows are toilers in the surrounding fields. Their scythes sweep within inches of each other's ankles, they stand closely in line abreast as their sickles take the seed heads from the grain, and they lie sweating together, swigging weak ale and swapping stories at every break. They share a deep and specialised knowledge of farming matters and country lore, and will readily converse on these subjects. Such potential for meaningful communication might exist only in a modern village if every resident was, say, an avid train spotter or stamp collector. This, however, is far from being an egalitarian community of like-minded individuals. Get to know them a little better and one will find a population that is highly conscious of social status and jealous of the distinctions that confer or erode it.

Village society is a class society. The class structure is not only complex, but also changes through time. The fundamental distinction is between those who are free and those who are in bondage. Even so, one cannot tell whether a householder is a villein in bondage by looking at his house. It might be larger and better-appointed than that of the free family next door. There is little to show that the free tenant has his tenure protected by the royal courts rather than it being subject to the jurisdiction of the manor court. Most villages have numerous 'tenements in villeinage', which are holdings whose tenants are obliged to perform work services on the demesne: the part of the manorial estate that is worked directly for the lord. Demesne services provide an eternal source of resentment and grumbling, though at the end of the day the tasks are, indeed, performed, if not to the total satisfaction of the authorities. The situation of freedom is amazingly complicated and, for example, an un-free man might become free through marriage to a free woman yet produce children that would then be villeins. Those who were free — and the proportions varied from region to region and from manor to manor – are immensely touchy about their status and a villein can be fined in the manor court for libelling a free neighbour by calling him a villein. Freedom can be bought, at a heavy price, or gained by residing for a year and a day on a royal demesne or in a chartered royal borough. Yet most free tenants toiled humbly in the cloying mud and driving rain and the arthritis that crippled their fingers and backs was no different from that afflicting the villeins.

After the Norman Conquest, the new legislators must have faced difficulties in fathoming the complexities of the much-stratified Saxon social order. As time passed, different classes became bracketed together into the two main classes of free tenants and bond tenants, or villeins. There were distinctions among the bondsmen based on the family home. The 'husbonds', who became our 'husbandmen', were bondsmen with houses of some (but probably not very much) substance, and they could look down upon the 'cottars', with their mean little cottages. Similarly, the cottar might hold a small cotland of a few acres that was incapable, on its own, of sustaining a family. In the south of England, the substantial villeins or *virgatarii* would tenant 'virgates' or 'yards' of around thirty acres (around twelve hectares) and were known as 'yardlings'. Unlike the poor cottars, the husbonds/yardlings owned draught oxen and could therefore negotiate between households to assemble plough-teams. In rambling around a village of the thirteenth century one might meet others, too. There were a few influential officials abroad; the king's tax collectors, the lord's steward and his parker. Anyone seen strutting proudly down the road might not be an important office-holder, but a franklin – a freeman or sokeman of more substance than any free cottars living in the village. If he passes any villeins grudgingly bound for service on the demesne, his bearing is likely to become even grander. However, he may not be entirely free of feudal duties – perhaps serving the district (hundred) court or supervising the reapers at harvest. At the other end of the hierarchy, wage-earning labourers are beginning to appear in some numbers on the demesne, mainly arising from the low orders that lack land. The lord's neatherd or cowman and his shepherd were normally cottars.

Thus, the village is far from being a uniform collection of witless yokels. Within the constraints of feudalism and tradition there lives a community that is intensely conscious of the status of people and the subtle divisions between the conditions of different groups. Short of enlisting in the priesthood or escaping from bondage in a town, there is very little scope for self-betterment on a grand scale. Because of this, people are desperately keen to make minute advances – even if this involves trimming away the edge of a neighbour's strip of ploughland or furtively rolling a boundary stone in the common meadow. It was through centuries of shrewd marriage-making, hard bargaining, tough hiring, calculated firing and explorations in the marchlands of legality that we got the farming dynasties of today.

A community as competitive and status conscious as the Medieval village had to be regulated. In the popular imagination of today, the feudal lord is seen imposing his cruel will on a cowed and servile set of peasants. It is true that the manor court or hallmote, held in the lord's hall, is the instrument for organising the community. Yet while the lord's steward presides over the court, judgements are reached by a jury that is composed entirely of villeins, though freemen are included in some places. Doubtless, the jurors are aware of the lord's interests and attitudes, as well as the ancient customs of the manor that are always so revered, but they also have an interest in seeing that things are done properly. The court intervenes and cajoles the villeins and cottars in attempts to enforce the feudal 'boon-works' on the lord's demesne, the trimming of obtrusive hedgerows and road repairs. It also seeks to curtail the acts of violence and hooliganism that are always ready to erupt. They also try the lesser crimes and arbitrate in the cases, like slander, which seem, so often, to sour relations between village neighbours.

Buttressing the work of the hallmote and facilitating the operation of intricate farming activities is the reeve or grave and his sometime assistant, the hayward. The reeve is a villein and is appointed for only a year. Yet he has the most onerous burden of duties and might even be likened to a village headman with responsibilities for farming, organising work on the demesne and for the community. He needs some special qualities

A landscape of desolation. When the Heath Chapel in Shropshire was built in Norman times, who could have imagined that the relatively balmy climate would decay and the village site would become above the limits of tillage and unviable?

of character for he has to command the respect of his fellow villeins and yet ensure that they perform their feudal impositions to the satisfaction of their master.

Women feature less frequently in the records of the Medieval village – not least because they were much less likely to commit misdeeds that caused their names to be recorded in the rolls of the manor court. Witches seem to have been unusual; scolds, less so. Women were not quite the downtrodden chattels of popular imagining and some tenanted holdings in their own right and performed all the farm work. Girls were not forced into marriages and the bond was normally only made after the prospective couple had undergone a trial courtship and the boy's father had surrendered his holding to the manor court and seen it passed on to his son. Occasionally, the lure of a generous marriage settlement would encourage a father to rush a pair into a child marriage, but such marriages were often frowned upon and seem to have lacked durability.

This, then, is our village. It is an extremely parochial place and this might deceive us into thinking that it is boring. It is a very tough place and those who live in it are the survivors of an amazingly harsh regime in which only the very fittest survive. The water supply is polluted by the graveyard and by half the village middens and cess pits. The skeletons in the graveyard are deformed by arthritis caused by working out in all weathers and the teeth in the skulls that the gravediggers unearth have had their enamel scoured away by grains of grit. The grit came from millstones and was baked into bread along with the flour, leaving many people tortured or even killed by dental infections. A closer analysis of remains would reveal checks to the growth of young bodies caused by famine or distortions brought about by diseases of malnutrition, like rickets. Thus, some of people seen walking to Mass have frail, bowed legs, while others have hands distorted by rheumatism and backs locked in the grip of arthritis. A very few deformities may be attributed to inbreeding, but contacts with people in neighbouring townships are more frequent than popular ideas about village introspection allow. With the call of death so close and insistent, life is grasped with both hands. At quite frequent intervals throughout the year, festivals blossom, wakes are held and bonfires are lit. Any of those holy days or rituals whose points and origins are long forgotten can bring little suspensions to the farming ritual and are greatly cherished. Each villager sees himself or herself mirrored in the village community. Working, praying, squabbling and conversing together, one knows who is a coward, who is weak and who is outspoken, whose opinions are to be valued and who often lies. There is no meritocracy in operation to cream off the intellectually gifted. Wise men, fools, men of great creative ability and others who are devoid of imagination: they all lunch in the open together.

If the villages of today are packed with 4 x 4 drivers who cannot tell a haycock from a peacock, the Medieval village was full of hard, rumbustious, colourful people, all accomplished experts on their setting, if not on the world beyond. Sometimes, the manor court rolls mention the 'blood of the village'. This does not mean that the villagers believed they were all related to each other – but they did see themselves as a unique communal entity and they took their identities from their membership of this group. Perhaps this is why the ructions during inter-communal games, festivals, fairs and processions had something of the character of international incidents?

So what of our village? If it existed around 1300 then the chances are that it still exists today. But its survival is far from certain. Should it lie in disaster-prone locations like the borders of Oxfordshire and Northamptonshire, the environs of Warwick or the Yorkshire Wolds, its survival must be in doubt. In Scotland, the map of much of the Highlands was wiped bare of hamlets. Some quite awful fates awaited the weaklings and the unfortunate members of the village fold, so that in no part of Britain was survival guaranteed.

The Elizabethan, William Harrison, was certainly aware that villages had perished and wrote:

> For albeit that the Saxons builded many towns and villages, and the Normans well more at their first coming, yet since the first two hundred years after the latter conquest, they have gone so fast again to decay that the ancient number of them is very much abated.

However, he greatly exaggerated the amount of destruction that had taken place since Norman times when he wrote:

> I find even in the time of Edward IV. 45,120 parish churches, and but 60,216 knights' fees [roughly, manors], whereof the clergy held as before 28,015, or at the least 28,000; for so small is the difference which he doth seem to use. Howbeit, if the assertions of such as write in our time concerning this matter either are or ought to be of any credit in this behalf, you shall not find above 17,000 towns and villages, and 9210 in the whole, which is little more than a fourth part of the aforesaid number, if it be thoroughly scanned.

In the chapters that follow, the progress of villages through the minefield of fate is charted. The traps varied greatly in their nature, though it was the case that the village that was weakened by one ordeal would tend to fall prey to the next. No village future was guaranteed.

CHAPTER THREE

HARRIED TO DEATH

Dilemmas of fear

The villagers were rooted; they could not flee. Through much of the Medieval era, and, perhaps for centuries before, they were legally bound to their manors. Not only were they in bondage to their master, they were also bonded to a place, a settlement, a set of tenures and commons. They were also in bondage to a body of customs and local traditions that gripped them like a vice. There was yet another form of bondage: a tie to crops and the earth that nourished them. Like bothersome brats, the crops demanded attention, competing for it with the animals that had to be pastured, stall-fed and generally kept out of mischief. Any villager fleeing the family home left not only a household and a group of dependents; he or she also left behind the products of farming – the supplies of milk, peas, bread, gruel and broth that might preserve life through the barren weeks of winter and spring. And in those days of bondage to place, if they walked out of their estate and township they left behind their identities, their very selves, too.

Faced with danger and invasion, the villager could not run very far before becoming a feudal fugitive as well as a parasite on the produce needed to sustain other communities. However, should the villager turn to face armed intruders the prospects were most discouraging. Villagers were not Highlanders; they were not given martial training – feudalism may have faced a swift and violent end if they had been schooled in swordplay. It is true that in the later Medieval centuries, archers of a low social status were encouraged to practice, but these were mercenaries or semi-professional soldiers of exceptional upper body strength and dedication. Unlikely to survive away from their townships and ill-equipped to confront intruders, the most that the villager could do in the face of armed intruders was to run to the nearest hiding place and hope that things would get better.

Whether the invaders were Norman horsemen with mercenaries loping alongside, the retainers of a baron from the Scottish Borders with their torches and train of plunder, foragers from some passing army or ruffians discharged from a distant war, the response was much the same. If you thought that there was time, you drove your cattle and sheep into whatever woods or marshes there might be in the vicinity. Probably, the cattle would expect to be milked or be driven in a different, more familiar direction, but you could not shout at them or that might betray your location. The family would have to be gathered together and in the panic you probably forgot to bring any food to tide them over the long vigil. And so you would head for the depths of the wood or marsh. Having got there, the silence and absence of any indications of the events outside would lure you to the woodland margins. If you had managed to keep with your cattle, you then faced the dilemma of what to do if the raiders came looking for them? There might be voices and the sounds of hooves, and by this time the baby – cold, hungry and disorientated – might start to cry, so you would retreat back into the depths of the wood where the crying was lost among the prattling of jays and trilling of songbirds. With the wean exhausted by its crying, there could be a return to the woodland margin. Then a seemingly interminable wait would follow as chills penetrated the deepest flesh and cramped joints craved movement.

At last, the long-awaited sign would appear: soaring plumes of black, spark-spangled smoke that signalled the imminent departure of the intruders. As likely as not, it had all happened before, so that as the villagers trudged back to where the homes had been, the man, with a pessimism born of experience, would eye any trees that seemed to offer useful house-building timbers. Of course, the village would have been razed, the hoppers emptied, the geese and chickens slaughtered and the pigs herded away along with any other livestock that had missed the trail to the woods. If the villagers were lucky, the raid would have come while the crops were still in the fields, yet still too green to be burned. Later, with the raiders gone, the community would fall back under the sway of the manor court. It would do all in its power to curb the brawls and the cudgel blows so freely traded between the villagers, but would do nothing to help them to resist the greater acts violence from outside.

The place would heal. Houses could be erected in a few days and everyone would lend a hand. Some villagers would starve, and if the pillaging had been widespread, then famine would affect the surrounding countryside and prices at market would be high for a season or two. But there was no doubt that the community would survive and probably recover its numbers within a century. The name of the village would be passed on and the brief incident of violence and excitement in its history of drudgery might well pass unrecorded. In a generation, the pillage would have become a skirmish; in two generations it may have been inflated as a great battle, but in three it might have been quite forgotten.

Village battlefields

There was a more frightening, though unlikely, prospect to be faced when a raid was sighted. It concerned the possibility that it was the villagers themselves, rather than their homes and chattels, that were the intended targets. Villagers had no reason to expect clemency since religious houses were frequently pillaged and the foreign mercenaries so often employed were oblivious to cries for mercy. When the defeated and retreating army of Henry Percy razed the Crossraguel Abbey, near Ayr, in 1307 it was simply enacting a ritual that would become commonplace in the Borders. Villages and villagers could become entangled in warfare in a variety of ways. Occasionally, an accident of history would locate the opposing forces, pincer-like, on either side of a village. This confrontation would never be of the village's making, although the consequences of the unfortunate juxtaposition could be severe. On the whole, commanders preferred to wage war in open country, where events were visible and could be responded to with speed. Villages interfered with the manoeuvres of forces and houses could become blockhouses or redouts and complicate a battle plan.

In one of the last battles of the Wars of the Roses in 1487, the village of Stoke, near Leicester (now East Stoke), found itself in the middle of the army of the rebels supporting the pretender, Lambert Simnel. The royal army under Henry VII advanced directly on the village and the outcome was decided by the victory of the king's archers over the German mercenary crossbowmen, who stood on ground directly to the west of Stoke. In the Civil War battle of Newbury, in 1644, Parliamentary infantry under Lord Manchester mounted a night attack on the village of Shaw, where King Charles and his leaders were based in Shaw House. The attack was repulsed by Royalist artillery and musketeers, with very heavy casualties on both sides. Earlier in the same year, the village of Long Marston, near York, found itself between the Royalist and Parliamentary cavalry at the eastern end of the Marston Moor battlefield, while Cromwell had his wounds dressed in Tockwith village, about two miles away at the western extremity of the fighting. The battle was confused and very costly of life, with skirmishing reaching beyond the battlefield as retreating Royalist contingents were pursued. Skirmishing in the aftermath of a battle greatly widened war's influence on villages; at Ripley, a few miles west of the battlefield, a green in a local track was, in local legend, stained red by the blood of Royalists massacred in the flight from Marston Moor and the scars of musket balls in the church wall are said to result from execution squads.

Damage of a much more widespread and deliberate nature was occasioned by the Anglo-Scottish wars that plagued the border country from the late thirteenth century until the close of the sixteenth century. On the one hand, the wars reflected Scottish resentment at the invasion of their country by Edward I and the attempts to impose a puppet monarchy, and on the other, English retaliation for incursions by Scots raiders. The actions exemplified the tyrannical powers of martial aristocracies and the armed retainers that they spawned and employed. Before long, retribution was the motive for war and raiding, ransom and wrecking became a way of life. On both sides of the border, 'reivers', whose lives revolved around raiding, arose among the communities living within a day's ride or so of the border. Political instability had given birth to the reivers and it became their legacy. In modern times, weird and quite inappropriate associations with romance and nationalism have been attached to these despicable people. Quite why anyone would wish to identify with those who rustled cattle from defenceless, struggling farming folk, who gave birth to the word 'blackmail' ('black rent') because of their extortion of tribute or protection money from peaceful villagers, townspeople and farmers, and whose acts of vandalism imposed starvation on the half-starved, is hard to comprehend. Whether originating in Scotland or in England, they became most active as the nights lengthened, when, mounted and in armour, they materialised from the murk and appeared in the midst of helpless communities. While benefiting from surprise, they did not hesitate to use their lances, crossbows or, particularly, daggers on any unarmed man, woman or child seeking to protect the family food stores. Far from being Scottish or English patriots, when enlisted as mercenaries, the reivers displayed a readiness to serve either side, to break away from battles in order to pillage, and to switch allegiances as a matter of convenience. Rather than being nationalists, they formed a community both united and divided by geography and would adopt whichever identity best suited the needs of the moment.

In time, the social deformations of the Anglo-Scottish borders became institutionalised. March Wardens presided over the geographical divisions or 'Marches' on both sides of the border. The habitual instability would be periodically punctuated by Days of Truce, with rumbustious entertainment and trading. In the high uplands of the frontier, near the heads of becks or burns, there were various 'gates' or crossing points which were used as meeting places for the appointed knights concerned, or outwardly so, with maintaining peace in the Borders. In reality these provisions often amounted to little more than a sham. The Scottish Wardens were often corrupt and watchful for chances to commit the same offences they were supposed to suppress, while the English were often chosen from the southern gentry, people traditionally indifferent to the plight of their northern countrymen. Where retribution for raiding did take place, it was frequently undertaken on a vigilante-like basis, whereby the victims of a raid had six days in which to launch an armed and noisy 'hot trod' or counter raid, with people on both sides of the border being required to join and assist the recovery of the booty.

One of the most evocative monuments from the age of Anglo-Scottish warfare is Langley Castle, Northumberland. It was built during the peak of border raiding in 1350 but later became a centre of Scottish, Jacobite loyalties under the Earls of Derwentwater. After the 1715 uprising, Viscount Langley and his brother, Charles, were beheaded on Tower Hill for their supposed treason. Those who could not rise to the castle-dwelling ranks sought safety where they could. Parsons and members of the local squirearchy had their pele towers, like Sizergh in the Lake District, Nappa Hall in Wensleydale and the Parson's Pele at Corbridge. It is also said that some church towers, like the one at Bedale in the Yorkshire Dales, served as refuges.

Built in 1350, Langley Castle was in the forefront of Anglo-Scottish warfare until its owners were beheaded at Tower Hill after the 1715 Jacobite uprising.

Nappa Hall in Wensleydale, a pele tower.

Raids could be invasions sanctioned by a monarch, major incursions masterminded by members of great feudal dynasties, like the Douglases from Scotland or the Percys from Northumberland, or they might be opportunistic overnight intrusions by a small pack of reivers. The damage caused was immense, although it is difficult to assess the toll on villages. The destruction imposed on market towns and great churches was normally recorded in some detail. Villages, however, were the relatively insignificant chattels of their feudal masters and their burning seldom troubled the scribes. All that one may find may be a terse record that a place has been relieved of tax in the year of its destruction. The Scots fell upon countrysides that were, as their own must have been, ravaged by torrential rain and famine, as described in Chapter 6. Following the English defeat at Bannockburn in 1314, a further defeat at Myton-on-Swale came in 1319, when 300 clergymen who had taken up arms were said to have been killed, while in 1322, a smaller scale English defeat took place at Byland. In 1318, Scottish invaders burned the town of Knaresborough under the gaze of the garrison established in the king's castle there. Some 140 of the 160 houses were said to have been burned. In the 1320s, the threat from the north was considered so great that Hull was fortified, and the deepest Scottish raid reached Pontefract, on the threshold of the Midlands. The old castle town of Appleby-in-Westmorland, located inside a meander loop of the River Eden, was exposed to cross-border raiding. A raid in 1388 destroyed the town. Appleby had its commerce and Knaresborough has its armaments and textile makers, its royal castle and its function as an administrative centre for the huge royal hunting Forest. Such places could be reduced to ashes but would surely rise again.

During their forays into North Yorkshire in 1318-22, the Scottish raiders seem to have been attracted to villages in the vicinity of the royal hunting park of Haverah, to the west of Knaresborough. Churches and religious houses had no immunity and the Church of Pannal, also in the Knaresborough locality, was burned. In 1318 the friary of St Robert in the town was fired and the king granted a remission of taxes to the friars. In 1320, a combination of Scottish raiding and murrain amongst its cattle caused the community of Bolton Priory in Wharfedale to abandon their monastery for five years. The entry in the *Lanercost Chronicle*, recording the burning of the 140 houses in Knaresborough, also recorded that houses had been burned in nearly every township in the vast Forest of Knaresborough. It also indicated the way in which countryfolk responded to such attacks and told of the intruders '… searching the woods… whither the people had fled for refuge with their cattle, they took away the cattle.' Otherwise, the burning of farmsteads, hamlets and even villages went largely unrecorded. They could be rebuilt and re-tenanted if necessary and there is little reason to believe that permanent extinctions were anything other than very few indeed.

One of the more credible casualties of war is Leake, in North Yorkshire, though its best link with Scottish raiding concerns the hoard of coins found here and dating mainly from the raid of Edward I. Presumably they were buried when a raid threatened. Leake has one of those churches linked with legends of satanic intervention, it being suggested that attempts to build a church atop neighbouring Borrowby Bank failed when the materials were mysteriously removed each night to the site of the surviving church. Such legends are found in various places, though their meaning is uncertain. In local legend too, Leake was an Anglo-Saxon town that was destroyed by Danes, and the locality was certainly devastated by the Normans. The Danish-based folklore claims that in Danes' Lane, near the churchyard, the women of Leake massacred as many as 500 Danes on one night – perhaps a folk echo of the St Brice's Day massacre of Danish settlers in England in AD 1002? The Church of St Mary is partly Norman, but incorporates Saxon material from a predecessor. Stone coffins that were periodically unearthed by gravediggers seem to tell of people of high status in the parish. More puzzlingly, during drainage work on the churchyard in 1852, a jumbled mass of human bones was discovered. Whether the unfortunates were casualties thrown into a hurriedly-dug plague pit or the dead from an unspecified battle, one cannot tell. The evidence of the church suggests the presence of a Saxon/English community, with the English recovering after the devastation inflicted on the region by the Normans and expanding to provide a sizable congregation to support a substantial church. What went wrong in the closing century or so of the Middle Ages is uncertain. Raiding, famine, plague and clearances presented so many unwelcome possibilities, and all were present in this locality.

Pickworth in Rutland is another strange case. All that remains of the church is the arch that might almost have been re-erected as an eye-catcher. Local legend and reports of a mass grave suggest that the village was destroyed by soldiers fleeing the Battle of Losecoat Field. The battle was the consequence of an uprising in Lincolnshire led by Lord Welles. The rebels were intercepted on the Old North Road about five miles from Stamford and defeated by a Yorkist army under Edward IV. The battle took place in March 1470, while Pickworth was not mentioned again after 1491. Even so, the region is strewn with the corpses of village victims of the Tudor sheep enclosures (see Chapter 8) and so caution is advised. Some ninety-nine local people paid the tax in 1377, so the downfall of Pickworth seems to have been abrupt, though seemingly occurring some years after the battle. The deserted Medieval village of Hardwick lies directly to the north of the battlefield.

A northern graveyard

The Scottish raids on the North of England had caused a temporary rather than a permanent destruction of villages. When these raids took place, an area of the North considerably larger than that ravaged by the late-Medieval war-bands and reivers was still carrying the scars of a far more systematic and ruthless invasion that had had genocide rather than plunder as its objective. The culprit was the king, William of Normandy, and the context was his frustration at a sequence of rebellions in the North of England. The defeat of King Harold's Anglo-Danish Godwinson dynasty at Hastings in 1066 broke the old, indigenous links of kinship between the English and their leaders. It gave, to most villagers, landlords who were both new and foreign.

It seems that the Norman invaders made their first marks on the English landscape in the weeks immediately before and after their victory at Hastings in 1066. At this time, the old estates had not been reallocated and the Norman army had no formal system of feudal obligations that could be exploited to extract food from those who produced it. Therefore, they must simply have seized whatever grain, peas, beans and livestock they could find, employing such violence as was necessary to remove it from the native farming communities. One might imagine that the effects of pillaging, even the effects of the calculated ravaging of royal estates and a burning of home-steads and settlements employed to draw King Harold into battle, would have been short-lived. However, two decades later, in 1086, *Domesday Book* revealed a trail of estates in the south of the kingdom, first occupied by the Normans that still seemed to display the scars of wasting and pillaging.

This destruction seems almost insignificant in comparison to the vengeance inflicted on the North. The Conqueror feared that the North could break out of his control, perhaps forming an independent country centred on York and supported by Scottish and Viking allies. In 1068, the popular northern earls, Edwin and Morcar, led a revolt against new taxation policies. William marched north and garrisoned the city, only to learn of the massacre of the Norman garrison in the following year. A re-taking of the city and massacre of dissidents soon followed, though in the autumn of 1069 there was another northern revolt with Danish support and a lesser uprising in Staffordshire. York was occupied again by the Normans, who negotiated for the Danish army to sail back home from its base in the Humber estuary leaving the dissident English and Danish-speaking communities to face their fates. William seems to have realised that whenever he withdrew from the North, and especially if he returned to visit his beloved estates in Normandy, a northern insurrection was likely. The 'Harrying of the North' from 1069-71 was his response.

It was a systematic and efficient campaign of genocide that was launched against northerners, whether they be rebels, bondsmen, women or infants. Perhaps the most striking aspect of the Harrying that comes down to us across the centuries is the fact that people living in the waning years of Viking attacks – people who were familiar with the brutality of war and the injustice of fate – were still shocked by the awfulness that the Norman armies perpetrated. A contemporary, Hugh the Chanter, told that York and the entire surrounding district perished by '… the French, famine and flames'. Symeon of Durham wrote that the harried lands lay desolate for nine years, the survivors being obliged to eat dogs and cats and the countrysides inhabited only by wild animals and bandits. He described how the Conqueror devastated the North throughout the winter and slaughtered the people, and told of the horrors of observing corpses rotting in the thoroughfares, '… for no one survived to cover them with earth, all having perished by the sword and starvation, or left the land of their fathers because of hunger.'

The most important source of information on these hideous times, Orderic Vitalis, (1075-c.1143), would have been just a small boy when the events took place. The son of a Norman father and an English mother, he was sent to the abbey at St Evroul in Normandy when he was merely ten years old. Wrenched from his family, he proved a credit to his order and established his own monastery at Shrewsbury. Working in the tradition of Bede, he had a mission to record history so, in 1123-41 he wrote an *Ecclesiastical History* that was largely concerned with the reign of

William I. Unusually, perhaps influenced by the plight of his mother's nation, he mounted a forceful critique of William for his instigation of the Harrying, deriving his account from a biography of the king by William of Poitiers, that was subsequently lost. He wrote:

> Nowhere else had William shown such cruelty. Shamefully he succumbed to this vice, for he made no effort to restrain his fury and punished the innocent with the guilty. In his anger he commanded that all crops and herds, chattels and food of every kind should be brought together and burned to ashes with consuming fire, so that the whole region north of the Humber might be stripped of all means of sustenance. In consequence so serious a scarcity was felt in England, and so terrible a famine fell upon the humble and defenceless populace, that more than 100,000 Christian folk of both sexes, young and old alike, perished of hunger.

Thus he wrote in recording the events of 1069, but he returned to the Harrying later in his text in an account of the death of the Conqueror, when, one imagines in rather fanciful terms, Orderic Vitalis has him racked by guilt and self-accusation that he did:

> … tremble my friends when I reflect on the grievous sins which burden my conscience, and now, about to be summoned by the awful tribunal of God, I know not what I ought to do. I was bred to arms from my childhood, and am stained from the rivers of blood I have shed… It is out of my power to count all the injuries that I caused during the sixty-four years of my troubled life.
>
>   … I caused the death of thousands by starvation and war, especially in Yorkshire… In a mad fury I descended on the English of the north like a raging lion, and ordered that their homes and crops and all their equipment and furnishings should be burnt at once and their great flocks of sheep and cattle slaughtered everywhere. So I chastised a great multitude of men and women with the lash of starvation and, alas! Was the cruel murderer of many thousands, both young and old.

As with most great historical events, the Harrying of the North has experienced its share of debunking, though in fact there are few events of the eleventh century that are so well documented, both in the archives and in the countryside. *Domesday Book* depicts northern countrysides and estates that were still crippled around fifteen years after the terrible events. Some of the controversy concerns the use in *Domesday* of the word 'waste', which can denote both pillaged and worthless land and commons. However, the book's many valuations that compare the value of estates in the time of King Edward (1042-66) and in 1086 leave no doubt about the widespread wasting of the northern territories. If the chroniclers presented the statistics of 100,000 victims in a rhetorical manner, the tax assessors compiling *Domesday Book* were not at liberty to employ rhetoric. It seems that Domesday Yorkshire may have contained only a quarter as many people and plough beasts as had been there on the eve of the Conquest. If this were so, Orderic Vitalis would have underestimated the carnage considerably.

The best landscape evidence for the extermination of villages and their communities derives not so much from what is missing as from what is there: hundreds of villages with precisely planned and rather stereotyped layouts. The most convincing scenario on offer is that in which the old English villages – many with sprawling, untidy layouts including farmsteads within their own paddocks – were firstly obliterated in the phases of scorched earth and genocide, and later replaced by purpose-built agricultural dormitories as estate owners struggled to get their lands back to work. There are grounds to think that bondsmen from outside were brought in to fill the vacuum. The historian, Trevor Rowley, has pointed out that about 370 places in Yorkshire were first recorded between 1067 and 1349, with one in six villages in the region coming into existence in the post-Conquest period. In the Vale of York, around the York focus for anti-Norman dissent where the Harrying seems to have most severe, the great majority of villages have aspects of planning (like straight building lines, right-angled boundaries or tofts behind dwellings that terminate in line at back lanes) showing in their plans, even almost 1,000 years after their creation. Further north, in Co. Durham, around two thirds of the villages, similarly, have planned layouts.

The corpses of the earlier villages, those that perished forever in the Harrying, are rather harder to detect. However, the planned Norman villages quite often contain parts or large portions of pre-Conquest churches, as at Middleton, near Pickering. This suggests that pre-existing churches often provided the nuclei for the new villages. Thus, it may well be that the traces of the Anglo-Danish villages may sometimes lie beneath their Norman successors. Had *Domesday Book* been compiled just twenty years earlier, then we would have the basis for a detailed inventory of what the awful Harrying of the North destroyed. Yet even without this, the accounts of the eleventh-century chroniclers, the repeated reference to waste on northern estates in *Domesday Book* and the landscape evidence of wholesale village redesign in the North all tell a truly gruesome story. The number of Anglo-Danish and English villages and hamlets destroyed by the Harrying will never be known, but in Yorkshire alone it must certainly run into hundreds.

CHAPTER FOUR

CURSED ARE THE MEEK

Heaven in mind

The landscape detective who is seeking to win an understanding of the patterns embedded in the countryside from earlier ages should try to enter the minds of those who made them. All human actions involve certain systems of reason and logic, even if those employed are ill-judged, bizarre or convoluted. The British heritage of prehistoric monuments is, as yet, poorly understood and the interpretations provided for features like stone circles or megalithic tombs are those currently fashionable in the seminar rooms of Departments of Archaeology. Of these explanations, the only near certainty is that soon, today's conventional wisdom will be deemed passé and will be replaced by some other short-lived consensus doctrine. However, if we could resurrect the people whose inspiration shaped Stonehenge, Callanish or Newgrange then they would provide us with accounts of precisely why things were done in the ways that they were – accounts that would probably be surprising, perhaps a little outlandish, but entirely self-consistent. Suddenly, the mysteries of yesterday would all become quite lucid – and doubtless all concerned would wonder why the answers had not occurred sooner. In other words, things make sense to those who make them even if their *raisons d être* prove elusive to those who follow.

Thinking is the key to unlocking the secrets of the historic landscape, but it can only be thinking that is intense, prolonged and informed by the facts. Concocting nonsense about crop circles, the Knights Templar, ley-lines, Merovingians and other lucrative items of mumbo-jumbo does not constitute serious enquiry. A very useful form of thinking is one in which one seeks to interpret patterns by seeing the landscape through the eyes of those who made it. If we think, for example, of landscape parks and of the kinds of people who commissioned them, it emerges that the flaunting of status, the trumpeting of a dynasty's rise or the demonstration of its antiquity, were generally more powerful motivations than any aesthetic considerations. However, aesthetics and fashion helped to establish the refinement of the family concerned and so helped to promote status. Stripped of any dynastic, hierarchical or aesthetic ambitions, the park designed by the average aristocrat would probably have comprised a cockpit for gambling on cock fights, a cricket field, also for gambling, limitless lawns for galloping thoroughbreds across and a racecourse. Statues and symmetry might easily have been overlooked.

Where Christian religious matters are concerned the task should be easier, for we retain roughly the same Bible as that which guided Medieval and Dark Age churchmen. The testaments that we use are around 2,000 years old, while those scrutinised by monks of the Plantagenet period had only circulated for around 1,200 years. Since they stood closer in time to the birth of the Christian era, we might expect that these monks must also have stood closer to the gospels and have pursued purer vocations. Modern attitudes emphasise the New Testament and the code of ethics that it contains. Most Christians emphasise the fundamental importance of loving one's neighbour, turning the other cheek to adversaries, reverence for the meek and the virtues of honest, unadorned life. However, when we look at the Medieval religious orders we see all these defining values flouted. We find that the supposedly subversive religion of outsiders, one that had contributed countless martyrs to their persecutors in the Roman Empire, had become locked into partnerships with the feudal ruling establishments of Europe and was shoring-up the causes of inequality and war. Dual standards endure and living by the sword is the practice of those who most decry it.

One might conclude that the bishops, monks, abbots and priors had reneged on their religious values and betrayed their Church. Most of them would probably have been deeply appalled and scandalised to hear such a claim. In their minds, they were loyal servants of their Church who employed measures of pragmatism to allow the faith to endure in a turbulent and threatening world. Over generations, churchmen had managed to twist and nudge their doctrines to make their lives compatible with success in unjust, class-ridden and often unstable and dangerous societies. The spin-doctors of the ecclesiastical mind had worked their magic until there were monks who could stand by benignly as their lay brethren did their bidding and dragged peasant paupers from their homes. They could sit enfolded in a blissful silence as, nearby, horses were harnessed to drag down the frames of wretched homes, or they could beam in admiration as they watched their abbot course, spear and slash the throats of gentle deer on lawns that were yesterday's village pastures.

Wretched were the meek

Lay communities were sometimes evicted from monastic lands for reasons of simple practicality: they intruded upon spaces intended for monastic farms (granges) or for deer parks. They were also evicted for reasons that seem more sinister and very deeply at variance with Christian principles: because the poverty-stricken villagers were seen as a severe form of social pollution whose mere presence contaminated the sanctity of a chosen site. This latter view was associated with the Cistercian order. The order was founded by St Robert, Abbot of Molesme, in Cîteaux (*Cistercium*) in France in 1098. At first, they first formed a seemingly pure and austere alternative to the ancient Benedictines, who were considered to have become lax, and the Cluniacs, with their focus on ceremony and liturgy. The first Cistercians sought an exacting return to monastic life as it had been in the day of St Benedict (AD 480-543). An Englishman, Stephen Harding, Abbot of Cîteaux from 1109-33, played a crucial role in shaping Cistercian ideals. Under St Bernard of Clairvaulx, (1090-1153) the white monks, in their habits of unbleached wool and their quest for lives of rigorous austerity, enjoyed great respect and popularity in continental Europe. They found success and learned how to cultivate it, so that by the close of the twelfth century, more than 500 of their houses had been established and half as many again would follow before the Medieval era was out. Strongly influenced by the conservative doctrines of St Bernard, the Cistercians placed great importance upon farming and the hard, open-air life. Their rules prohibited the establishment of monasteries in cities, by castles or on manors. In their rural missions they were assisted by their very extensive use of *conversi* or lay brethren, minimally educated workers who shared their houses and undertook the hard work. Up to 500 lay brethren may have been accommodated in and around Rievaulx Abbey in the twelfth century, representing a phenomenally potent workforce. Before very long, the commercial success of farming (primarily, but not entirely, shepherding) and the appeal of their ideals to powerful lay benefactors produced remarkable successes – with the expansion and development of Cistercian estates underlying the corruption of the earlier ideals. By 1335, Pope Benedict XII, a Cistercian, was seen attempting to restore the austerity and integrity of the order, though by this time the monks were facing ridicule in England for their corruption and avarice.

Learning of the potential of England for monastic development, Bernard of Clairvaulx wrote to Henry I (1100-1135), 'In your land there is possession of my Lord and your Lord... I have arranged for it to be taken back, and have sent men from my army who will (if it is not displeasing to you) seek it out, recover it and restore it with a firm hand'. Cistercians arrived at Waverley in Surrey in 1128, but the soft southern heartlands of England offered little of the rigour that had so successfully established the order's image and success. However, a couple of hundred miles to the north lay a country still, in places, desolate from the terrible Norman Harrying of the North half a century earlier. In 1131, Walter Espec, the Lord of Helmsley and a religious activist who had established Kirkham Priory for the Augustinians, planted a colony of thirty Cistercian monks at Rievaulx in the Rye valley and the epic of the Cistercians in Britain began. A dispute at the Benedictine abbey of St Mary's in York in 1132 resulted in the departure of thirteen dissidents. They settled on the fringe of the Dales in the Skell valley on land donated by Thurstan, the Archbishop of York, and thus another community, Fountains, in a supposedly rigorous setting was established. As the Cistercian houses proliferated, so more monks and lay brethren were recruited and as many of the monks took their names from their native estates and townships, we can see that they were largely northerners from the more privileged of social backgrounds.

Leaders of the order had already discovered the image-building values of rigour and self-sacrifice and various 'foundation myths' were carefully cultivated in order to exaggerate or, indeed, invent, the hardships undergone by the founding monks. If potential benefactors concluded that only divine intervention had allowed the community to survive and prosper, then this was to be encouraged. In the case of Jervaulx Abbey in Wensleydale, which nestles in its fertile vale, it was said that John de Kinstan and a dozen monks left Bolton Priory, in Wharfedale, in 1156, became lost in a dense forest but were guided to Yorevale (Jervaulx) by a vision of the Virgin and Child. However, despite this colourful myth, Jervaulx seems to be the daughter of a daughter house of Rievaulx, while Bolton Priory was an establishment of Augustinian Canons, not Cistercians. Moreover, an archaeological survey by English Heritage at the end of the twentieth century showed that far from being established in a wilderness, Jervaulx Abbey was planted in working farmland with roads, ploughlands and dwellings then in place. Presumably, the monks removed the previous occupants and took over a place that was far from being a desolate waste.

Rather than being placed in the hearts of dangerous wildernesses – locations St Bernard described as '… fearful desert places' – the great Cistercian abbeys were sited in settled, cultivated areas or just on the fringes of such lands. St Bernard described Rievaulx as an outpost that his monks would occupy and restore. To the contemporary Cistercian chronicler, Serlo, it was a place of horror and great solitude. In fact, this was a rather pleasant setting in the Hambleton Hills to the west of the upland of the North York Moors and populated by settled agricultural communities. This 'topographical demonisation' served several purposes.

It led to the belief that the Cistercians were fulfilling their pledges to return to the fundamentals of ancient Benedictine austerity and to experience the hardships endured by the early hermits in their mountains and deserts. If the visitors found these places to be rather tame and inviting they begged the retort that they had been wildernesses until the remarkable energies, sacrifices and labours of the monks pacified them and made them fruitful. This reminds me of the myths perpetrated about Native Americans by later waves of European settlers in the eastern USA. The seemingly primeval appearance of the woods was attributed to their virgin status, rather than to the extermination of all the indigenous communities that had previously used and occupied them.

Much was made of the hardships, some doubtless real, experienced by the starving pioneers who founded Fountains Abbey. It was told how they had huddled through their first winter under a leafless elm, yet within a generation the abbey would be the hub of a rich and expanding estate and be wielding immense political influence. The lay villagers, living at places like Herleshow and Cayton, less than a brisk stroll away, did not accord with this image. Firstly, they were associated with social pollution, but secondly and more deviously, the presence of any time-mellowed settlement on the doorstep of an abbey must contradict foundation myths about the monks' pacification of a desolate wilderness. It is a strange wilderness that contains villages and village tillage and a strange myth that invites one to believe in privations endured amongst dwellings, meadows and barley fields. Not many mountain hermits could inhale the wood smoke from village fires, listen to the sounds of children at play and watch the women go nutting.

Kirkstall Abbey (now in a suburb of Leeds) was originally established at Barnoldswick, near Colne, where the feudal community was evicted and the abbot paved the way for Cistercian piety by pulling down the village church. Meaux Abbey was a great Medieval Cistercian foundation, though its estates were devastated when the waters of the Humber estuary invaded them during the climatic deterioration of the later Medieval centuries. The Cistercians derived their estates by bequests from nobles who were usually anxious to atone for sins and save their souls from eternal damnation. Such concerns focussed the mind of William le Gros, who admitted to being both too old and too gross to redeem his fate by travelling to the Holy Land as a pilgrim. He was, therefore, an easy target for a monk, Adam of Fountains, who persuaded him not only to donate land for a new daughter abbey of Fountains, but to hand over the best portion of his estate. It so happened that Adam was engaged in enclosing land for a deer park in this choice area around St Nary's Hill, so his feelings on parting with it may have been mixed. Monastic evictions and deer parks became

Fountains Abbey.

the greatest threats to village life in the centuries following the Norman Conquest and both were attracted to lands partly emptied and communities weakened by the Harrying.

There is one story of village removal that is as strange and seemingly as improbable as any foundation myth. In this case, the monks concerned had travelled far, originating in a colony of monks that left Furness Abbey, a Savignac foundation, in 1134 and had founded a house at Calder, in Cumberland, in the following year. However, four years later, Scottish raiders ravaged the county and the monks returned to Furness, where, for unknown reasons, they were rejected. Then the colonists headed for York, hoping to find favour with Archbishop Thurstan, who had assisted the founders of Fountains Abbey. On the way to York they encountered an official of the noblewoman Gundreda d'Aubigny whose son, Roger de Mowbray, had estates in Nidderdale and the Thirsk region and became their patron. Roger endowed them with numerous lands and they were settled beside a hermitage at Hood.

By 1142, the first Byland Abbey had been established in Rye Dale on a site close to Rievaulx Abbey and it had established its first grange at Wildon. As tended to be the case, the arrival of the monastic community was the occasion for the removal of a lay village. These villagers were unusually fortunate, for instead of being put on the road they were re-housed in a purpose-built settlement, Old Byland. Then things became complicated, for the proximity of the two substantial but separate communities of monks and lay brethren produced problems. One of these was the confusion caused by the tolling of two different sets of bells which were issuing conflicting commands. Byland Abbey had to go, and so in 1147 the monks claimed a new site, also on the de Mowbray estates, about five miles away. This move endured, with the much-travelled community being absorbed into the Cistercian order. Old Byland village was built on an elevated site on the plateau of the Hambleton Hills to a neat and simple square plan around the core formed by a rectangular green. Like its predecessor, it was furnished with a church and after the trauma of the removal it proved remarkably stable. The visitor today would have no difficulty in navigating around the present village using the map drawn by Christopher Saxton in 1598 – a map that doubtless closely mirrored the original village layout.

The first phase of Cistercian evictions concerned the removal of settlements that lay, according to Cistercian values, too close to the site of a new abbey. The ruthless efficiency of monks of the order in acquiring estates and then developing them to their greatest commercial efficiency won them many enemies. The satirist, Walter Map, who lived in the years around 1200, seems to have been embroidering a true story when he told how monks (who he referred to in code as 'Hebrew brethren') slaughtered a knight, his family and household. The wife fled, but when she returned three days later, all traces of dwellings had gone, the old field patterns had been erased, the trees felled and the land had been ploughed over. This seems to echo the fates of the villages and hamlets that lay in the path of monastic expansion. The contemporary chronicler and critic of the Cistercians, Gerald of Wales (1147-1223), seems to have been reluctant to attribute the assault on helpless villagers to anything but the monk's misplaced desires to be generous to their guests and to give alms freely to the poor – but he could see the injustices that were being done. He wrote:

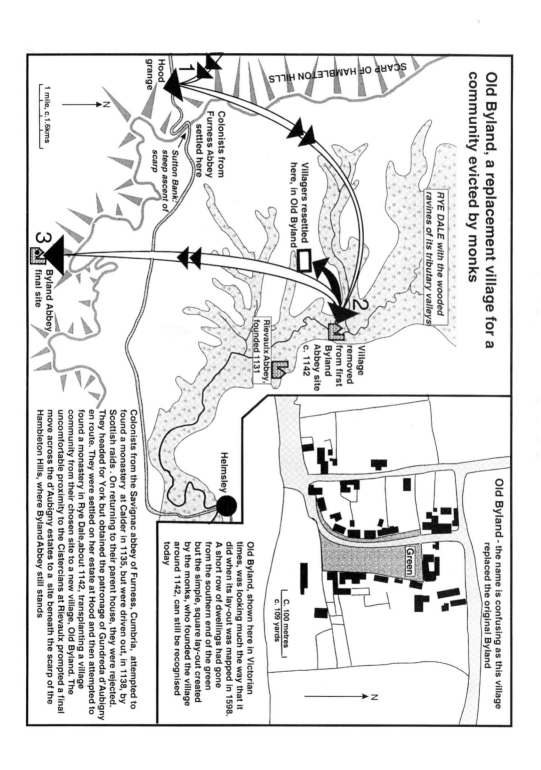

Old Byland, a replacement village for a community evicted by monks

SCARP OF HAMBLETON HILLS

RYE DALE with the wooded ravines of its tributary valleys

Hood grange

1

Colonists from Furness Abbey settled here

Sutton Bank: steep ascent of scarp

1 mile, c.1.6kms

N

Villagers resettled here, in Old Byland

Village removed from first Byland Abbey site c. 1142

2

Rievaulx Abbey, founded 1131

3

Byland Abbey final site

Helmsley

Colonists from the Savignac abbey of Furness, Cumbria, attempted to found a monastery at Calder in 1135, but were driven out, in 1138, by Scottish raids . On returning to their parent house, they were rejected. They headed for York but obtained the patronage of Gundreda d'Aubigny en route. They were settled on her estate at Hood and then attempted to found a monastery in Rye Dale,about 1142, transplanting a village community from their chosen site to a new village, Old Byland. The uncomfortable proximity to the Cistercians at Rievaulx prompted a final move across the d'Aubigny estates to a site beneath the scarp of the Hambleton Hills, where Byland Abbey still stands

Old Byland - the name is confusing as this village replaced the original Byland

Green

N

c. 100 metres
c. 109 yards

Old Byland, shown here in Victorian times, was looking much the way that it did when its lay-out was mapped in 1598. A short row of dwellings had gone from the southern end of the green but the simple, square lay-out created by the monks, who founded the village around 1142, can still be recognised today

What shall they answer who seize other men's goods and have given them away in alms? They will say: 'Oh Lord, in thy name we have done charitable deeds, we have fed the poor, clothed the naked, received the stranger at the gate.' The Lord will answer: 'You speak of what you have given away, but you do not mention the fact that you have stolen it in the first place. You are mindful of those whom you have fed, but you have forgotten those whom you have destroyed'.

Byland gained a special reputation for avarice, but Fountains seems to have accounted for several older settlements near to its abbey site. Cayton village lay about three miles to the south of the abbey and was removed and replaced by a grange about ten years after the monks gained control of the estate there in 1135. Soon, the abbey was pressurising its feudal neighbours in Ripley to surrender rights of way and damming their boundary stream to create a large fishpond for the abbey beside the former village. Herleshow lay closer to the abbey precinct at the foot of How Hill, a prominent landmark that signals the proximity of the great monastery. According to Dr R.A. Donkin, six villages and hamlets were probably destroyed, and up to sixteen more may have been removed by Fountains. These removals were normally terminal, with the village lands being absorbed into the abbey estates and often being created into a grange worked by a small squad of lay brothers. Baldersby, near Ripon, seems to have had a very lucky revival. The village appears to have been levelled by the monks of Fountains and converted into a grange. However, around the time, in 1336, that an impoverished abbey estate was ravaged by Scots, a monastic rehabilitation of the lands at Baldersby seemed unsustainable and so a resettlement of the site by a lay community was sanctioned. The reborn village persists to this day.

The second eviction stage occurred as successfully-established Cistercian abbeys attracted generous endowments from nobles, some of them bullied into parting with lands but most of them happy to grant resources and estates in the hopes that their much-sullied souls might yet be saved. Often, the new holdings were worked directly by the abbey, developing them as granges cultivated by a handful of lay brethren under the guidance of a monk. On the granges the social divisions of the lay world were perpetuated, with the monks tending to be drawn from the gentry and the lay brothers coming from the ranks of the bondsmen and being provided with the most frugal education. In the more remote territories, the granges sometimes controlled subsidiary lodges. This creation of granges led to a second wave of clearances affecting the lay villages that preceded the granges on their sites, though in cases like Cayton, the two modes of destruction overlapped. The village of Meaux, just north of Hull, was

East Witton – the village removed by the Cistercians of nearby Jervaulx Abbey. The uniform house style results from a rebuilding of the village at the start of the nineteenth century.

converted into a grange by the Cistercian abbey that took over its site and name. One unusual case where a replacement village is known to have been provided was East Witton, in Wensleydale. Here, the site of nearby Jervaulx Abbey is known to have been cleared of settlement when the abbey was founded. East Witton survived and became a flourishing village standing just outside the pale of the abbey's home park and by its Church of St Martin. During the thirteenth century, Jervaulx Abbey steadily increased its holdings in the surrounding countryside and gained control of almost all its parish. It is probable that at the start of the fourteenth century, the existing village was removed. A replacement was built further from the abbey on a track leading to a crossing on the River Cover. This new East Witton still preserves the layout provided by the monks, having an elongated green pointing eastwards towards the abbey, lined on both sides by dwellings with their plots or tofts running back to terminate together neatly at boundary lines. The East Witton that is seen today has pleasant but uniform houses and a new church, all commissioned by the Earl of Ailesbury in commemoration of the jubilee of George III in 1809. The underlying pattern is of about 1400, with the special chartering of a market and fair for the village in 1307 representing an unusual degree of patronage by the Cistercian founders.

A number of factors made the North of England such a magnet for the Cistercians. The Harrying had created empty spaces and yet the very strong pre-Conquest Benedictine presence left powerful religious undercurrents

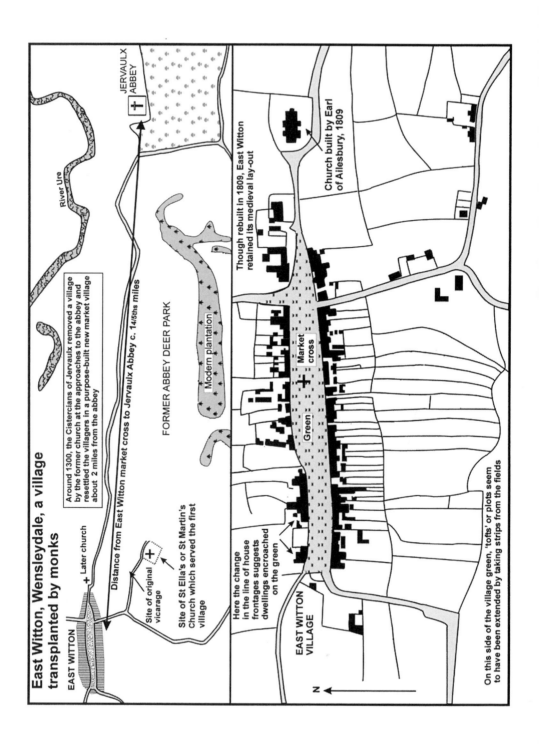

East Witton, Wensleydale, a village transplanted by monks

Around 1300, the Cistercians of Jervaulx removed a village by the former church at the approaches to the abbey and resettled the villagers in a purpose-built new market village about 2 miles from the abbey

EAST WITTON

+ Later church

Site of original vicarage

Site of St Ella's or St Martin's Church which served the first village

River Ure

JERVAULX ABBEY

FORMER ABBEY DEER PARK

Modern plantation

Distance from East Witton market cross to Jervaulx Abbey c. 1⁴/₅ths miles

Though rebuilt in 1809, East Witton retained its medieval lay-out

Church built by Earl of Ailesbury, 1809

Here the change in the line of house frontages suggests dwellings encroached on the green

Market cross

Green

EAST WITTON VILLAGE

N

On this side of the village green, 'tofts' or plots seem to have been extended by taking strips from the fields despite the destruction wrought by Viking invasions. The Norman North also contained more than its share of magnates seeking to make their marks and save their souls. The generous levels of the endowments of land that were given will have undermined many incomes, yet the association with the monks did provide important contacts and access to the centres of power. The Cistercians were not confined to the lands north of the Humber, and neither were their evictions, which also took place in Lancashire, Nottinghamshire and Leicestershire. The West Grange of the Cistercian abbey at Pipewell in Northamptonshire stood on the site of a hamlet. Other orders also evicted communities, though less frequently or systematically. The Benedictines of Crowland Abbey in Lincolnshire were involved in depopulating their far-off estates at Elmington in Northamptonshire in the fourteenth century, the conversion of tenanted lands to sheep pasture being the motive. The monks of Chalcombe priory seem to have followed the same course at the same time at Appletree, also in that county. Meanwhile, in neighbouring Oxfordshire, the Augustinians of Osney Abbey were involved in depopulating land for sheep runs on their estates at Hampton Gay and Fulwell, whilst the Benedictines of Eynsham depopulated lands at Brookend and Caswell. There were a great many other depopulations by monks of various orders.

The story of the monastic assault on 'Village England', and the lands beyond, contains warnings that we might still do well to heed. It reminds us of the frightening might of institutions: those institutions which, by controlling our behaviour and reorganising our values, can persuade us that values of right and wrong, duty and compliance, conscience and belief are flexible and can be controlled by the prevailing winds of power. It tells us that that the promotion of a seemingly worthy organisation can be made to appear to be a goal superior to the honouring of the dictates of one's conscience. It also shows that when institutional advancement is allowed to become the paramount objective then all manners of evil and injustice may follow. The abbots, bishops and priors had risen to the tops of their institutional worlds and yet they presided over organisations that were as corrupt and unjust as they were successful. The homeless, penniless and half-starved friar was a far better ethical role model than most members of the Medieval ecclesiastical establishment. Any thoughtful person who was living in the twelfth and thirteenth centuries must have been aware of the crushing social pressures and frightening powers of coercion that were being mobilised in support of establishment goals. In this age of spun news, invasive government and diminishing rights, these lessons are as relevant as they ever have been.

CHAPTER FIVE

A SPORTING MISCHANCE

One man's meat

Sometimes, the mist hung over the summit of Baile Hill and at other times, when the wind whooshed into the iron furnace, the hill was streaked with smoke. Normally, though, the conical hill offered a prospect across a rumpled patchwork of working countryside. This landscape was so very varied. Lordships marched with royal estates; monasteries and priories glowered across their boundaries, sometimes distrustfully and sometimes with greed; the Knights Hospitallers had their 'commanderies' slotted between the lay manors; there were Honours and berewicks and Liberties, and all the kinds of feudal holdings than one might imagine. One factor energised the entire landscape, irrespective of the identity of the owners, their titles, privileges or tenures. The energy came from the sweat of the bondsmen and smaller free tenants. They formed the overwhelming majority of the population, owned next to nothing and bore the weight of feudalism and the unfurling panoply of chivalry on their shoulders.

The windy hilltop that had attracted the gust-hungry smelter was girdled by the slumped ramparts and silted ditches of an ancient hill fort. This was not the only stronghold to be seen hereabouts, for if one peered down among the cornfields, woods and meadows there was the pimple on the plain that was a Norman castle. Two centuries had passed, and so the village stories about its origins had become ragged and improbable. They were accurate insofar as they recalled the arrival of one of William's conquerors, almost alone in a watchful and unwelcoming setting. They told how he and his few mercenaries had dragged the men from their houses and forced them to heap-up an earthen mound and crown it with a palisade of stakes. This motte soon gained a defensive compound or bailey with some stores, stables and a manor house, but though it might cow the villagers, it never was much of a castle. Now it had a new owner. There had been one of those stillborn rebellions – the villagers were not sure what it was about – and their lord, suspected of plotting, had forfeited his estates as a result. 'So what?' thought the families of the bondsmen. A new name to learn, a new face to bob and bend to, that was all. This new man seemed to be one of the grander kind. He arrived with a string of palfreys and pack-horses, a mad-eyed warhorse, liveried servants and his own cooks. Moving like a slow, brightly-speckled serpent, the retinue could be seen weaving the lanes from miles away. When the lord stopped to chat and point, all stopped. From time to time there would be a longer pause as riders careered across the young corn or when a lady released her kestrel at a songbird. No sooner had the party arrived at the tired old castle than the lord set about giving orders in English and French. Villagers materialised in many shaded places and observed the gesticulations. Lost on none of them was the fact that when lords had plans, hard work for their tenants would shortly follow.

Soon, a reluctant village was hard at work. All the pressing work on shares in the common ploughland and meadow was set aside. Cattle broke into the green hay and gorged along with the bloated sheep. Eggs went uncollected, garden vegetables ran to seed and the whole village pulsed to the tune of complaints and resentment. To make matters worse, nobody had thought it necessary to explain what the changes were about. Villagers found themselves barrowing and basketing soil from one place and dumping it, seemingly without purpose, in another. All the while they could hear cows bawling to be milked. The shifting of earth had not lasted very long when a team of masons appeared and, after a measure of pacing, pointing and squinting along taught lengths of twine, began working on a new castle of stone. The mound of the old fortress was not trusted to bear the weight, so a new site was chosen nearby. The place did not seem to have much to commend it apart from a fine view and the villagers were not slow to recognise spots from which a good bowman could sweep the battlements. They could not have cared less about the problems of holding the castle, but were much more concerned about the presence of masons billeted in their houses and the threats this posed to their womenfolk. Those who thought themselves lucky to have been given one of the older men then found they were kept awake by their coughing, silicosis being the fate of most Medieval masons.

As the walls rose, orders came to excavate a new set of fishponds on higher ground, while the shifting of earth was creating a saucer-like depression around the new castle. Several villagers were very good at gauging levels, and had used their knowledge to convey water around the setting in carefully graded leets, drains and culverts. They were not slow to point out the absolute folly of the current operations, for the next time the river flooded, the environs of the castle would be inundated. The arrival of November proved them right – but it also vindicated the deductions of the clerk in charge of the works. For as the morning breeze wafted the rain clouds away, they saw the castle walls rearing up like silvery cliffs above the steely sheet of floodwater. The castle was mirrored in the lake, a fabulous Gibraltar, linked to the land by a slender, serpent-like causeway. This was an other-worldly experience every bit as stunning as going to the painted church, but village minds could not connect with the underlying mythology. They had not read the idylls of Arthur or listened to the troubadours. They could not locate the reality before their eyes in the context of Avalon, romance and courtly love.

And so the works went on. The highest level of the castle gained a hog-tooth pattern of crenulations, as though poised to take a bite out of the sky. It stood on an island within its silver lake – a lake that generations of later historians would mistake for a moat. The road that approached its causeway and drawbridge wove around the locality in a devious manner, so that in just one instant, visitors were confronted with the scenic tour de force of the lake-girt fortress. There were no hints, distant glimmers and peeps. At one moment one was riding through the pleasant lawns and tree clumps of the landscaped setting, while the next, one emerged from a grove and the scene filled the whole view ahead, a visual detonation, an arrival at Camelot.

The lord's family and his guests were housed in a suite of chambers on the south side of the castle. From windows rather larger than a military engineer would have preferred, or from the battlements above, they could gaze across the lake, shimmering as the approaching sunrays met the ripples, and towards the neat garden. This was placed on the sunny south side of the castle and was set out for dalliance, with bowers, turf benches and tubs for bathing. Beyond the garden there was a 'wilderness' of a less formal design, and then an expanse of lawn where the horses belonging to visiting retinues could graze.

Villagers had expected that, with the completion of the castle and its landscape, they might be allowed to tackle the many tasks that had accumulated. However, one task remained. The steward and a couple of servants were seen riding out with a bundle of hazel rods, pausing occasionally to set one in the ground. At dusk, the villagers stole out to see what was afoot. The rods formed a long, arcing chain. Some were set on the level, but others seemed to have been judiciously placed at the break of steep slopes and along the edges of outcrops. A few curious bondsmen followed the rods for a couple of hours, until the last few had melted into the night. They saw that the line of rods came back upon itself to mark out a great pear-shaped loop. Curiously, not only were the castle and a few dozen acres of farmland included within the loop, so too, at its narrower end, was their village.

Then the work began again. Immense ditches were dug around the inner face of the loop, while on the up-cast from the ditching, a solid fence of upright cleft oak palings was set. The logic behind the construction was clear to all, for while ramps set in certain places would allow a deer to leap the palings and get into the great enclosure, those deer inside could not breast the ditch and the bank with its paling, beyond. They were there to meet their fate

When the deer park was finished, the fate of the village was sealed. The new park, with its five-mile perimeter, had taken a massive bite out of the village wood pasture, ploughlands and meadows. Fewer tenants were now required. There was a little work for servants, though most of the erstwhile villagers were judged too uncouth to be seen around the hunt. One of the free tenants became the parker and he gave employment to a servant – but the rest of the community were either settled into hamlets elsewhere on the estate or put out on the road.

The parker's fortunate servant, looking out from his lodge on the loftiest swell of the park, saw his childhood home loose its thatch, saw the mud crumble and slump from its walls and saw a carter haul away the posts and beams for the castle hearth. Veils of smoke and swarms of flies hung over the other villages of the district, and in them, things went on much as before, and much as before that, too. He could picture each house and where it had stood. The features of every occupant of every dwelling in the village were fresh in his mind. He missed the gossip and grumbling and games. Yet outrage burned like a furnace in his innermost being. These things happened. You could not argue with fate. Lords were lords, after all.

The burden of the hunt

For all that they energised their world, the village toilers had little influence on fate. The events that shaped their lives owed much to their lords, but much, too, to the accidents of history. It is no wonder that fatalism was the cornerstone of peasant culture. Historical accidents were largely responsible for the facts that some communities might endure for generation after generation, while the villagers on the next estate or township might be evicted by monks, displaced by some castle-building operation or otherwise cast out at their lord's pleasure. This last phrase is more apt than one might imagine, for in the three centuries after the Norman Conquest, the lordly pursuit of pleasure accounted for an uncertain but not insignificant number of village demises. For quite some time, it has been known that several communities were removed during the Norman enlargement of the New Forest. Only recently has it been appreciated that the manipulation of countryside to compose more 'tasteful' scenery was not invented by the great landscapers of the eighteenth century. Rather, it was avidly pursued by the Medieval aristocracy and by the promoters of the ideal of courtly love. The Forest and the deer park were not isolated features of the countryside, but components of 'designed landscapes' – landscapes designed for pleasure and the proclamation of status. Sometimes, an existing village had no place in the idyllic vision.

In terms of Medieval blood-sporting, we have been taught to make a distinction between the Forests (not 'forests'), which were royal game reserves spanning many different kinds of terrain and land-use and thousands of acres; the chases of the greater nobles, and the enclosed deer parks of the greater and the lesser nobility. Forests were immense, had no walls, earthworks or palings to control the movements of game, but were subject to the Forest Law, which imposed restrictions on poaching and the urge to poach. The chases were also large and lacked peripheral defences, but were regulated by the courts of their feudal masters rather than by the Forest Law. Deer parks were smaller than Forests or chases and were bounded and confined. Their proliferation was regulated by the requirement for a 'license to empark'. The sale of such licenses provided the monarchs with useful revenues. Sometimes, the license to empark was preceded by a 'grant of free warren', which entitled the recipient to hunt small game, like foxes, on his own estate. The distinction between Forests, chases and deer parks is a handy one to bear in mind, though the Medieval documents show they were used rather interchangeably and with less discrimination than they are by the experts of today.

The establishment of Forests and the introduction of Forest Law soon entered into popular mythology as epitomising the cruel impositions of the Medieval kings on a servile peasantry. Yet, like some other aspects of Norman rule, they involved the formalisation and institutionalisation of practices already existing. Canute, an earlier conqueror of England, controlled hunting territories and fined those found poaching in them, while Edward the Confessor, the penultimate English king, had appointed Forest Wardens. In Saxon England there were some royal hunting reserves, but their nature is shadowy. *Domesday Book* records various places as *haia*, *haga* and *parcus*. Some of these will have been hunting parks, but the *haia* and *haga* places would sometimes be other sorts of hedged enclosures or just small woods. These names often survive today, in placenames like Hay-on-Wye, Haywards Heath and Roundhay. Saxon nobles could hunt boar, the shy roe deer of the woods and the red deer of the open land. The dappled fallow deer was the favourite game of the Normans and they reintroduced the animal to a land that it had not roamed since before the last glaciation. That deer were widespread in Medieval England is another myth. They shunned the clamour of the crowded village fields and were much scarcer than they are in the lonely countrysides of today. Deer were greatly valued and the gifts of Forest deer were a principal form of royal largesse granted

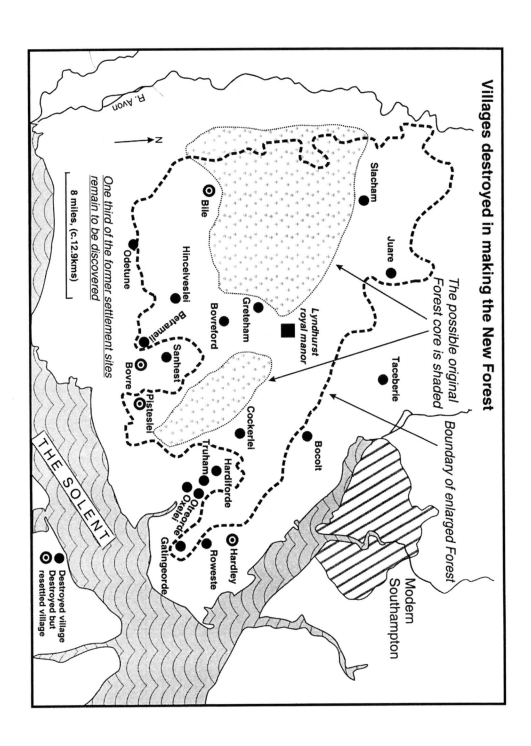

Villages destroyed in making the New Forest

The possible original Forest core is shaded

Boundary of enlarged Forest

Modern Southampton

THE SOLENT

R. Avon

N

8 miles, (c.12.9kms)

One third of the former settlement sites remain to be discovered

● Destroyed village
◉ Destroyed but resettled village

Slacham
Juare
Bile
Odetune
Hincelveslei
Betrameli
Bovreford
Greteham
Lyndhurst royal manor
Sanhest
Bovre
Pisteslei
Cockerlei
Truham
Hardliforde
Otreorde
Oxelei
Gatingeorde
Roweste
Hardley
Bocolt
Taceberie

to subjects to whom favours were owned or from whom they would be welcomed. The Normans brought a new perception to bear on hunting reserves. They were not seen, as the Saxon aristocrats had probably seen them, as places sharing the countryside with the neighbouring cultivated area, but as places set apart. They stood apart from the common law that governed other places and they had their own special system of law – one that prioritised the conservation of game and the interests of the royal hunt.

The popular ideas that Domesday England was a place of vast woods derive from oft-repeated myths. In 1086 the kingdom was a little more wooded than today, but the woods that did exist were familiar rather than secret places: working woods producing fuel, browse and materials for wood turners, house wrights, cartwrights and the 'colliers' who made charcoal. It was not possible for hunting parties to vanish into wildernesses, for hunting had to exist alongside farming and a host of commercial woodland pursuits. In the years following the Norman Conquest, countryfolk would have been well advised to keep out of the paths of the hunts and to avoid being found poaching or even disturbing the game, though there may have been no actual evictions. In 1079, William the Conqueror declared that the region of heathland, woodland and farming in south-western Hampshire that came to be known as the New Forest would be a royal domain. However, it would not to prove to be a place of happy associations for this, the harshest of kings. A son, Richard, was gored and killed by a stag, an illegitimate nephew of the same name was killed when his mount trapped him against a tree and in 1100, thirteen years after William's death, his successor, William Rufus, was mysteriously killed – probably assassinated – in a hunting 'accident' in the New Forest.

There was no shortage of people in Hampshire who attributed these misfortunes to divine retribution for the Conqueror's oppression of the communities that had inhabited the Forest territory. Legend claims that when a charcoal burner found the king's body and took it by cart to Winchester, no bells were tolled and no prayers were said. Today, legend and fact coil together and one cannot tell the one from the other. In 1841, the Warden of the New Forest erected a new Rufus Stone to replace an earlier three-sided inscribed stone. It claimed to mark the spot where the tree that deflected an arrow fired by Sir Walter Tyrell, a Norman visitor, had stood. Instead of striking a stag, the deflected arrow was said to have killed the king instantly. Other accounts claimed that the fatal arrow was fired by a huntsman on the orders of the king's younger brother, Henry, and that Tyrell, who fled to Normandy via the port of Poole, was merely a scapegoat.

There can be no doubt that the first Norman kings had caused much resentment in Hampshire. The circumstances of the king's death will remain mysterious, while as for the origins of the New Forest, they are more

complicated than the legends (as such things so frequently are). The core
of the New Forest, amounting to about 75,000 acres (around 30,352 hectares) was composed of thinly-populated heathland and woods lying to the
west and south-east of the royal manor of Lyndhurst. Lyndhurst was a royal
manor before AD 980 and the area may very well have existed as some form
of Saxon royal hunting reserve. The Conqueror's crime was not to have created the Forest, but to have extended it to the north and the south and to
have imposed the unpopular Forest Law, with its restrictions and its despised
enforcers. Perhaps 500 families were obliged to abandon their villages and
hamlets as their farmland was converted into a hunting reserve, and then
up to twice as many people were removed from the fringes and from the
temptations to trespass and poach. It is hard to know which of the places
concerned were villages, which hamlets and which mere farmsteads. Also,
once deserted, it is very hard to identify the sites of lost settlements, for without dwellings to attach to, placenames could soon be forgotten and lapse. The
names of thirty-four destroyed or largely devastated settlements are known,
though the sites of a third of them are undiscovered. The land concerned was
not of the best agricultural quality, population must have been fairly thinly
spread and villages of the fatter kind will have been few and far between.
Perhaps twenty villages and a dozen or so hamlets were destroyed in the initial expansion, and an uncertain number of little settlements perished in the
depopulation of the fringes. A few fragmented communities somehow managed to endure inside the Forest at places such as Brockenhurst and Fawley.
A few other destroyed places, like Pisteslei, which became Pilley, were resettled, but the plight of most of the uprooted families are uncertain. Many must
have looked for tenancies on Hampshire manors outside the Forest and some
could have gravitated to the seaports of the Solent.

Perhaps the most remarkable feature of this massive disruption of the
region's communities is the fact that it seems to have been unnecessary.
During the thirteenth century, when Forests covered around one fifth of
the kingdom, England contained almost seventy of them, though the Forests
had reached their greatest extent in the previous century, under Henry
II (1154–89). These Forests covered all manner of terrain, from heather
moors and high fells to lowland heaths and vales. Yet on the whole, their
creation does not seem to have involved wholesale evictions of population.
By the time of *Domesday Book* in 1086, at least nineteen counties, apart from
Hampshire, had Forests and under the Plantagenets, the English obsession
with Forests would grow and greatly exceed the development of Forests
in other realms, such as Scotland or France. In the many places where
ancient reserves became Forests, or where new Forests were established,
the system functioned quite smoothly without evictions being involved.
Under the Forest Law, communities went on with their day-to-day chores.

They generally resented bullying and extortions by corrupt foresters and other officials. Also, they might not like having their working dogs 'lawed' by the removal of claws to prevent them from chasing deer. Periodically, the Forest tenants would be summoned to account for their misdeeds at the Forest court. This was not exceptional, for elsewhere, tenants found themselves at their mercy of their manor courts and Forest justice was not usually significantly harsher. Forest folk will have watched with impotence and smouldering anger as deer slipped from the woods at dusk to devour their crops. Sometimes the royal hunt would flatten the standing crops that had escaped the deer. And then the Forest dwellers may have resented the impositions of work connected with the hunt, like kennelling hounds or setting up the hunting camp – though meanwhile, their brethren living under the common law were obliged to toil on their lords' demesnes. In short, Forest life certainly had its irritations, yet it was perfectly possible for ordinary communities to co-exist with the Forest Law. Unfortunately, this does not seem to have been realised in 1079, or if it was realised, William chose to do away with the communities of the New Forest anyway. A man who had waged genocide against the North of England would not have been troubled by the fate a few dozen bond households in the south.

The impact of parks

A more general threat to village life arose after the Forests had reached their twelfth-century zenith. In 1086, the existing deer parks may only have numbered around forty, but by the beginning of the fourteenth century their number may have approached or exceeded 4,000 (more are being recognised all the while). Many of these parks were around 100-200 acres (around forty-eighty hectares) in extent, so they were far smaller than the Forests. There were some far larger examples, like the 2,000 acre (around 809 hectares) Shottle Park in Derbyshire, or the royal Haverah Park near Knaresborough, which occupied an entire parish. The deer that they contained were unable to escape. They would either die inside the park after coursing by dogs or being shot with arrows or bolts fired from hunting towers, from the flanks of courses or by disguised archers – or else they might, less commonly, be released and hounded across the adjacent countryside. There was a ritualistic character to hunting in deer parks. They were quite small and everyone knew where the deer were hiding. Privileged members of a society ruled by martial values would display their prowess to the audience gathered on battlements, peering from apartments or perched in towers or 'touresses' to watch the slaughter. When Harewood Castle, near Leeds, was built or rebuilt in 1367, its principal rooms were placed on the upper floor and a walkway on the roof gave an additional opportunity to admire the vistas of the Wharfe Valley. There were four towers, including two tall ones that gave elevated views over the gardens, ponds and park of the setting. At Middleham, in Wensleydale, the castle was surrounded by a constellation of deer parks that were commandeered from villagers' ploughland and commons. A paved walkway around the parapet offered spectacular views southwards across the gardens and lake to the deer park beyond. In some cases, a part of the park that was well visible to onlookers would function as a deer course, with deer being driven from a gathering ground along a defile or a valley flank. There, they would be coursed by greyhounds and shot by bowmen and crossbowmen lining the course – for the delectation of spectators whose sensibilities must have resembled those of present hunt followers. Such a course is thought to have flanked a valley in the deer park at Ravensdale in Derbyshire.

Only in quite recent years has it been realised that deer parks were frequently located in 'designed landscapes' that were spread out around focal castles and the palaces of kings and leading churchmen. Castles like Bodiam in Sussex, Framlingham in Suffolk, Stokesay in Shropshire, Manorbier in Dyfed, Ravensworth in North Yorkshire and many more examples were provided with contrived settings featuring surprise views, mirror-like lakes, causeways, gardens, 'wildernesses', lawns and spinneys. In 1367, Harewood Castle, now lost in the landscape park of Harewood House, near Leeds, was rebuilt in a designed landscape that offered views across the River Wharfe and its valleys. In 1414, the retiring Justice of the King's Bench, Sir William Gascoigne of Gawthorpe Hall, Harewood, was granted four bucks and four does every year for his deer park from the Royal Forest of Pontefract. Such gifts of deer were an important form of patronage and will not have been wasted on Sir William, who had lent money to the king. Fortunately for the monarchy, he only lived to enjoy five years of retirement.

Recently, there has been some disagreement among experts concerning the roles of deer parks. Some see them as arenas for the practice of bloodsports while some see them as venison farms, whose main function was to provide meat for the lord's table. In reality, given that the deer that were slain in the course of a hunt would end on the table anyway, providing meat for the gatherings associated with the hunt, the distinction is not particularly clear. The creation of a carefully designed setting, along with elevated vantage points, show that the hunt was regarded as a spectacle. The park pale defined the area within which the slaughter was enacted; it removed the ability of deer to disperse and possibly vanish into cover, and it made poaching much more difficult. There is plenty of evidence that the threat posed by poaching was taken very seriously, not least because park-breaking was seen as a potent means of insulting a rival. Medieval poachers

We have only recently realised the importance of expensively landscaped settings for Medieval castles. Bodiam is one of the best examples.

have been stereotyped as wretched peasants seeking meat for their starving families. In reality, they came from all manner of backgrounds, including gay young blades and members of respected professions who were seeking surges of adrenalin. When the mighty Earl of Northumberland wrote to his relative, Sir Robert Plumpton, in the reign of Henry VII (1485-1509), 'I of late had in ward [prison] two servants of Thomas Myddleton for hunting in my parke of Spofforth', one suspects plotting by the master rather than the servants. Occasionally, poaching may have been prompted by resentment at the emparking of common land, as occurred during the creation of a girdle of parks around the royal castle at Knaresborough. However these events had passed far back into history in 1505, when an apparently mindless urge for excitement brought Sir John Robinson, the serving vicar of Knaresborough, into Haya Park on the fringes of his parish. He came with a mob of ten or twelve others, armed with bows and accompanied by greyhounds. They killed four deer and injured two or three more that died later – all this in a royal park and in the reign of one of England's most brutal kings. In other cases still, the motives of the poachers seem to have been purely commercial, as in 1621 when the poachers who broke into another royal reserve, Bishopdale Chase, near Wensleydale, and killed a doe and fawn were found to be a local butcher and two labourers.

It has generally been imagined that deer parks were slotted into voids in a gradually filling countryside. However, my own work in the Yorkshire Dales shows that this was far from being the case. On the whole, examples from the multitude of parks there shunned the open expanses of fell and

Manorbier Castle, Pembroke, stood in a designed landscape.

moor. The parks were generally sited on the very doorsteps of the castles and mansions of their owners, and these were situated on the lower valley slopes and on the choicer agricultural land. This being the case, it was inevitable that peasant communities would be uprooted and evicted as thoughts in the thirteenth and fourteenth centuries turned, increasingly, towards the establishment of hunting parks. The lord of modest to middling stature might have a single deer park to provide entertainment and buttress his status. But the greater lords – the Nevilles at Middleham, the Cliffords at Skipton and the Scropes at Castle Bolton – surrounded their castles with constellations of deer parks, while the Abbot of Fountains had two deer parks and the Prior of Bolton, one. Often, the presence of earlier Medieval ridge and furrow ploughland inside a deer park demonstrates the theft of peasant farmland. Indeed, the tranquillity and stability of some deer parks has allowed them to survive as open air museums of peasant farming. Studley Royal, near Ripon, contains furlong upon furlong of ridged ploughland, a deserted village site and all the field details that went with it.

Although the heyday of the deer park came a couple of centuries or more after *Domesday Book*, the surviving records are still full of gaps. While a license to empark was normally essential to the creation of a deer park, many of these licenses cannot be traced. Far less evidence remains of the impact that the new parks had upon their settings. Given that the parks were carved out of settled, working countryside, the impacts must have been very considerable, and a few documented examples exist to show this. Today, it may seem strange that a community could vanish without trace, but in the Middle Ages, people of substance did not consider the removal of a village to be of sufficient relevance in itself to be recorded. Yet parks that were scores of acres in extent could not be hidden in quiet corners of the countryside and their creation was a cataclysmic event at the levels of the township and parish. At the end of the fifteenth century, William, Lord Conyers, was engaged in improving his castle at Hornby, near Bedale, in North Yorkshire. A large deer park appears to have figured in the scheme and the superimposition of the 700 acre (around 283 hectare) park upon the working countryside was said to have involved the casting down of forty 'husbandries' or farm holdings.

It was an under-privileged bishop or abbot who lacked a deer park and many priors, like the Prior of Bolton in Wharfedale, also had hunting parks. Furness Abbey, a Cistercian house in the Cumbrian Vale of the Deadly Nightshade, demonstrates the difficulties of recognition resulting from the northern habit of using 'park' to describe both parks and enclosed pastures. Work on the abbey began in 1147 and soon a large hunting park was extended across nearby countryside. Its divisions were Low Dale Park, Middle Dale Park and High Dale Park, 'dale' being a Scandinavian word for a valley. However, there were also stock-rearing parks, like Oxen Park and Stott Park (its name shows its use for young livestock) as well as outlying sheep granges at Abbot Park, Lawson Park and Park-a-Moor. To complicate matters further, a new deer park was set out by the current abbot in 1516; it was short-lived and divided into three farms after the Reformation. All this shows that a 'Park' placename seen on a map does not necessarily reveal an old deer park.

The deer park of the Bishop of Winchester at Highclere in Hampshire was one of the earlier examples and existed in the thirteenth century. An abandoned church marks the site of the village of Burghclere, removed in the creation of the park. Linked to the church were extents of arable land and other good farmland, and at the beginning of the fifteenth century, the current Bishop of Winchester was engaged in annexing this land and negotiating arrangements with a local landowner about pasturing sheep. Parks were not only attractive to landowners because of their resources of hunting and venison, but also because of the lucrative rents that could be obtained for 'agistment' or the renting of grazing. The deer parks associated with the royal castle and Forest of Knaresborough had controversial origins, which, at the very least, involved the theft from the local communities of some ancient commons. However, they not only provided entertainment for visiting royalty and their guests, but also produced significant revenue. In the mid-1370s the parks of Haya, Haverah, Bilton and the little park that faced the castle from across the river Nidd, yielded a very substantial annual income from agistment of £34 11s 4d (around £34.56). To put this figure in perspective, in 1307-12, the demolition of an old tower at the castle and its replacement by a massively fortified great keep under the supervision of master mason, Hugh of Titchmarsh, cost £2,175 – with four interventions being needed to obtain the wages of the workmen from the king. Parks had grazing, browse, pannage of acorns or mast of beech for swine, timber, fuel, minerals and water power and so they would usually have great commercial attractions. However, people, apart from the parker and his servants, were unwelcome. The more hungry and impoverished they were, then the more likely they were to pillage the game and assets.

Similar evictions to those at Hornby and Burghclere continued in the seemingly more enlightened times that followed the Reformation. During the reign of Charles I (1625-49), Sir John Cutts depopulated the amalgamated parish of Childerley, in Cambridgeshire, in order to enlarge his deer park. The enthusiasm for bloodsports remained undiminished for a century and more after the end of the Middle Ages. Nobody seems to have been greatly concerned for the parishioners, though the archbishop was outraged that Sir John had seized the church tithes. New deer parks did not have to result in mass evictions to impact on their settings. In scores of cases the park wall or pale cut across existing routeways and necessitated time wasting diversions, as when an inter-village route in Wensleydale was diverted around the new park at Little Bolton in 1314. There must have been many villagers who were firstly displaced by a new park and obliged to settle in some neighbouring community, and then forced to waste hours of precious working time each week plodding along diversions around the park pale. Also, ordinary people could be removed from places in which they had enjoyed common rights to take firewood, pasture swine, lop leafy browse, dig clay, cut turf or gather sticks. Given the near self-sufficiency of village household economies, these losses could have serious consequences. Such impositions could give rise to much grumbling, but they seldom attracted the sympathy of the authorities.

However, the higher authorities would tend to take an interest if the proposed park seemed to pose a threat to royal game which might 'accidentally' stray into it. At such times, the interests of common people might suddenly be invoked to support opposition. Thus, in 1473, Sir William Plumpton gained a license to enclose an expanse of land on the estate, near Knaresborough, that shared his name. It was plainly working countryside, comprising meadows, 'feedings', pastures and woods as well as various tenements. Two years later, however, the Chancellor of the Duchy of Lancaster revoked the license, claiming that the park would interfere with the free run of deer and also curtail the free grazings enjoyed by the tenants. Sir William held his manor by feudal service and was expected to serve as a warden for the Forest of Knaresborough deer. Some may have feared that he would 'ward' some of the deer into his own park, a problem that was probably taken more seriously than the threat to peasant husbandry.

Virtually every Medieval deer park must have disturbed the community of its setting to some degree. Evictions must have been commonplace, but evidence of popular opposition is very rare indeed. It is forthcoming from Wilstrop, by the junction of the Rivers Ouse and Nidd (and not very far from Plumpton). Here, too, the emparking dynasty shared their name with their setting. As Professor Beresford discovered, in the 1490s, the Wilstrops enclosed farmland to make their park and one may suspect that that may have been the end of the story had they not made themselves unpopular with other members of the local gentry, as well as with their tenants. A case alleging that pasture and corn fields had been enclosed along with the common was heard by Star Chamber, but the lessons of the contemporary sheep enclosures argued against a reliance on officialdom to rectify matters. Thus, in the April of 1497, a gang of eight began demolishing the posts and rails of the park pale, with a neighbour, Sir William Gascoigne, orchestrating the operations. This seems to have encouraged a mob to materialise among the wet heaths, farms and woods of the Vale of York, and on the day after the attack on the pale, a party of 200 marched from Marston Moor to Wilstrop Park to renew the assault on the pale. Perhaps it was restored, but the following January a body possibly numbering 4,000 tore down 100yds (91.4m) of park pale. Repairs were made, but then a crowd 200 strong gathered and again a section of pale was levelled. Rioters cut up the boards, chopped down 100 walnut trees and apple trees that seem to have been planted in a fringe around the park, as well as destroying a length of hedgerow planted alongside the pale. Still the attacks continued, for in the autumn of 1498, the park warren was invaded and burrows were dug up, while in the January that followed, 100 tenants from the Gascoigne estate demolished 200yds (183m) of the pale, hunted Wilstrop's deer and tried to attack him in his own house. One suspects that resentful but otherwise cowed tenants were being used as tools in a feud orchestrated by neighbouring landowners and that without such incitements they would have mounted no serious opposition.

The enthusiasm for slaying the beautiful, gentle animals continued through the era of the Stuart kings and new deer parks continued to be created, even if the growing climate of antipathy towards the sheep enclosures made depopulation a little more difficult. If the centuries around the close of the Middle Ages marked a slight lull in emparking, a lull was all it would be, for while some values changed, a new onslaught was in store for many of those village communities slumbering close to a great mansion. Numerous settlements perished during this relative lull. Examples noted from Hampshire include the settlement that was served by the remarkable Saxon church at Breamore, which was emparked in 1579, and Bramhill, Deane and Elvetham, also emparked in the sixteenth century. Like vultures drawn to wounded game, the park-makers of the sixteenth century seem

Deer parks were sometimes created in breathtakingly dramatic settings – like the Prior of Bolton's park in the 'Valley of Desolation' (a later name referring to a disastrous flood).

to have been drawn to the settlements that had declined in the previous century. There was no clear cut break between the creation of Medieval or seventeenth-century deer parks and the establishment of landscape parks in the late seventeenth, eighteenth and early nineteenth centuries.

The Medieval parks were frequently set within designed landscapes and hunting in parks persisted long after end of the Middle Ages. The Dissolution of the Monasteries and the sale of the monastic estates introduced a class of particularly hard-nosed landlords into the English countrysides, and any communities that were small and vulnerable were particularly at risk. One process that can be recognised is that village communities that had been greatly reduced and weakened by Medieval emparking for deer, or by enclosures for sheep, would be relatively easy prey for the great ornamental park-making operations of the Georgian era. In the summer of 1981, a survey of about seventy rural parks in Hampshire found that almost fifty of them contained traces of former villages, rural churches, or both. In this county, more than 100 deserted settlements have been identified, in addition to the thirty-four lost settlements associated with the creation of the New Forest. The deer parks of the Plantagenet and Tudor eras would sometimes become landscape parks in Jacobean and Georgian times. Workmen carefully grading a bowling green might stumble upon the footings of a village house demolished centuries earlier, the ancient holloway of a road linking extinct villagers could become the course along which terrified deer were raced and then the way to a romantic temple or grotto, while the members of the squire's cricket team might be cracked about their heads by balls flying from the faint corrugations of Medieval ridge and furrow underlying the pitch. Such would be more revenge than most displaced villagers could enjoy.

CHAPTER SIX

BACK HOME TO ROOST

On the edge

Like an indigo curtain, dusk was descending from the high vaults down to the horizons. The man standing at his door looked along the shoreline and out to sea. The moon, now a great malevolent presence, was dragging in the waters. He knew that this was a dangerous time. He was looking for signs of any gale from the east that might, like some burly carter lending his shoulder to the wheel of a creeping cart, drive the bulging tide against the low shore. The sky seemed clear and uneventful. As he lowered his gaze, he saw the coastal pastures traversed by darker lines, a succession of small, parallel sea banks. Recent generations had been engaged in reclaiming farmland from the creeks, mudflats and salt marshes by 'warping' or building banks and barriers of brushwood to trap the shifting silts. Each time that the rain and freshwater streams flushed out the salt and the nutritious grasses supplanted the salt-tolerant plants, so the realm of dry land took another small step seawards. Every new bank marked the frontier of this progress. Population had been growing remorselessly, so each acre wrested from the tidal marshes and mudflats became essential. Population was like a great engine, never stopping or reversing, forcing people from the seething centres further and further into the fringes. Nobody stopped to think that one day, there might be nowhere left to go.

Comforted by the settled sky with its motionless streamers of cloud, our man huddled by the hearth and fell asleep. As he slept, the sky cleared and the stars sparkled more sharply than city dwellers can ever imagine. Then, a slight shudder rippled over the land, awakening breezes that began to twitch. Whispering to each other, they frisked and twined, flicking up dry stalks and wafting dead leaves into corners, where they rustled and gathered. Soon, the light-hearted breezes became surly; contorted with turbulence, they bullied the clouds, which, angered by all the bluster, spat showers here and there. Finally, the jinking, writhing and gusting currents were overrun by a wind that drove across the seascape like a great, roaring wall.

The children heard it first and tugged at their deeply sleeping parents. Their grandmother gathered them together and herded them into a corner. Above them, the rafters repeatedly flexed and straightened like the pole of a wood turner's lathe. The bundled reeds of the roof strained to be free. Slits of light appeared between the bundles, the stars shone in, and then the wind ripped out a whole section of timbers and thatch. The roof was opened like the door of a threshing barn. Now, the gale curled into the house, scooping ashes from the hearth and rushes from the floor and blasting them into the sky. The parents awoke into this maelstrom and were pounded into confusion by noises from every quarter. Their returning senses were shaped by an overwhelming terror that the children might have been swept away by the spiralling blast that rearranged the home. Then they saw the little huddle in the corner, a crush of bodies, each one trying to burrow into the shelter of the wall. The father began to build a barricade in that corner, struggling against the squalls with a harrow, the frames that carried the table and whatever heavy household items he could find.

It was there that they spent the night. The door crashed remorselessly against its bar throughout the long hours of darkness; eventually the predictability of the raps became reassuring. Above, as night melted into day, they watched the ridge beam, now stripped of any swathes of thatch, as it bowed and trembled against the slate and charcoal-streaked sky. Steely bursts of rain swirled around the landscape like squadrons of light cavalry on a battlefield. They lashed around the naked home, peppering the cowering bodies with splatters of wetness. A plume of spray breasted the gable and the man took a blast full in his face; he rubbed his eyes and they were stinging. He licked a trickle as it ran down his cheek and it tasted of salt.

At last, as the sky paled and the tortured clouds became more shapely, the wind dropped and voices could be heard again. For hours, the man had repeated a Latin phrase he had learned from the clerk but never understood – and at last it seemed to have done its work. But now he must do the thing he dreaded and step out to survey the wreckage. He was thinking of re-roofing, some ditching and, perhaps, patching a sea wall, but what awaited him was unimaginably worse.

He had expected to see thatch and poles from the roof littering their yard, but he had not expected to step out into a lake of brine. He raised his gaze and saw the pastures transformed. The successive lines of sea walls were now hyphenated, with the portions breached by the sea being far wider than the surviving fragments. The pastures were now dappled with puddles and elsewhere, the grass had a sheen of wetness. At once he realised that the entire shoreline swathe of grazings was effectively poisoned

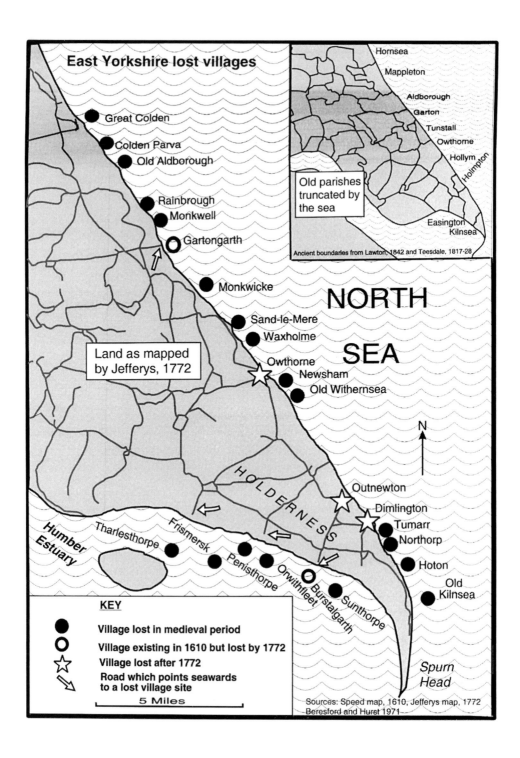

East Yorkshire lost villages

Old parishes truncated by the sea

Hornsea
Mappleton
Aldborough
Garton
Tunstall
Owthorne
Hollym
Holmpton
Easington
Kilnsea

Ancient boundaries from Lawton, 1842 and Teesdale, 1817-28

Great Colden
Colden Parva
Old Aldborough
Rainbrough
Monkwell
Gartongarth
Monkwicke
Sand-le-Mere
Waxholme

Land as mapped by Jefferys, 1772

Owthorne
Newsham
Old Withernsea

NORTH

SEA

N

HOLDERNESS

Outnewton
Dimlington
Tumarr
Northorp
Hoton
Old Kilnsea

Humber Estuary
Tharlesthorpe
Frismersk
Penisthorpe
Orwithfleet
Burstalgarth
Sunthorpe

Spurn Head

KEY

● Village lost in medieval period
○ Village existing in 1610 but lost by 1772
☆ Village lost after 1772
⇗ Road which points seawards to a lost village site

5 Miles

Sources: Speed map, 1610, Jefferys map, 1772
Beresford and Hurst 1971

by the salt water. Ages would pass before the salt would flush out. Then he raised his eyes a little higher and saw the line of flotsam, stranded seaweed and driftwood that marked the limits of the sea's incursion. It was punctuated by what seemed like thistle plumes or bloated grey bumblebees. That was the village flock. Looking beyond, he saw that the entire coastline had been redrafted. Great bites had been taken from the fields behind the sea banks. Gullies, like miniature canyons, now carved up the land and creeks had started to form between the new mudflats. Some of the mud banks and creek channels had strange, whiskery surfaces, a patchy stubble formed by clumps of turf and dry grass washed away from the fields. He looked in horror, unable to assess the consequences of what had happened, unable to gauge the amount of effort needed to put it all right again.

And then a new thought dawned, more awful in its implications than those that had gone before. This was the hour of low tide.

What do households do when the grinding pressures of a mindlessly growing population deprive them of resources? Why, they become pioneers and colonise new lands of their own. But what do they do when those new lands and all the efforts invested in them are destroyed? What do they do when there are no lands left for pioneers? They steal, they die in ditches or they end their days sweating, shaking and heaving in the gutter of some disease-ridden town. The Medieval kingdoms had no protective services of any note, no health provisions, no universal state pensions – no safety nets. The best that a suddenly landless community could hope for from the state would be relief from the taxes that they were, in any event, unable to pay. It was in the years around 1400 that people found that there was nowhere left to run to and that even the safe old places could no longer be relied upon.

Climates of change

Science is exposing the minutiae of the human make-up, yet the broad view is largely ignored. Having realised that our distant ancestors took to the ground when a drying of the southern African climate caused the jungle to become savannah, anthropologists have variously attributed evolutionary progress to the development of an upright stance, a larger brain, meat-eating or the employment of tools. Each explanation is flawed, while the real key to human success has been adaptability. We belong to a species uniquely successful by virtue of its ability to enter ecological regions as diverse as the equatorial rainforest, the tundra and the sub-tropical sand desert – and to dominate them all. Some animal species have been able to command a single habitat, but we have out-competed them all and exerted universal ascendancy. At first, this dominion over the planet did not have profound environmental consequences, for humans remained within the controls of their ecosystems. If a community exterminated the caribou or antelope it fed on, then it, in turn, would face annihilation. But then humans seemed to outgrow natural controls and to dictate the course of planetary events. At first, this was regarded as a triumph of human will and genius. Even for people living in the middle of the twentieth century, the course of human progress seemed to be summarised by a line that went ever upwards. This was an almost universal, but yet a witless, vision. Not only was it blind to the ecological disasters, most of them predictable, that lay in the decades ahead, but it was also blind to the multitude of man-made environmental disasters embedded in the past.

In the course of recent millennia, human communities have been devastated by natural disasters that were not of their making – and also the guilty victims of many that were. Yet instead of the human species gaining in humility and caution with each failure and act of folly, our arrogance has only increased. Lessons of history abound, but learning from them has been an absent or transient experience. When, in the course of a few generations or a few centuries, the lifespan of our species ends, this termination will be due to causes the very opposite of our success. It will be caused by a failure to adapt. Already, the clear signs of the consequence of the lifestyles of the developed world are apparent. We see them, we hear the predictions, but have lost the flexibility and vitality to respond. We have become unable even to forego luxuries and inessentials in order to prevail. The first species to dominate the whole world may perish, ignominiously, for the sake of its addiction to oil, inefficient personal transport and cheap jet flights to places already bludgeoned into similarity by the tourist industry.

That natural 'disasters' can affect human societies should not surprise us. After all we seem to have originated in the climatic calamity that caused the desiccation of sub-Saharan Africa and its rainforests. Once modern humans had moved out of Africa and made the phenomenal adjustments needed to survive another 'disaster' – the glaciation of Europe – they then faced the immense challenge of reorganising their sub-Arctic big game hunting culture to cope with a pronounced amelioration of climate and the unwelcome expansion of woodland across the old, open hunting ranges. Eventually, the diffusion of farming from the Middle East and the adoption of the new technologies in the Atlantic outposts of Europe allowed for a massive increase in the number of humans. Yet farming, in its way, had more rigidities. One could not just up and go in an opportunistic way, as one could when one area was fished- and hunted-out, or when herds changed their migration routes. Hard-won land and growing crops tied the household to one place. Also, the crops that were adopted were often growing at the northern limits of their range. They could not respond to changes in the environment, could not re-specify their toleration of moisture and cold or re-define their patterns of growth. Very slowly, new strains might be developed, but farming was filled with constraints and impediments. Gradually, a community might develop a method of farming that was in harmony with their setting. Then, their numbers would swell quite swiftly to consume the entire sustainable yield of the place. Next, they might court disaster by increasing their numbers still further and thus outstripping the farming potential, culminating in land wars or over-cropping and over-stocking. Equally, the environment might change a little. A few more cloudy days in summer, late frosts delaying the onset of growth in the fields, or a few more inches of driving, leaching, waterlogging rain each year might tip the balance towards failure and migration. In farming, the natural margins were quite small and just small shifts in climate could make the difference between satisfaction and famine.

Human recklessness and natural catastrophes took their toll on prehistoric populations throughout the world. Energetic visitors to Britain's western uplands, particularly to the mist-hung moors of the South West, cannot fail but notice the profusion of stone monuments on display – the rings that were once the walls of round houses and persist as 'hut circles'; the petri-fied fingers that are 'longstones', menhirs or standing stones and that mark boundaries, burials and places of note, and the mysterious stone rows that link anonymous places. Could one hack down the heather, bracken and coarse grasses with a gigantic mower, it would be seen that entire landscapes are preserved, with field networks outlined by walls spanning the horizons, with villages, hamlets, farmsteads and compounds, and with trackways and droves to tie the settlements and fields together. These are fossilised country-sides, and the key to their fossilisation lies in the fact that after their desertion, no really substantial communities have returned to scour away the earlier landscapes or to bury these, the Bronze Age layers of creative endeavour, beneath layer after layer of later activity. The great slumber that overtook these uplands in the Bronze Age has never quite been lifted.

For Dartmoor, Exmoor and Bodmin Moor, it is as though life ended in the Bronze Age, between 3,000 and 4,000 years ago, and all that have hap-pened since have been ghostly wanderings across the desolate canvas of life. Such desertions may seem most pronounced on the moors of the South West, but the same pattern was repeated across the uplands of Britain and Ireland, up to Skye, and far beyond, to the Faroes. The uplands may have been somewhat marginal environments, being less able to tolerate small fluctuations in climate, but many of the countrysides that experienced desertion were not thinly populated backwaters. They were not character-ised by the bleak, soulful emptiness that we associate with uplands today.

Dartmoor was patterned by a detailed network of field boundaries of walls and hedgebanks known as 'reaves': it was a finely-partitioned and productive fieldscape. Today, around 5,000 hut circles are known on the moor, representing the circlets of low walls that remain after their conical roofs of thatch have decayed. Most of them were homes. Many such circles must lie overgrown or have been robbed for stones by later stone-wallers, yet sufficient remain to tell of a numerous, and doubtless vibrant, population.

The empty countrysides created by the wholesale desertion of the uplands in the Bronze Age endured. Rainfall increased and beds of peat advanced across the waterlogged fields as the landscapes became tinted rust, mauve and charcoal by bracken, heather and bog. Few households settled the moors until an inviting warming of the climate brought a few early Medieval colonists to settle, sometimes building their long-houses within the tumbling walls of a prehistoric compound. Now, the oldest survivors of these farm sites are the Ancient Tenements, dating from the fourteenth century or, occasionally, the twelfth and thirteenth centuries. The establishment of Ancient Tenements did not signify a wholesale re-colonisation of Dartmoor. There were forty-four of them in the moor's central basin in 1344-45 and just thirty-five in 1702. They, in their turn, would often contribute to the landscape of desertion, the most informative being the excavated settlement of Hound Tor, a small village dated by ashes from a hearth to 1235. It was a place where the households huddled together with their livestock in a manner that was already archaic. The bustling fruitfulness of Bronze Age Dartmoor was never recovered. The evidence of massive desertion has been recognised for centuries, but the cause of desertion remained unknown.

If modern history had been coloured by triumphal visions of the irresistible advance of humans armed with industrial technology, by the latter part of the twentieth century disillusionment had surfaced and such notions seemed increasingly like mirages. At the very time when societies were being alerted to the consequences of industrial modernity, interest in the phenomenal potency of natural catastrophes began to command more attention. The awesome natural hazards had always been there, greedy for human life, but the global communication of images of earthquake devastation, drought and volcanic eruptions now made distant calamities instant and immediate. Meanwhile, too, the realisation that humans were contaminating their only world led to research into many aspects of the environment – and these revealed both natural and human-made disasters on spectacular scales.

Many aspects of research contributed to an understanding of the Bronze Age desertions. It was seen that partly-fossilised oaks from Irish bogs showed narrowing of their rings in certain sections. These corresponded to crises of growth, which might line-up with geological and cosmic events. Volcanoes seemed capable of hurling sufficient ash into the atmosphere to create the effect of those 'nuclear winters' that were so prominent in public imagination in the later days of the Cold War – but so too could impacts by asteroids and comets. A comet or meteor impact was the most popular explanation for the extinction of (most) dinosaurs and the phenomenon of cosmic catastrophe had captured the public imagination. Models developed by astrophysicists suggested that some twenty to thirty catastrophic impacts had probably affected the Earth during the last 6,000 years, though in some cases the catastrophic experiences were fairly localised. A gigantic oceanic comet impact in 2807 BC was recognised and a cosmic explanation was favoured for the mysterious Tunguska Event of 1908, when trees in a vast area of the Siberian taiga were flattened. For a while, the finger of guilt seemed to point in a cosmic direction. Archaeologists had noted that simultaneously, around 2300 BC, the major civilisations of the world had collapsed, with 1,000 years of recovery being terminated by another great collapse around 1200 BC. The conjunctions of disaster had been noted by the French archaeologist, Claude Schaeffer, in 1948, though he attributed the blame to vast earthquakes occurring on a 1,000-2,000 year cycle. In the late 1970s, the British astronomers, Victor Clube and William Napier, replaced this with a cometary explanation. They believed that occasionally the outer planets would divert comets into the inner solar system. There, their debris could affect the earth when dust blocked out sunlight, while sometimes there would be more dramatic collisions, followed by 'impact winters' when the earth was veiled in dust.

No fewer than seven impact craters from asteroids or comets on the Earth were attributable to the third millennium BC, the era of the Bronze Age desertions, according to the advocates of cosmic catastrophe theories. However, in the event, volcanoes would prove to be the more likely culprits, most particularly Mount Hekla in Iceland. In fact, the explanation had been lying unnoticed since 1784, when Benjamin Franklin noted a persistent fog and an associated chilling:

> The cause of this universal fog is not yet ascertained. Whether it is adventitious to this earth, or whether it was the vast quantity of smoke, long continuing to issue during the summer from Hecla in Iceland, and that other volcano which arose out of the sea near the island, which might be spread by various winds over the northern part of the world, is yet uncertain.

Hekla, the persistently violent Icelandic volcano, produced an eruption, known as 'Hekla 4', around 2200 BC and another, 'Hekla 3', around 1120 BC, while Santorini in the Aegean erupted sometime in the decades around 1600 BC. These eruptions seemed to relate to the tree ring evidence and Hekla 3 matched the abandonment of the British uplands. The last major eruption of Santorini in 1450 BC was known to have destroyed the entire Minoan fleet in Crete, but there were suggestions that an earlier eruption, around 1600 BC, might have destroyed the rich Wessex culture in England, the creators of Stonehenge and many other remarkable monuments.

Modern researchers then realised that each volcano leaves its 'fingerprint' on the scene of its crimes in the form of microscopic, glassy particles of volcanic ash, known as 'tephra'. Excavations on Skye, on North Uist in the Faroes and on the uplands of mainland Britain from Caithness to the South West discovered the distinctive tephra of Hekla lying upon the remains of Bronze Age settlements like an invisible shroud, with tephras from other Icelandic volcanoes sometimes being found as well. Ash from Hekla was deposited after the close of the Middle Ages and into the modern era. The volcano is still active and an eruption in 2000, the first for nine years, jetted a column of ash upwards for four miles and into the upper atmosphere. That March, Reuters reported that ash from the latest eruption of the volcano would be drifting over Shetland and the Orkneys, crossing country where Hekla's ash had floated in times long before. Though pilots were instructed to avoid a large area of North Atlantic airspace, no serious threat to humans was anticipated.

The most interesting of the numerous eruptions is Hekla 3, now generally seen to be responsible for the destruction of Bronze Age settlements in the Atlantic uplands of Europe. The deposition of the tephra, which fell like an invisible shower, will have been accompanied by the arrival of dark clouds in endless succession. Perhaps the only colourful relief from the grimly overcast skies may have been brilliant red sunsets associated with the ash particles in the atmosphere. Rain will have increased, saturating the fields, while crops will have failed to ripen before summer drew to an end. If one season of sodden meadows, failed crops, murrain in the cattle and foot rot in the sheep was insufficient to break a household, a succession of such seasons certainly would have been. And so the families will have retreated, never actually seeing the thin film of volcanic ash that coated their roofs, dusted their pastures and sealed their fates.

Into the Little Ice Age

The Bronze Age refugees were not the first people to be driven from their homes and lands in Britain, though most other prehistoric catastrophes were more localised. Some migrations may have been caused by changes in the climate, but in many cases bad farming technique had fouled the family nest. Given the accumulation of such experiences in the popular memory, one might imagine that societies would develop rational and responsible approaches to their settings, adjusting their population numbers to the available resources with proper allowances for the fact that climatic downturns could occur. In reality, nothing was learned. The Depression of the late 1920s and 1930s years saw the Dustbowl refugees streaming out of the broken farmlands of Oklahoma, Arkansas and Texas. They became icons in the unending saga of environmental abuse and human culpability. A generation or two removed from the family crofts and small-holdings of Europe, they knew little about proper farming techniques in dry country and nothing about the drought phases that punctuated the climate of the Great Plains. In recent decades, humans have acquired the ability to recognise the volatility of the natural environment, though without adopting the facility to respond to the challenge. Global warming is the subject of much discussion, if little action, but it was back in the mid-1960s that scholars became aware of a Medieval shift in climate. It became known as the 'Medieval Warm Period', and it preceded the more widely known 'Little Ice Age'.

Scientists debate what the warm period was, which parts of the world were affected, and how, as well as its time span. There is a loose consensus that it ran from around AD 1000 to around AD 1400 and that, though it may have had some worldwide aspects, the greatest effects seem to have been experienced in Europe. The peak in warming seems to have been experienced near the start of the period, after which the climate gradually cooled. Thus, after destructive sea storms presaged its ending, from 1400 it dipped into the cooler zone and continued to cool until the depths of the Little Ice Age were reached around 1650. The Little Ice Age seems to have had three low points that were separated by slightly warmer interludes, with the minima dated to 1650, 1770 and 1850. In Britain, the warming of the climate was never sufficient to sustain a thorough re-colonisation of the upland moors, but the earlier springs and later autumns did encourage a drift of surplus population to areas too marginal to be cropped by previous generations. There have been suggestions that, as the climate improved towards its optimum, Danish Vikings mounted expeditions across ice-free seas in the North Atlantic. Meanwhile, European glaciers retreated in the years before AD 900, and again, for a while, after 1250.

The causes for the warming are debated, though the phase from 1100-1250 of the 'Medieval Maximum' coincided with a peak in solar activity. However, some scientists argue that this would not affect all areas equally and only some regions would have been warmed. The time of the Medieval Maximum was also a time of frequent volcanic eruptions, and the ash in the atmosphere might have led to milder winters. However, volcanic activity is also blamed for triggering the Little Ice Age! It is pointed out that ash clouds cause cooling by blocking incoming radiation from the sun, while the sulphur emitted by eruptions becomes sulphuric acid particles in the stratosphere, and these particles also reflect the rays of the sun. The causes of the deterioration after the Medieval Maximum are much disputed, some blaming a 'quiet sun' with a lack of sun spot activity. However, Professor L.H. Nelson has quoted contemporary accounts of auroras of great intensity in flaming skies, indications of a sun that was far from subdued. In 1192, for example, Baldric, a monk at Nivone Monastery, Aalst, in eastern Flanders, recorded that '… throughout Gaul, a fire was seen in the night sky such that each person thought the neighbouring village was on fire'. Those who wrote of these things saw them as harbingers of a severe famine that followed in 1197.

In general, the historical changes of climate tend to be regarded as natural, rather than human-made, occurrences. However, there have been hints that the sharp decline in human activity (such as farming, for example) after the Black Death could have accelerated the Little Ice Age, as well as suggestions that when the world emerged from the Little Ice Age after 1850, with the Industrial Revolution a century old and human population rapidly beginning to expand and migrate, the warming climate change could have been induced by humans. This might have been the initial triggering of the current global warming crisis. Much remains to be learned and the Medieval Warm Period in Europe may have been no warmer than the conditions at the start of the twentieth century. There may well have been short-term fluctuations that we have not recognised, while differences between regions could have been considerable. Yet all this considered, the consequences of a warming and then a decaying climate were profound for the societies that experienced them. Small shifts in climate can produce great shifts in human prospects.

A rational species would have seen the period of warmth as a time when health could have been built up, production consolidated and provisions made for the time when the climate would swing again. Instead of being able to see the climatic boom time as a period of relief from famine and hardship, the human race simply exploited every emerging niche in its habitat and multiplied, so that the threat of famine never left its side. Then, when the pendulum began to swing away from optimum warmth, all the extra mouths still cried to be fed and the roads to disaster were thrown open. In the thirteenth century, far from the gaze of the feudal villagers in Britain, the glaciers in Greenland ended their retreat and slowly began to advance; within a few decades most other glaciers in the world would also begin to creep back down their valleys. The pack ice in the Atlantic had also begun to spread, jostle and grind. The contemporary generation of British villagers knew nothing of glaciers, pack ice and such things. In spare moments they basked, savoured the sweet smell of well-dried hay, mopped away the droplets of sweat before they could reach their eyes and gazed at the red, sinking orb that gave life to all. But then, as the fourteenth century arrived and began to take root, they came to know it as a century of less dependable summer warmth. Where summer had been predictable, now it was not.

The century was but fifteen years old when the great rains came. They drove down crops, swamped pastures that should have been baking brick-hard, drove the hay down in mouldering heaps, set the cows coughing and the sheep hobbling. And so there was a hideous and remorseless famine of unheard-of severity. Communities and households that had struggled ever harder to sustain a rising population now had to strive even more to maintain a population from a shrinking resource pool. It could not be done.

When disaster came, was it caused by the changes in the climate or by the collapse of an environment that had long been over-stressed by excessive demands from its farmers? Both were probably to blame, but the rain was more obvious. In 1315, the spring was worryingly wet. Villagers were slow to begin the customary negotiations that swapped the household oxen or horses around to combine into plough teams. The designated plough-lands were sodden, waterlogged in some cases. Some loud and impatient voices demanded that a start be made. Hooves squelched, mouldboards were caked in clay and the severed sods did not lie ready to be crumbled by the frost – rather they slumped, glistening with moisture, into the saturated mass. Seed was broadcast after the first drying winds, but then it started to rain again, so that much of the seed grain rotted as it lay. The harvest was bound to be poor, so the nutting and berry-picking in autumn became desperate endeavours rather than the garnishing of a harvest safely home. Most people survived, but the spring that followed was every bit as chilly and sodden as the one before. People who had entered into winter emaciated and weak had no chances to recover their strength. Those that lingered into the spring of 1317 were now desperate; they looked at their plough beasts and saw steak for the pot, just as they saw bread and gruel in their seed corn.

According to a near-contemporary report by the monk, Johannes de Trokelowe, in 1315:

> The summer rains were so heavy that grain could not ripen. It could scarcely be gathered and used to bake bread down to [the feast of the nativity of the Virgin, 8 September] unless it was firstly put into vessels to dry... Bread did not have its usual nutritious powers because the grain was not nourished by the warmth of summer sunlight... the poor wasted away while even the rich were constantly hungry... Four pennies worth of coarse bread was insufficient to feed a common man for one day. The usual kinds of meat, suitable for eating, were too scarce; horse flesh was precious; plump dogs

were stolen. And, according to many reports, men and women in many places secretly devoured their own children.

With the shortages came price rises, with the price of wheat grain and beans rising fourfold. In its turn, the inflation undermined the other aspects of the economy. These horrors fell on communities that were about to be assailed on the land as well as from the heavens. In the June of 1314 a massive English army with Scottish contingents, combining in a force around 20,000 strong, was surprisingly but utterly routed at Bannockburn, beneath Stirling Castle. With the feudal forces of Edward II in full flight, the northern marches of England lay exposed to Scottish armies and raiding parties. Soon, the Scots came and returned time after time to take the stock, raze the crops and burn the homes of village, hamlet and farmstead communities, all so sadly reduced by famine.

Sea storms and sand storms

Famine and raiding might deplete and exhaust a community but they were unlikely to exterminate it. As population was driven down to a level that the local farming resources could sustain, then the situation should stabilise. However, when the wind, the moon and the sea combined, the environmental forces did have the might to exterminate a community overnight. Sea storms were not confined to the Little Ice Age when weather conditions were at their worst; villages could be carried away when the climate was in a relatively benign phase. During the balmy twelfth century, the village and parish of Whimpwell, offshore from the currently eroding parish of Happisburgh, in Norfolk, was swept away along with the parish church. In 1183, only one of Whimpwell's fields remained. In 1987 members of a local sub-aqua club thought that they had traced the outlines of the village's Medieval quay on the seabed.

   The decay of the climate during the fourteenth century will have been associated with cooler, wetter and more cyclonic conditions. Gales will have become much more frequent, and when such gales drove behind unusually high tides then incursions into cultivated and settled areas could be expected. Along the low-lying seaboards of Atlantic Europe the effect was often to reverse centuries of slow progress in reclaiming land from mudflats and salt marshes, driven by the need to feed relentlessly growing populations. On the Channel coast near the Kent/Sussex border, reclamation had been practised for centuries. From the launching pads of the old Saxon and Norman sea walls it had advanced seawards, snatching and cleansing coastal sands, salt creeks, mud banks and shingle ridges and converting them into

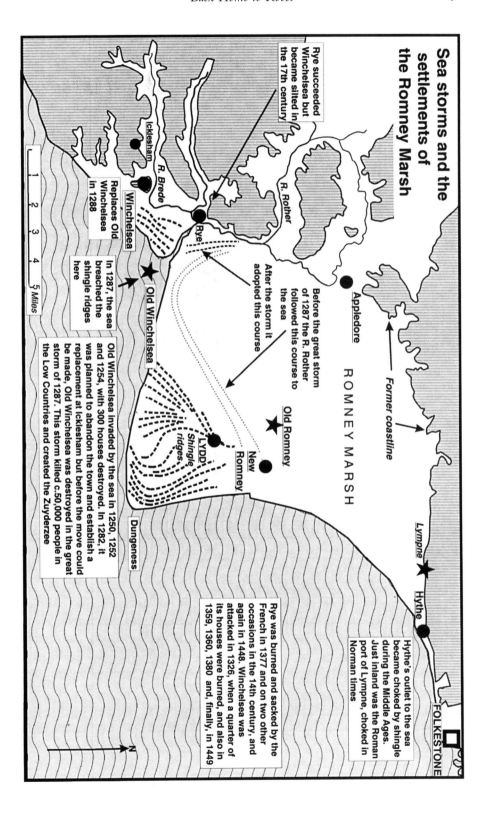

Sea storms and the settlements of the Romney Marsh

Rye suceeded Winchelsea but became silted in the 17th century

Icklesham

R. Brede

R. Rother

Winchelsea

Replaces Old Winchelsea in 1288

Rye

In 1287, the sea breached the shingle ridges here

Old Winchelsea

Appledore

Before the great storm of 1287 the R. Rother followed this course to the sea

After the storm it adopted this course

Former coastline

ROMNEY MARSH

Lympne

Just inland was the Roman port of Lympne, choked in Norman times

Hythe's outlet to the sea became choked by shingle during the Middle Ages.

Old Romney

New Romney

LYDD

Shingle ridges

Old Winchelsea invaded by the sea in 1250, 1252 and 1254, with 300 houses destroyed. In 1282, it was planned to abandon the town and establish a replacement at Icklesham but before the move could be made, Old Winchelsea was destroyed in the great storm of 1287. This storm killed c.50,000 people in the Low Countries and created the Zuyderzee

Dungeness

Rye was burned and sacked by the French in 1377 and on two other occasions in the 14th century, and again in 1448. Winchelsea was attacked in 1326, when a quarter of its houses were burned, and also in 1359, 1360, 1380 and, finally, in 1449

Hythe

FOLKESTONE

N

1 2 3 4 5 *Miles*

pasture and crop land. The port of New Romney, a sea port so valued that its people were relieved of all feudal services bar service at sea, could, in the twelfth century, provide the king with five ships and 120 sailors to crew them. It lay a couple of miles seaward of Old Romney, a port probably badly clogged with silts by the time of the Norman Conquest. New Romney, with its quay, great Norman church and long Saxon history, was overtaken and stranded by the changes caused by the advance of reclamation. Its townspeople created a canal, 'The Rhee', which gathered water, ponded-back from the River Rother and from land drains, and released it at low tide to flush away the silts clogging their harbour and its approaches. Settlers, meanwhile, moved into the reclaimed lands, establishing trackways among the saltings on the gravel ridges that marked former shorelines, building their farmsteads beside them and raising varieties of crops and livestock.

While all this optimistic colonisation was taking place, the climate was becoming increasingly unstable. Old Winchelsea, a town and port that had been granted to the monastery at Fécamp by Canute (1016-35), stood, precariously, on low shingle islands in the estuary of the River Brede by Rye Bay. It was a port of considerable value – so much so that in 1247 the gift of the port to the monastery was revoked and Winchelsea became owned directly by the Crown. However, its misfortunes had scarcely begun. In 1233, a violent storm in the Channel presaged the events to come and in the 1240s, well before the time of the Great Famine, the storms and strong tides had degraded Winchelsea's shingle footings. While the cyclones increased in ferocity, the supply of fresh shingle being washed along the shore diminished and so the damage could not be restored by natural drift and deposition. Shore defences had been cast up, but a succession of storms, in 1244, 1250, 1252 and 1254, battered the town and destroyed 300 dwellings and several churches. Even so, the Winchelsea of the 1260s was still a thriving town, said to be pretty, and with 700 houses and fifty taverns and inns. About a tenth of its population, which may have been as high as 5,000, comprised sailors who were available for royal service. In 1271, the quay to the south of the Church of St Thomas was reportedly borne away by 'tempests of the sea' and most of the church had collapsed in the flood. By 1280, much of Winchelsea lay underwater and Ralph of Sandwich was instructed to establish a replacement settlement on Iham Hill, Icklesham (see map on previous page). The last of these storms, the notorious Great Storm of 1287, appears to have forced the River Rother to change course, signalling the end of New Romney as a seaport. By the end of the century, Old Winchelsea had gone and the waves were coursing across the once-reclaimed lands in the Romney and Walland marshes, while Romney saw its channel and lifeline to the sea choked with sediments and eventually, around 1400, completely clogged, useless and abandoned.

Old Winchelsea had enjoyed the advantage of a short Channel crossing in one direction and proximity to the growing London market, with its appetite for French consumer goods like wine in the other. Its seamen also had a liking for piracy. Edward I (1272-1307) reacted to a pessimistic report in 1282 with the decision to replace the stricken port. A rigidly planned new town of New Winchelsea was established by Icklesham and the Brede Estuary, with as orderly a grid-iron layout of streets as might be found in any North American city today. But before an orderly switch could be accomplished, Winchelsea was drowned. A breach in the old shingle sea defences at the successor port opened into the new harbour, ships sailed in on the tides and, for a while, the town prospered. However, the fate of New Winchelsea would prove no more secure than that of its namesake and the port declined in the face of plague, silting, competition from Rye and cross-Channel raiding. The town was virtually stillborn for, in 1342, just fifty-four years after receiving its official title, New Winchelsea contained some ninety-four unoccupied houses, though it struggled doggedly on. In 1637, the retreat of the shoreline resulted in nearby Camber Castle being left stranded and ineffectual while in 1652 the diarist, John Evelyn, described the hovels and cottages of New Winchelsea as being few and despicable. In the reign of William and Mary (1689-94) the diarist, Celia Fiennes, came to Winchelsea and seems to have been mostly impressed by the traces of its chequerboard layout:

> In ye middle you see it has been a fine place for there were 36 Large Squares of building, the remaines of pieces of walls in most places you see, or else a hedge supplys that you see ye streetes were very broad and long and divided these squares, ye Cross streetes ye same… Remaines of Churches and halls are to be seen but Else grass grows now where Winchelsea was as was once said of Troy. There are but a very few houses now.'

In about 1724, the imaginative writer, reporter and spy, Daniel Defoe, complaining about the electoral corruption of what would become known as 'rotten boroughs' wrote:

> … Winchelsea, a town, if it deserves the name, which is rather the skeleton of an ancient city than a real town, where the ancient gates stand near three miles from one another over the fields, and where the ruins are so buried, that they have made good corn fields of the streets, and the plough goes over the foundations, nay over the first floors of the houses, and where nothing of a town but the destruction of it seems to remain…

A more celebrated victim of the unstable maritime environment is Dunwich, perhaps because of the evocative myth of the undersea tolling of bells from a lost church. Dunwich differed from its south coast counterparts in that it was not sited on vulnerable shingle ridges, but on soft, sandy cliffs, having its harbour facilities in the mouth of the River Blyth. It was, however, like Winchelsea, a seaport of the first rank. An important port in Saxon England, Dunwich had around 3,000 townspeople, six churches and two chapels at the time of *Domesday Book*. It gained borough status at the end of the twelfth century, continued to grow and its fleet in the reign of Edward I (1272-1307), comprised thirty-six merchant vessels, eleven fighting ships and twenty-four fishing smacks. Attempts to create coastal defences gathered urgency during the thirteenth century, though the end for Dunwich came a little later. The Great Storm of 1287 provided a violent warning of things to come and another great storm in 1328 choked the mouth of the harbour and diverted the access to the sea. A terrifying wind drove waves against a shingle spit known as the King's Holme and beds of shingle were piled into the harbour entrance. As the harbour on the Blyth began to choke, so the river developed a new mouth, where Walberswick exploited the volatile geography. In 1342, the sea began to assail the town of Dunwich as well as its harbour and 400 dwellings, two churches (St Martin's and St Leonard's), shops and windmills slumped into the waves as the storm surges undermined the soft cliff on which they had perched. The main Church of the borough, St Nicholas's, was left so precariously perched above the surf that, in 1352, it was abandoned. Another church had to be abandoned in the 1540s, another in the 1650s and yet another in 1755. In 1677, the market place, so symbolic of the town's prosperity, was transgressed by the sea.

Dunwich and Winchelsea were not the only ports of prominence to perish in the onset of the Little Ice Age. Ravenser and Ravenserod, the neighbouring 'Raven towns' of the Humber's mouth, were also victims. In 1256, a storm severed the spit on which the latter stood, yet it continued to function as a commercial centre and traded through its partner. In 1346, its inundation began; in 1355 corpses were being washed from its churchyard, and by the end of the century, it was gone. Ravenser, its outport, was reduced to a manor house.

A combination of the erosion of the town's site and the silting of its harbour resulted in the capture of Dunwich's commerce by Southwold and Walberswick; Defoe explained that the merchants of Dunwich had sought other outlets and:

> … what little trade they have, is carried on by Walberswick, a little town near Swole [Southwold], the vessels coming in there because the ruins of Dunwich make the shore there unsafe and uneasy to the boats; from whence the northern coasting seamen a rude verse of their own using, and I suppose of their own making; as follows,

Swoul and Dunwich and Walberswick
All go in at one lousie creek.

Defoe had visited the town before the terminal storm and told how its people were still clinging to the vestiges of trade; shipping out local butter, cheese and corn. He wondered that a town could decay 'of itself', rather than being the victim of conquest, yet he realised:

> … this town is manifestly decayed by the invasion of the waters, and as other towns seem sufferers by the sea, or the tide withdrawing from their ports, such as Orford… Winchelsea in Kent and the like: so this town is, as it were, eaten up by the sea, as above; and the still encroaching ocean seems to threaten it with a fatal immersion in a few years more.

And thus it would prove, for in 1740, a severe storm devoured what was effectively just the dismembered corpse of a once great town. In 1904 the Norman Church of All Saints, a shell since its rector departed in 1755, surrendered to the sea, apart from its tower which resisted until 1919. A buttress from the church that had witnessed the rise and fall of the town was rescued and erected beside the new Church of St James. Rubble from All Saints could be seen on the beach until the 1950s.

In the realms of evocative monuments, those at Dunwich must have been surpassed by the amazing sight, enjoyed in the nineteenth century, of a cylindrical flint church tower standing, intact, like some great lighthouse on the shore at Eccles in Norfolk, between Cromer and Great Yarmouth. At Hickling, about four miles to the south, some 180 souls were reported to have been drowned in 1287. In 1338, it was recorded that the village church at Eccles was threatened as the sea had destroyed a part of its churchyard, though the end was delayed. Tim Pestall, a researcher, noted that while burials in the churchyard at Eccles continued into the 1560s, by the end of the century, parishioners were requesting burial in the neighbouring churchyard at Hempstead. At the start of the next century, the village was reduced to just fourteen households, around a sixth of the former population, with the bulk of the village supposedly being flooded in 1604. In 1643, the survivors claimed that merely one-twentieth of their land then remained. Then, both the village and its church seem to have been deserted. In the nineteenth century, as the sea drove away dunes that had carpeted the site, tourists arrived to marvel at the soulful Norman tower until it, too, surrendered during a gale in 1895, leaving but a slight stump and some occasionally surfacing bones from the churchyard. Recent excavators of the site noted that the original villagers had chosen a site that was remarkably low. Perhaps they had felt protected by the coastal

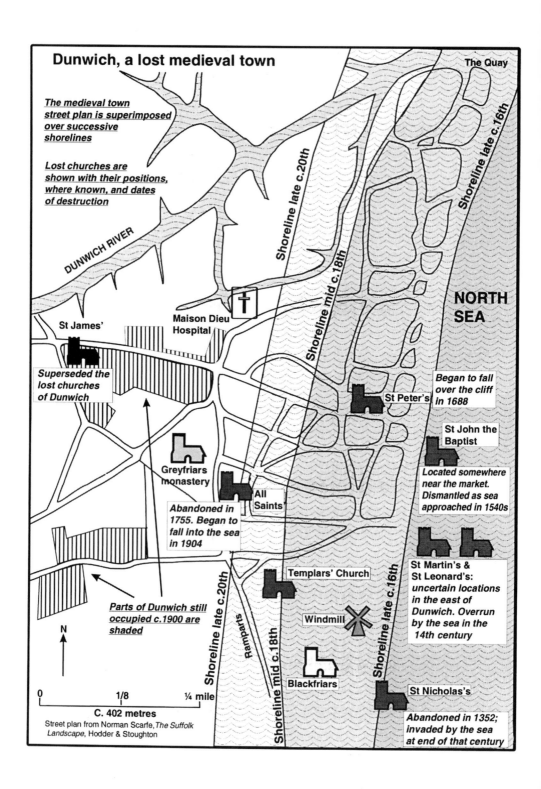

Dunwich, a lost medieval town

The medieval town street plan is superimposed over successive shorelines

Lost churches are shown with their positions, where known, and dates of destruction

The Quay

DUNWICH RIVER

Shoreline late c.20th

Shoreline mid c.18th

Shoreline late c.16th

NORTH SEA

Maison Dieu Hospital

St James'

Superseded the lost churches of Dunwich

St Peter's

Began to fall over the cliff in 1688

St John the Baptist

Located somewhere near the market. Dismantled as sea approached in 1540s

Greyfriars monastery

All Saints

Abandoned in 1755. Began to fall into the sea in 1904

Templars' Church

St Martin's & St Leonard's: *uncertain locations in the east of Dunwich. Overrun by the sea in the 14th century*

Windmill

Parts of Dunwich still occupied c.1900 are shaded

N

Shoreline late c.20th

Ramparts

Shoreline mid c.18th

Shoreline late c.16th

Blackfriars

St Nicholas's

Abandoned in 1352; invaded by the sea at end of that century

0   1/8   ¼ mile

C. 402 metres

Street plan from Norman Scarfe, *The Suffolk Landscape*, Hodder & Stoughton belt of sand dunes and the higher ground to the north and seaward? Once any gaps had been made in these defences, the community was vulnerable to flooding and their lands to contamination by salt water.

The threat of flooding was experienced further north along the North Sea shores, wherever soft cliffs and low coasts were exposed to storm surges driven landward by easterly gales. On the northern shores of the Humber estuary, the reclaimed fields on the estates of the Cistercian Abbey of Meaux were poisoned by salt and scoured away in the 1320s, along with the villages of Sunthorp and Orwithfleet, followed by three more settlements on Sunk Island, which vanished completely from view between the fifteenth and seventeenth centuries. Tharlesthorp, in the same locality, subsided into the Humber in 1400. Further north on Yorkshire's North Sea coast, the villages perched on the crumbly boulder clay cliffs have surrendered in a historical sequence. Furthest out to sea are the graves of at least fourteen Medieval villages; places like Rainbrough, Monkwell, Waxholme and Old Withernsea. Then there is Gartongarth, lost between the mapping of the coast by Speed in 1610 and by Jefferys in 1772, while Owthorne, Outnewton and Dimlington have gone since Jefferys completed his *Atlas of Yorkshire*.

In addition to the places that were obliterated by storms and tides, there are several that were reduced and debilitated and yet survive. Aldeburgh in Suffolk is famous for its music festival, but its area is but a portion of that occupied when Drake's ships, the *Greyhound* and *Pelican* (later *Golden Hind*) were built there in what was then a significant port and shipbuilding centre. Its outlet, the River Alde, silted and closed the port to larger ships and the town declined to become a mere fishing village and a rotten borough, stripped of its representation in Parliament in the reforms of 1832. The Moot Hall survives as a symbol of Elizabethan greatness. To the south of Aldeburgh, the great spit of Orford Ness was growing as the tides and currents swept sand and shingle southwards. The River Ore was forced further and further southwards by the growing spit, until the old town of Orford, itself still a thriving town when Drake's ships were being built, became obscured and cut-off. By the eighteenth century, the waters behind the spit were of interest only as a place of shelter from storms. Walberswick grew as Dunwich was diminished and it shared its peak years with Aldeburgh. But at the end of the sixteenth century, the accumulation of shingle at the harbour necessitated the cutting of a new navigable channel. Attempts to develop a strong fishing industry in the two centuries that followed were unavailing. Walberswick had capitalised on the decline of Dunwich, and being located at the new outlet of the River Blyth, it took over some of the commerce from the ailing port (it is also believed to have put the old town's protesting customs officers to the sword), while developing fishing and embedding some of its prosperity in the

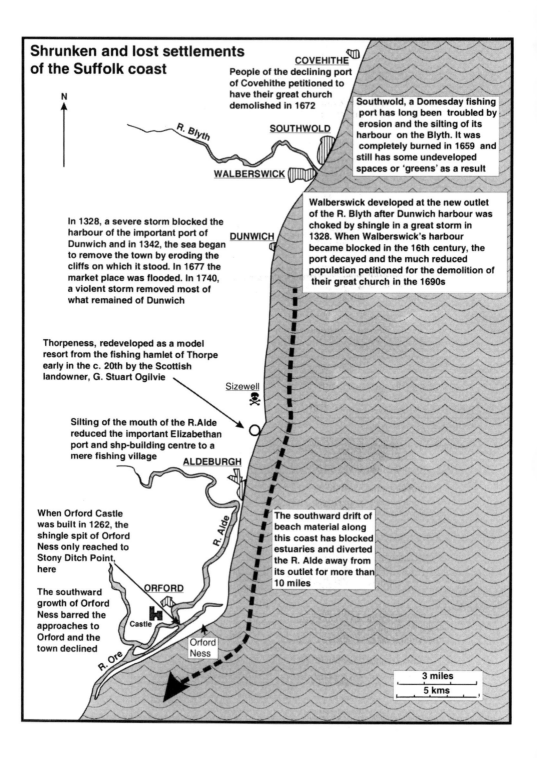

Shrunken and lost settlements of the Suffolk coast

N

COVEHITHE
People of the declining port of Covehithe petitioned to have their great church demolished in 1672

SOUTHWOLD

Southwold, a Domesday fishing port has long been troubled by erosion and the silting of its harbour on the Blyth. It was completely burned in 1659 and still has some undeveloped spaces or 'greens' as a result

R. Blyth

WALBERSWICK

Walberswick developed at the new outlet of the R. Blyth after Dunwich harbour was choked by shingle in a great storm in 1328. When Walberswick's harbour became blocked in the 16th century, the port decayed and the much reduced population petitioned for the demolition of their great church in the 1690s

In 1328, a severe storm blocked the harbour of the important port of Dunwich and in 1342, the sea began to remove the town by eroding the cliffs on which it stood. In 1677 the market place was flooded. In 1740, a violent storm removed most of what remained of Dunwich

DUNWICH

Thorpeness, redeveloped as a model resort from the fishing hamlet of Thorpe early in the c. 20th by the Scottish landowner, G. Stuart Ogilvie

Sizewell

Silting of the mouth of the R.Alde reduced the important Elizabethan port and shp-building centre to a mere fishing village

ALDEBURGH

When Orford Castle was built in 1262, the shingle spit of Orford Ness only reached to Stony Ditch Point, here

The southward drift of beach material along this coast has blocked estuaries and diverted the R. Alde away from its outlet for more than 10 miles

R. Alde

The southward growth of Orford Ness barred the approaches to Orford and the town declined

ORFORD

Castle

R. Ore

Orford Ness

3 miles

5 kms

Covehithe ruined church – a monument to the vagaries of the sea.

spectacular fifteenth-century Church of St Andrew. As the tide of Walberswick's fortune turned, the townspeople, who had been able to boast one of England's finest Perpendicular churches, were humiliatingly obliged to petition for its demolition in the 1690s. The church tower was preserved as a landmark for sailors. The same had been the fate of Covehithe, about six miles north along the coast. Its dwindling population could no longer fund their great church and petitioned for its demolition in 1672. All along the eastern shores of England one encounters hopeful little resorts, some with the last vestiges of a fishing fleet but quite a few with a rather distant history of urban commerce as well.

Sand dunes had protected Eccles and some other coastal communities, but dunes are not always stable and do not always protect. Rocks, eroding from sea cliffs, are gradually ground into sand between the pebbles and boulders of the shore. There, these products of diminution are joined by other grains, eroded from the land and washed to the sea by rivers. When the winds are strong, sand can be blasted from the beaches, to accumulate above the strandline in chains of dunes. Such dunes can form protective belts, guarding a shore or screening an inlet. However, their loose soils are slow to be colonised by plants. Until humus levels build and allow the dense and deep-rooted growth of vegetation, fields of dunes are liable to migrate before a driving gale. An acquaintance with lost villages reveals that lightning is, indeed, likely to strike in the same place, with one assault on a community eventually provoking another one from a quite different direction. While building his great state-of-the-art fortress at Beaumaris, on Anglesey, Edward I uprooted an established Welsh commercial community in the township of Llanfaes. They were removed to Newborough, a new, purpose-built settlement on a royal estate in the south of Anglesey in 1303. Of the original townlet only the parish Church of St Katherine survived, yet Newborough proved a poor choice, though merchants were originally attracted and commerce and a leather tanning industry survived beyond the Middle Ages. The main impediment to growth was sand. At the time of Newborough's foundation, the town was set in good farmland. In the fourteenth century, however, a succession of very violent storms caused sand dunes to migrate across the countryside to the south and west of the town. The problem persisted through the Medieval period, with the only agent for stabilising the dunes being the drought-tolerant marram grass, which bound the unconsolidated sands with its roots. However, the marram was regularly being cut for the making of mats. When Elizabeth I introduced a ban on this mowing, the sands became more stable. By this time, the rabbit, a Norman introduction from the continent, had acclimatised and had gravitated from being a delicate luxury to become common fare and locally, a pest. Rabbits colonised the dunes and Newborough gained a new function as a warren; rather less of a destiny than had been hoped for. Around six miles to the north-west of Newborough lay the ancient capital of the Welsh Princes of Gwynedd, Aberffraw. Here, too, the dunes became active as the Little Ice Age approached, and a warren developed to the east of the old palace and capital, now reduced to a modest village.

Wales has an impressive endowment of sand-afflicted places. One of the most striking is Llandanwg, about two and a half miles to the south of the remarkable castle town of Harlech, where an old church lies half entombed in the dunes. The simple, rectangular building is of the thirteenth and fifteenth centuries, but the inscribed stones of the sixth century and the dedication to the ancient Breton saint, Tanwg, suggest a much longer history of devotion here. Burials in the churchyard continued through to modern times, though in 1841 the church, where the sand level varies according to the vagaries of the winds, was superseded by its neighbour at Harlech. Kenfig, three miles to the north of Porthcawl, was altogether a more substantial place and lasted rather longer than Newborough. When the Normans penetrated Wales, the indigenous lord was supplanted by Robert Fitzhamon, the Earl of Gloucester. Robert's earthen fortress was in turn soon superseded by a stone keep, to the south of which the feudal borough of Kenfig coalesced. Kenfig was formally established in 1183 and had a stormy existence in the centuries that followed, being an inviting target for Welsh patriots. Two centuries of insurgencies and burning were not complete before the migrating dunes of Kenfig Burrows posed a very different challenge. The problem of drifting sand arose in the thirteenth century, and by 1471 the town church had been rendered unusable. By the seventeenth century, many areas inside the old town's stockade had been buried by sand and at the start of that century, a new Town Hall was built to replace the original hall, by then entombed. Kenfig was by this time no more than a village. A solitary family was recorded left living among the sand-swathed ruins of the castle in 1665.

Wales was not the only country with settlements overwhelmed by drifting sand. At the Sands of Forvie, around the estuary of the River Ythan in North East Scotland, the vagrant dunes have entrapped both an Early Iron Age settlement and a Dark Age/Medieval village. Among the sand, grasses and wild herbs lie the remains of a church dating back to AD 704. Beneath the sands nearby are the relics of the stone- and clay-walled houses from a village that perished in a sandstorm in 1413; the consequence of a curse by a noble daughter cheated of her inheritance, or so the story goes. At the other end of Britain, the ancient Church of St Piran lies engulfed by dunes near Perranporth in Cornwall. In indigenous Cornish eyes it has an iconic status, being of immense national significance, while also being one of the oldest of Christian monuments in Britain. St Piran is the patron saint of Cornwall, and also of tin miners, of which the Duchy once had a great many. Some date the oratory to AD 450 and others to the following century. The stone building probably succeeded others of timber and is likely to post-date the legendary saint by quite some time. It may have been abandoned as the Penhale Sands advanced in the tenth century and then replaced by St Piran Old Church with its attendant graveyard, itself abandoned in 1805. Tin miners, ironically, were blamed for disrupting a stream that had previously swept the sand away. The antiquarian, William Camden (1551-1623), knew of the existence of a buried church dedicated to St Piran, but it was not until the late eighteenth century that the oratory was rediscovered. It was recovered from the sands and in 1835 was said to be remarkably well-preserved, but then its appears to have deteriorated considerably. Because of the erosive effects of wind-blown sand, it was returned to a protective entombment. In the spring of 2004, hundreds of Cornish people marched across the dunes as part of a campaign to have the oratory of Cornwall's national saint uncovered and restored.

Despite being assailed by floods and blowing sand, British settlements face a relatively narrow range of natural hazards. Avalanches do not afflict them, earthquakes are not terminal in their effects and volcanoes only exert indirect attacks. Landslides are seldom a challenge, though a few quite brutal instances are known. In 1664 a landslide destroyed almost the whole of the Yorkshire coastal community at Runswick Bay, sparing but a single cottage. The dwellings of the small fishing community were

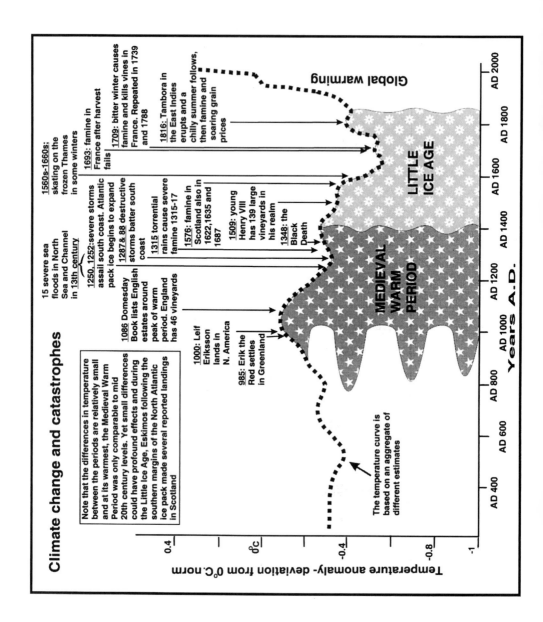

Climate change and catastrophes

Note that the differences in temperature between the periods are relatively small and at its warmest, the Medieval Warm Period was only comparable to mid 20th century levels. Yet small differences could have profound effects and during the Little Ice Age, Eskimos following the southern margins of the North Atlantic ice pack made several reported landings in Scotland

15 severe sea floods in North Sea and Channel in 13th century

1250, 1252: severe storms assail south coast. Atlantic pack ice begins to expand

1086 Domesday Book lists English estates around peak of warm period. England has 46 vineyards

1287 & 88 destructive storms batter south coast

1000: Leif Eriksson lands in N. America

985: Erik the Red settles in Greenland

1315 torrential rains cause severe famine 1315-17

1576: famine in Scotland also in 1622, 1635 and 1687

1509: young Henry VIII has 139 large vineyards in his realm

1348: the Black Death

1560s-1660s; skating on the frozen Thames in some winters

1693: famine in France after harvest fails

1709: bitter winter causes famine and kills vines in France. Repeated in 1739 and 1788

1816: Tambora in the East Indies erupts and a chilly summer follows, then famine and soaring grain prices

Global warming

MEDIEVAL WARM PERIOD

LITTLE ICE AGE

The temperature curve is based on an aggregate of different estimates

Years A.D.

AD 400   AD 600   AD 800   AD 1000   AD 1200   AD 1400   AD 1600   AD 1800   AD 2000

Temperature anomaly - deviation from 0°C norm

0.4   0°C   -0.4   -0.8   -1

huddled near the foot of an unstable cliff. Fortunately, two mourners at a wake recognised the initial movements and the village was evacuated. Learning from mistakes and natural disasters is not a human trait, for another movement on the unstable cliffs destroyed a small iron smelter there in 1858. Victorian Yorkshire seems to have harboured ambitions to become the landslide capital of Britain. During a storm in the depths of the winter of 1829, the village of Kettlewell, an alum working settlement near Runswick Bay, began to slump from its crumbling cliff. The cliff was too steep for the villagers to escape upwards, but many found refuge on an alum transporting boat that was fortunately anchored just offshore. Then at the other end of the Broad Acres, at the end of the nineteenth century, the village of Fewston, near Harrogate, began to slip. This became a local tourist attraction for visitors to the spa, following a slumping of the slope on which it stood causing the dwellings to become cracked and distorted. The blame lay with the construction in the direct vicinity of two reservoirs to serve Leeds, the works having affected the drainage patterns in the locality.

The onset of the Little Ice Age brought many dramas as settlements were toppled from their perches or engulfed by storm tides. A trawl through the evidence leaves us with many images of terror and violence. These, however, were just symptoms of a much more serious and pervasive malaise, for while the coastal fringes of Atlantic Europe were being remodelled by the gales and waves, the lands that they contained were suffering slower, but remorseless, fates. The sheep bleating across a sodden fell or the horses hock deep in a squelching morass; the oats sagging on stems speckled black with mould; the wheat that yesterday stood shoulder high but was now driven flat; the smoke and steam from a newly-built corn drier, or the hay that stank mustily of rot: these signalled much more pervasive problems. The map of village farming had to be redrawn. The warmth had gone from the upper margins, and so too must the cultivation of cereals. The hopeful little settlements budded-off into farming's margins were but a summer's folly. The clay vales stayed dank and cold in April and were now better suited for livestock than for crops. Less grain could be grown, so fewer calories were produced. Settlements must retreat and shrink. Famines trimmed the population and the survivors were more poorly nourished. They were less well prepared to survive the next famine, and the next. People already starved of calories and vitamins, and bowed by the struggle to maintain yields from a decaying environment, were ill-placed to survive the next epidemic. One would come, one always did.

CHAPTER SEVEN

A GREAT DYING

The Pestilence amongst us

This is a rather short chapter. Since it concerns the Black Death, its brevity may seem surprising. However, those villages that are known to have been exterminated directly and permanently by the terrible disease are quite few in number. The majority of rural communities tend to be unaware of the existence of a deserted village in their parishes or townships. There are many, though, that are aware of such places. Whenever one invites local opinions, the virtually invariable response attributes the death of the settlement to 'the Black Death'. That today's villagers should believe that the Black Death was a great slayer of settlements should not surprise us, for this was believed at the time of the first epidemics. The chronicler and canon of St Mary's, Leicester, Henry Knighton (d. 1396), wrote:

> After the pestilence, many buildings, great and small, fell into ruins in every city for lack of inhabitants, likewise many villages and hamlets became desolate, not a house being left in them, all having died who dwelt there; and it was probable that many such villages would never be inhabited.

The plague has left a persisting legacy of horror. It was not so much an event as a long period of devastation and foreboding that haunted communities from the arrival of the Pestilence in the late 1340s, through the era of Shakespeare and even into the times of Daniel Defoe (1660-1731). Even the nightmarish recollections of the Black Death cannot acquaint us with the terrors and mind-warping experiences undergone by the people who saw their worlds of kinship, work and fellowship torn apart before their eyes.

In seeking to comprehend a little of this, we need to appreciate that our fourteenth-century villagers were extremely tough people in every respect. Natural selection, driven by virulent diseases, terrible working conditions, extreme poverty and malnutrition, ensured that only the most robust individuals survived infancy. If we could enter a village dwelling and sit on a rustic form beside one of the occupants, we would be in no doubt about the lack of soap and bathing. He seems oriental, but his complexion is a concoction of sunburn, sweat and earthen dust. He wears his homeland on his face. This grubbiness is not our villager's fault; his house has no plumbing, no wash basin and no bath. The closest approach to bathing comes on the hottest days, when the men, goaded by exhaustion, dash from the fields and plunge into disease-ridden rivers or ponds; it comes again on the wettest days, when the driving rain seeps through sodden garments to weave channels through the grime. Only after the most sustained of downpours are the village men reminded that their workmates have pink complexions. In our villager's bowels, parasitic worms are slowly writhing; little twitching movements flick the hairs on his scalp, and he habitually and involuntarily slaps and scratches the bites of fleas and the itches of the lice. Grit from the millstones is scouring the enamel from his teeth and creating pits where infection and excruciating pain will be born. Under his coarse woollen clothes, themselves an anthology of invertebrate life, his taught muscles pull on joints and bones weakened by childhood famines and before he has been an adult for long, the cold mists will set half a dozen old injuries aching.

He, and the members of his village community, survive on a doctrine of fatalism. For Fate, they substitute God, and whenever a tragedy occurs then they tell each other that it was God's will. Each calamity in the community sets heads nodding in a way that underlines resignation and the inevitability of misfortune. This is their way of saying that there is nothing to be done about it so they might as well get on with life. Dead cattle, miscarriages, war bands, butter that will not churn and harvest downpours, all are God's will or the Devil's work. Pickled in adversity and shielded by fatalism, our villagers seem to be as defiant and resilient a bunch as one might ever meet. There are, however, small chinks in their mental and physical armour. The progressive deterioration in the climate has exposed the weaknesses of over-population, the vulnerability of communities that out-number their resources. Famines have become more common, and each famine leaves a legacy of debilitation, making those affected more susceptible to the bloody flux or some other colourfully-named disease of mysterious origins. Still, epidemics are a part of life, not ogres from outside. They are there in the ditches, in the thatch and around the hearth. The nature and consequences of their visitations are familiar; they are parts of village life. Their tap on the shoulder comes as no surprise.

There was not a villager in the realm who had not seen death enacted, seen the tortured corpse carried away and seen the body, sagging in its shroud and without a coffin, lain to rest. Yet how can we enter the consciousness of a not-unusual villager who saw (say), his two brothers die in agony just inches from his sleeping place, who then lost his mother, his sole surviving grandparent, an aunt, three cousins and five of his dozen best friends? How could he cope with the successive mental blows of seeing all these deaths take place within just a fortnight? And how could he survive in a village where every corner and plot was haunted by the faces of dead friends and neighbours? The land next to his in Town Pond furlong was Robin Lidgate's. Sometimes he could still hear Robin hoeing behind him, would call to ask if he had any weak ale to spare – then turn and remember that Robin was laying black and bloated in the plague pit. Then he might see widow Atwood stooped at the flank of her little milk cow, milking. But as he gazed, she would reform as a thistle clump, for she, too, was in the pit.

He might lose his senses and wander in aimless disbelief. Many did. But a day would dawn when the village was plague-free, if only for a while. Then, there would be those who would realise that their days of extreme poverty were over. The plague had ended the years of sullen obedience and perpetual hunger. Now, more than a third of the holdings in the village were empty and available on easier terms. They might be haunted by their recently dead tenants, but now these lands, empty as none had been for much more than a century, beckoned to the survivors. Now, the only limit to a household's land holding might be set by the level where they surrendered to exhaustion. Households with none bar paupers in their ancestries might now rise to the dignity of thirty-acre holdings and employ their own downtrodden landless cottar.

Not only were holdings lying empty, but so, too, were some villages. These were usually rather sad and struggling places where the special awfulness and potency of the disease had reduced the population below the numerical or psychological levels where recovery was possible. Sometimes, the dwellings and perhaps the corpses, too, were left to the dogs and the flies as the survivors departed to sleep under hedgerows or lodge with relatives and in neighbouring villages. Normally, however, colonists would return within a few years, if not before, setting up their houses upon or near to the wreckage of the former village. A place might be infested by hideous memories and stalked by ghosts, but if it was a village it would have village land – and if it had land it would be resettled and the settlers would need somewhere to live.

The blackest of deaths

About Midsummer Day in 1348, just before the feast of St John the Baptist, a little pot-bellied sailing ship carrying goods from Gascony gently pitched and rolled into the anchorage at Melcombe in Dorset. The plague, known at the time as the Pestilence, had arrived. Its arrival was inevitable. It had burst out of Asia to reach the Crimean Black Sea shores in 1347, and had rampaged through Italy in the following spring. By 1352, the whole of Europe would be in its grip as it invaded the easternmost shores of the Baltic and Finland. Melcombe could not satisfy the ravenous disease and it soon spread through Southampton and thence to Bristol, an international port and England's second city. Among the open sewers, cess pits, roadside middens, waste-strewn fish quays, fly-infested food stalls and urban pigsties of this vibrant, affluent and stinking port, the disease found its metier. It would have been during the violent culling of Bristol's townsfolk, out-stripping the ability of the burial parties, that an awareness of the unique potency of the new disease would have travelled across the kingdom. By 1349, fifteen of the town's fifty-two councillors were dead. Before the autumn of 1348 was much advanced, the Black Death had arrived in London. In the spring of 1349 it had entered the Midlands and Wales and the northern marches of England, and in 1350, it raged like wildfire in Scotland. Henry Knighton described the impact of the Pestilence on the East Midlands:

> There died at Leicester in the little parish of St Leonard more than 380, in the parish of Holy Cross more than 400; in the parish of St Margaret of Leicester more than 700; and so in each parish a great number. Then the bishop of Lincoln gave general power to all and every priest to hear confessions, and absolve all with full and entire authority except in matters of debt, in which case the dying man, if he could should pay-off the debt while he still lived, or others should certainly fulfil that obligation from his property after he died.

What was the disease that could cause such carnage in populations so hardened to infectious diseases? The people affected had no certain answers, but the notion that foul miasmas or vapours caused infection to spread was widespread. Fires were lit in the streets to purify the air, fragrant herbs were burned to refresh the atmosphere indoors, and bakers were sometimes required to keep their hot loaves in the bakery until the aroma of baking had dispersed. There was a very widespread belief that the Pestilence was divine retribution. Given that organised village worship was so heavily coloured by doctrines of sin, guilt and retribution, such ideas were scarcely surprising. Some sought to appease the Lord through prayer and sacrifice and a few thought that communities living lives of purity and abstinence in isolation might enjoy His protection. Others still took an apocalyptic view of the Pestilence and pursued missions of debauchery in anticipation of the end. However, zealots in holy orders claimed that it was aristocratic debauchery at tournaments and the like that had brought the Great Mortality down upon Christendom.

There must also have been an awareness that the disease spread from person to person, as suggested in Geoffrey the Baker's account of the arrival of the Pestilence in the West Country, 'From [the Dorset ports] it passed into Devonshire and Somersetshire, even into Bristol, and raged in such sort that the Gloucestershire men would not suffer the Bristol men to have access to them by any means'. This understanding persisted, so that in 1665, Daniel Defoe wrote of seemingly healthy people who acted as carriers for the disease, 'Such a person was in fact a poisoner, a walking destroyer perhaps for a week or fortnight before his death, who might have ruined those that he would have hazarded his life to save...'. Even so, more than three centuries after the arrival of the disease, preventative medicine strategies amounted to little more than keeping away from the victims. The disease, however, seemed capable of spanning most divides. Relatively sanitary communities, like monks and friars in their houses and nuns in convents, do not seem to have fared notice-ably better than the people of the filthy villages – and the tentacles of Pestilence reached the solitary hill farms as well as the seething ghet-toes. Later medical experts knew from earlier accounts of epidemics that a swelling of the lymph glands had been a feature of the disease, and in the late nineteenth century it seemed certain that the guilty disease could be identified as bubonic plague, which produced similar swell-ings or 'buboes' in the armpit or groin. Bubonic plague, which still kills around 2,000 people a year, is a disease of rodents caused by a bacterium named *Yersinia pestis* after Yersin, its discoverer, which is passed between rats by infected fleas. When their hosts perish, the fleas may then transfer to human hosts, spreading the infection with their bites. Then, it seemed that the accelerated virulence of the Black Death as it spread across England was caused by a mutation of the bubonic form of the disease into a yet more lethal pneumonic one that could be spread by sneezing. Symptoms of the pneumonic form were rather different, but death was still more certain.

Recently, however, it has been recognised that while the Medieval Black Death had some of the features of bubonic plague, there are others that do not seem to be shared. A team of anthropologists, three from Penn State University and one from the University of Washington, have been study-ing English church records and other documents that reveal the pattern of the deaths of priests in the first plague years. They reveal the remarkable rapidity of the spread of the disease; during the plague months these priests faced risks of death that were forty-five times greater than in normal times. Other researchers, too, have pointed out that the Black Death seems to have been far more virulent than bubonic plague, spanning countries more quickly than rats ever could. Also, the massive mortality in the rat population that must be part of a bubonic plague epidemic does not seem to be indicated in any Medieval accounts, although modern experiences tell that the appearance of thousands of rodent bodies marks the beginning of bubonic epidemics as fleas desert their dead hosts. Moreover, while the Pestilence returned again and again, bubonic epidemics should come to an end once the rat population has been killed-off by the disease. Then, as Christopher Duncan and Susan Scot have pointed out, rats live within small, confined territories and so a wildfire spread of disease across countrysides should not be possible, while fleas could not multiply in cold northern European climates. In addition, the conventional explanation that the endemic ended when the brown rat replaced the black now seems unsure. There may even have been no rats in the Medieval countryside and the expansion of the brown rat, the successor to the plague-carrying black rat, was not effective until six decades after the Pestilence had left Europe. Where detailed records of the spread of infection are known, as at Eyam in Derbyshire, the patterns do not match those of bubonic plague. Finally, the symptoms described by Medieval chroniclers do not match those of bubonic plague. Prominent on the chests of Black Death victims, were the 'God's tokens', reddish spots caused by haemorrhaging beneath the skin.

So the cause of the Black Death must once again be mysterious. The bacterium or virus responsible may be extinct or it may be dormant, waiting to return again. The disease might have been a form of the terrifying ebola, or a more potent mutation of bubonic plague – one that spread by human contact – or it might be an unknown disease. Bubonic plague still has the ability to mutate and a form resistant to antibiotics has recently emerged. With a mortality rate of almost 100 per cent and an ability to exterminate in one great attack and in a hideous, agonising and humiliating manner about 40 per cent of the British population, the Black Death's assault is the most loathsome event in all British history. By the end of the fourteenth century, the number of its victims amounted to about half the British population. Soon to die in the spring of 1349, the Welsh poet Jeuan Gethin wrote:

Woe is me of the shilling [the buboe] in the armpit; it is seething, terrible, wherever it may come, a head that gives pain and causes a loud cry, a burden carried under the arms, a painful angry knob, a white lump. It is of a form of an apple, like the head of an onion, a small boil that spares no-one. Great is its seething, like a burning cinder, a grievous thing of an ashy colour. It is an ugly eruption that comes with unseemly haste. It is a grievous ornament that breaks out in a rash. The early ornaments of black death.

Quite swiftly, these 'ornaments' would spread to all parts of the body and black or purple spots would appear on the chest and other places; sometimes few but large and sometimes many and small. They signalled that a merciful death would soon arrive. It came about three days after the appearance of buboes.

Plague in the village

The experts agree that the first great eruption of the Pestilence removed between a third and a half of the British population. If, say, 40 per cent of people died we can begin to gauge the impact on Village England – but it was not the case that every village lost four out of every ten inhabitants. Some might suffer just a few mortalities, while other communities might be virtually exterminated, or some age groups in a community might be almost wiped out while others were lightly touched. Various complications seem to be at work, including the possibility, described below, that genetic immunity may have spared some people, even those in close contact with infectious corpses. It is very difficult to identify villages exterminated by the plague – in part because they were probably rather few. The evidence available is far from being conclusive. Because ordinary people were not normally worthy subjects for the clerks, our best evidence of human impacts concerns the records of the death and replacement of priests, mortality rates in religious houses and the replacement of tenants. Thus, if 45 per cent of the priests in a diocese died in 1348-49, and if we deduct a value for normal mortality, then we are left with a figure for plague deaths of over 40 per cent, that is likely to be roughly representative for the population of the diocese as a whole. However, we must be cautious. The death rate for priests could have been higher than average and this might be explained by infections some received when administering the last rites to plague victims. The second source of evidence comes from relief from taxation granted to communities so reduced that they were unable to pay their taxes (reliefs could be granted for other reasons, and in 1349, both Scottish raiding and the Pestilence devastated the country around Durham). Records of the vacation of holdings can reveal great epidemics and in the king's Forest of Knaresborough about 45-50 per cent of tenanted holdings were vacated in 1348-49, the great majority being the tenancies of plague victims.

The great Pestilence fell upon communities weakened by famine and confused by the adversity of the climate. In the church at Ashwell, in Hertfordshire, frightened villagers huddled around their priest in the base of the church tower while the clerk, perhaps fearful that the world was ending and anxious to leave a record, diverted their attention by

Graffiti inside the church tower at Ashwell. The bottom line translates as: 'On St Maur's day it thunders on the earth'.

scratching a message in the soft clunch (chalk) that lined the tower. Others had done the same, so that a chronicle of hardships remains. There are stark announcements of the eruption of the Pestilence in 1349 and of a different epidemic in 1300, and also longer inscriptions telling how the surviving dregs of humanity witnessed a great tempest in 1350 and, 'On St Maur's day this year 1361 it thunders on the earth'.

When all this is taken into account, the popular vision of the plague village – with the screams of the dying issuing from the dwellings, bereaved friends and relatives standing stunned and weeping, new orphans made homeless, the byre waiting in a doorway, the gaping plague pit with the attendant clouds of flies, and no priest remaining to mumble the right words as the earth is shovelled into the pit – all this must have happened in thousands of places. Henry Knighton described the scenes in villages reduced to chaos by the epidemic:

> Sheep and cattle wandered over fields and through crops, and there was no one to go and drive them or gather them for there was such a lack of servants that no man knew what he ought to do. Wherefore many crops perished in the fields for want of someone to gather them.

However, villages were much harder to kill than people. Some communities abandoned their settlements and sought safety in isolation and, as Boccaccio, a survivor or the ravaging of Florence in 1348, wrote in *The Decameron*:

> Others still held a yet more cruel opinion... They said that the only medicine against the plague-stricken was to go right away from them.

Men and women, convinced of this and caring about nothing but themselves, deserted their own city, their own houses, their dwellings, their
relatives, their property, and went abroad or at least to the country round
Florence, as if God's wrath in punishing men's wickedness with this plague
would not follow them but strike only those who remained within the
walls of the city, or as if they thought nobody in the city would remain alive
and that its last hour had come.

There must also have been various British villages that were abandoned in
similar ways, for weeks, months or even years. Such abandonments could
have taken place without ever surfacing in any surviving record. Medieval
villages entered the record at landmarks in the accounting cycle, like the
levying of poll taxes. One could quite easily 'vanish' for three years or so
without its absence being recorded. At Eyam, the famous Derbyshire village, the reverse decision was taken: to suffer self-imposed isolation for
the protection of others. Partly because of the relative recentness of the
events, Eyam has captured the popular imagination, though the death of
260 people from a population of about 800 was less than the average village toll in 1348-49. The popular version of the events records that the
plague was brought to Eyam in a box of infected cloth by the local tailor,
George Viccars, in 1665 (the year of a great Pestilence eruption in London).
He soon died, but the epidemic spread in the village. Then, under the
leadership of their rector, William Mompesson, the members of the community took the courageous step of imposing a voluntary quarantine and
remaining in the plague-stricken village to face their fate. Money to pay
for supplies was left in a stream outside the village, while coins circulat-
ing in the community were (hopefully) cleaned with vinegar. The Earl
of Devonshire arranged for provisions to be left on the southern limits
of the village. However, this received version may be misleading and the
historian, Patrick Wallis, has recently pointed out that Eyam:

> … attracts tens of thousands of visitors each year, making it an epicentre of
> Europe's plague heritage. The story of Eyam's plague is told as an exemplary
> narrative of heroic self sacrifice, in which the villagers suffer in self-imposed
> isolation to save the county from disease. It is, however, largely a fiction,
> a romantic tragedy constructed on a slender basis of evidence in the late
> eighteenth and early nineteenth centuries.

The role of Mompesson, who sent his own children to the relative safety
of Sheffield just before the village was quarantined, and who, according to
a later account, also urged his wife to leave, has been questioned. He was
a relative newcomer and seems not to have been taken into the hearts of

The church at Eyam. The village is the most famous plague victim, though unlike some others, it survived.

the villagers. His predecessor, Thomas Stanley, who was a previous rector at Eyam in 1644-60 and curate there in 1660-62, had moved back to the village in 1664. He had replaced an exceedingly unpopular and corrupt incumbent, he was highly regarded, and he appears to have been at least as influential as Mompesson. However, he was tainted in the eyes of authority with Puritan practices while Mompesson was a 'safe' Anglican. Still a popular local preacher, Stanley could well have had more influence than his successor. There are other fascinating aspects to the Eyam story, including a pattern of infection that does not seem compatible with bubonic plague and also the suggestion that some of those who survived at Eyam may have owed their good fortune to a gene mutation 'CCR5-delta 32' which has been found to be present in 14 per cent of people descended from plague survivors, though this proposal is disputed by subsequent research. There are documented cases of people who were in close and prolonged contact with plague victims and yet survived, and they are intriguing.

Once struck by the Pestilence, a settlement might, as mentioned, lose a handful of its population or the greater part of it. The village community that was killed stone dead, leaving nothing whatsoever but dwellings strewn with corpses, probably belongs in the realms of fiction. There is a hint of a total mortality in a record left just before he died by a friar, John Clyn, in Kilkenny, who was writing as though he was the sole survivor of a dead religious community. He wrote, 'I, seeing these many ills, and that the whole world encompassed by evil, waiting among the dead for death to come, have committed to writing what I have truly heard and examined...' He added that he would leave parchment so that his work could be continued if anyone should escape the Pestilence and be alive in the future.

We cannot doubt that villages were temporarily abandoned but it is difficult to discover examples of settlements that were permanently extinguished. Maurice Beresford found a small cluster of such places (coincidentally?) in Oxfordshire. Standhill or Standelf was one. In 1446 a generous relief from taxation was given, apparently because the community had been devastated by a plague. In the next year, the rector reduced his visits to the village chapel from thrice a week to once a week, claiming that there were no inhabitants remaining on account of the plague (so why did he need to go at all?). Tilgardesle was a second and the village seems to have been a victim of the initial invasion by the Pestilence, for in 1359 it was reported that nobody had lived there for ten years. Tax collectors hoped that a community might return, but in 1422 this cause was seen to be lost and the land was parcelled-out into leaseholds. Tusmore was a third Oxfordshire plague victim, being given a total relief from taxes in 1354 and four years later it was recorded that all the bond tenants had died. In the same county there are several settlements, like Wretchwick and Chalford, which were greatly debilitated by the plague and perhaps exposed to attacks by greedy landlords. Plague victims are hard to detect and the task is made complicated by the blaming of depopulations on the plague by those lords who were really responsible for the removal of tenants and enclosure of village lands.

Across the kingdom in Norfolk, archaeologists found the evidence of their abandoned churches. Until the sixteenth century, the pattern is fairly steady, with an abandonment rate of about seven for every half-century. It may be significant that the exception is the half-century 1350-1400, which, with fifteen abandonments, is twice the 'norm'. This is probably an effect of the recurrent pestilences of that century; a proportion of them might have been caused by the Black Death, but only three of them can be unequivocally attributed to that notorious plague of 1349.

The Black Death was a killer that covered its traces very well – or rather, the paucity of surviving documentations often obliges the landscape detective to accept an open verdict.

The village resurgent

There was not one Pestilence epidemic, but many, the famous Eyam outbreak occurring more than 300 years after the initial outbreak in Britain. The initial occurrence, killing around 40 per cent of the population, fizzled out after 1350. The Pestilence returned in 1361 in an epidemic known at the time as 'the plague of boys' or 'mortality of children', which took its heaviest toll on males and young people. This plague raged until 1364, after which there was a respite of only five years before another epidemic occurred, one that was again particularly voracious of young lives. The Pestilence erupted again in 1374, when London suffered severely. Before the wretched century was over there were major outbreaks in 1378 and 1390 that again seemed to target the young. Disease seems to have been evolving in a direction that made adolescents and children particularly vulnerable. It would be a source of terror, and sometimes death, until the eighteenth century.

For those who survived one or more assault of the Pestilence, life could never again be the same. Villagers who came through the torments with their minds intact would come to realise that paralleling the terror, grief and awfulness was a different universe of freedom, sufficiency and opportunity. The bloodstreams of villagers might be infested by bacteria, but the 'blood of the village' had a far stronger life force. This point was emphasised each time a stricken community returned to the site of its joy, companionship and bereavement. There must have been hundreds of occasions when a band returned to the tattered-roofed dwellings after the stench of the plague had died down and the abandoned dogs had scavenged away any unburied corpses. Cublington in Buckinghamshire was such a place. It was completely abandoned late in the fourteenth century, the thirteen dwellings standing empty. However, by 1410, the community had returned and a new incumbent had been installed in a brand new church. The earthworks on the site tell of an original village sited on low, damp ground that was replaced by a new one on a better, more elevated site that overlooked the old one. In 1519, the Bishop of Lincoln was outraged that the original churchyard still existed, but in a desecrated condition, and he demanded that it be secured against animals. Before the Black Death, Cublington was a weak and declining village, but after the ravages it was reborn and the ties with the past were neglected.

That the plague could actually invigorate a locality or community can only be explained in terms of the severe overpopulation and scarcity of resources that had cursed the countrysides of Britain for many decades. The mortalities, awful though they were, created openings, spaces, windows of opportunity. Things could never be the same; some plague-hit towns, like Boston or Winchester, could not attract sufficient recruits from the countryside, with its empty and inviting holdings, while as families reformed after the traumas there seems to have been less room for relatives

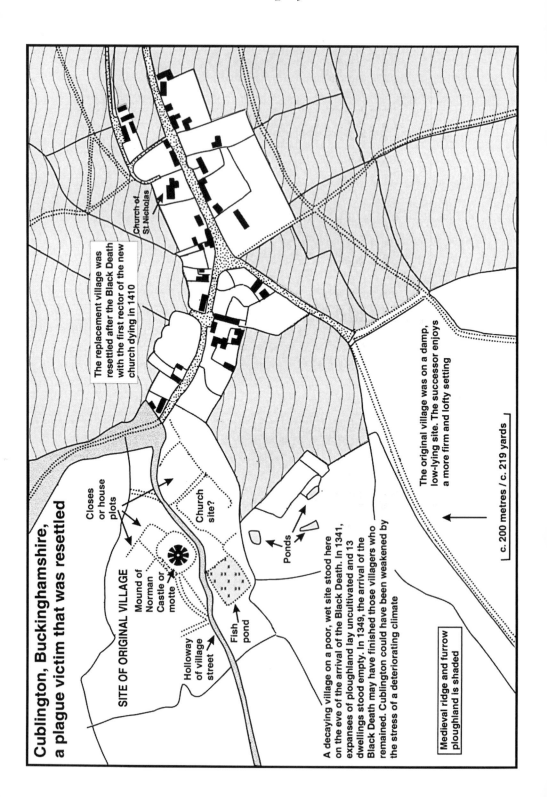

Cublington, Buckinghamshire, a plague victim that was resettled

The replacement village was resettled after the Black Death with the first rector of the new church dying in 1410

Church of St Nicholas

SITE OF ORIGINAL VILLAGE

Closes or house plots

Church site?

Mound of Norman Castle or motte

Holloway of village street

Fish pond

Ponds

A decaying village on a poor, wet site stood here on the eve of the arrival of the Black Death. In 1341, expanses of ploughland lay uncultivated and 13 dwellings stood empty. In 1349, the arrival of the Black Death may have finished those villagers who remained. Cublington could have been weakened by the stress of a deteriorating climate

The original village was on a damp, low-lying site. The successor enjoys a more firm and lofty setting

c. 200 metres / c. 219 yards

Medieval ridge and furrow ploughland is shaded

and a shift from the extended to the nuclear types. Henry Knighton wrote of the post-traumatic opportunities:

> … the king sent proclamation that reapers and other labourers should not take more than they had been accustomed to take (in pay). But the labourers were so lifted up and obstinate that they would not listen to the king's command; but if anyone wished to have them he had to give them what they wanted, and either lose his fruit and crops, or satisfy the wishes of the workmen.

The strangest case that I know of derives from my own research at Ripley, North Yorkshire, where I devoted three years to an intense study of the local landscape. In a township that was just one third of a parish I discovered a substantial deserted village, Owlcotes, a smaller, pioneering village, Birthwaite, that was probably budded-off from Owlcotes to establish settlers on the woodland margins, and several deserted hamlets and farmsteads. The church, serving three townships, lay some distance away and was situated on a narrow terrace on a steep river bluff – a topographically awful site that could be explained by the springs rising at either end of the church, for they must have been considered holy in pagan and early Christian times. A bungled modern pipe-laying operation exposed the closely packed skeletons in the Medieval graveyard on the level ground directly above the church, and archaeological rescue work suggested that a settlement from the middle Saxon period lay beneath this graveyard. Thus far, the little township revealed a complicated history, but matters became much more complicated when I demonstrated that Ripley, the surviving village, had been built on top of working Medieval ploughland.

Gradually, a picture began to form. The evidence of pottery from the site suggested that Owlcotes had flourished in the twelfth and thirteenth centuries, when its name was frequently mentioned, though pottery from later eras was sparse. Ripley was plainly the deliberate creation of the Ingilby family of rising lawyers, the first of whom married the local heiress in the mid-fourteenth century and was buried in the old, though seemingly recently-renovated, church in 1369. Then, and at the very time when the Pestilence was tormenting the region, the next Ingilbys set out to make their mark in a very big way, stamping their authority and their modernising designs on the erstwhile backwater. Around 1390, a brand new church was built near to the manor house and the bodies of first Sir Thomas and then his wife were removed from the old church and installed in the new one. At the same time, or within a few years either way, the brand new village of Ripley was set out to a 'Y'-shaped plan that incorporated the church. Tenants lost numerous shares in the ploughland

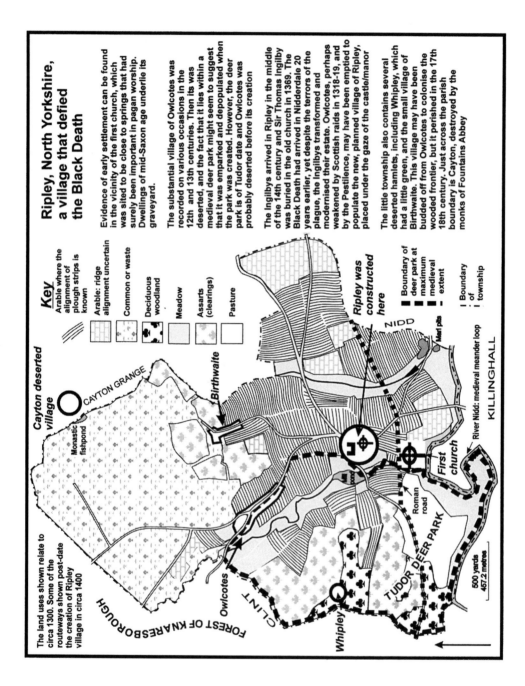

Ripley, North Yorkshire, a village that defied the Black Death

Evidence of early settlement can be found in the vicinity of the first church, which was sited to be close to springs that had surely been important in pagan worship. Dwellings of mid-Saxon age underlie its graveyard.

The substantial village of Owlcotes was recorded on various occasions in the 12th and 13th centuries. Then its was deserted, and the fact that it lies within a medieval deer park might seem to suggest that it was emparked and depopulated when the park was created. However, the deer park is of Tudor date and Owlcotes was probably deserted before its creation

The Ingilbys arrived in Ripley in the middle of the 14th century and Sir Thomas Ingilby was buried in the old church in 1369. The Black Death had arrived in Nidderdale 20 years earlier, yet despite the terrors of the plague, the Ingilbys transformed and modernised their estate. Owlcotes, perhaps weakened by Scottish raids in 1318-19, and by the Pestilence, may have been emptied to populate the new, planned village of Ripley, placed under the gaze of the castle/manor

The little township also contains several deserted hamlets, including Whipley, which had a little green, and the small village of Birthwaite. This village may have been budded off from Owlcotes to colonise the wooded frontier, but it perished in the 17th or 18th century. Just across the parish boundary is Cayton, destroyed by the monks of Fountains Abbey

Key

Arable where the alignment of plough strips is known

Arable: ridge alignment uncertain

Common or waste

Deciduous woodland

Meadow

Asserts (clearings)

Pasture

Cayton deserted village

CAYTON GRANGE

Monastic fishpond

Birthwaite

FOREST OF KNARESBOROUGH

Owlcotes

CLINT

Whipley

NIDD

Marl pits

Ripley was constructed here

Roman road

First church

TUDOR DEER PARK

KILLINGHALL

River Nidd: medieval meander loop

Boundary of deer park at maximum medieval extent

Boundary of township

The land uses shown relate to circa 1300. Some of the routeways shown post-date the creation of Ripley village in circa 1400

500 yards
457.2 metres

that vanished beneath the village. However, this coincided with the last great eruption of the Pestilence in the fourteenth century so we have to wonder why the Ingilbys were pursuing such ambitious ventures at a time when one would expect retrenchment and searches for sanctuary from the recurring horrors?

One wonders why a sizable new village with a very expensive new church would be built at a time when population must have been tumbling? Surely the plague gaps opening in the old village of Owlcotes would accommodate any extra population on the estate? A major reorganisation of the Ingilby territories was plainly in hand and it might be that the new lords wanted to have their tenants gathered together under the gaze of the manor. This might suggest that Owlcotes was deliberately emptied in order to populate the new Ripley. If old Owlcotes had been severely battered by the Pestilence the argument for a forced migration to a replacement village is still more inviting. Since Owlcotes lay partly just inside the boundary of the Ingilby deer park, the explanation that it was emparked is more obvious, yet not a hint of the creation of such a park occurs before 1488 and it is only for the early sixteenth century that we find convincing records of the park. Owlcotes seems to have been gone well before then.

The case of Ripley reminds us that even in the most tragic and desperate of times there were those – some lords, some freemen and some bondsmen – who could respond to the most daunting of threats in a bullish and opportunistic manner. Ultimately, for every tenant who perished in agony from the Black Death there is likely to have been a household that could then see more beans and grain and cheese set aside. They probably did not thank the Pestilence for relieving the pressure on the overcrowded fields (they might well have thought that to do so would invite infection into their own home) but one thing that the successive mortalities achieved was to release the little entrepreneur hidden within each husbandman and his household. After all, the successive epidemics had probably halved the British population by the time that the fourteenth century was over. Many decades would pass before most villages could swell to fill their old ground plans, yet the villagers who survived would have done well to let their optimism be tempered by the sound of distant bleating. A far more potent village slayer was poised and waiting.

CHAPTER EIGHT

THE SCARLET FLEECE

Pictures of the past

The flames had retreated into the embers and Robert could not be sure if his grimy toes were among the ashes or on the bakestone. At its best it had not been much of a fire, just a few dried turfs cut from the edge of the bog. The un-seasonal chill was keeping him awake. He became aware of the tiny stirrings in the hay bag that was his bed and then of things gently twitching in the seams of his cloak. (Scarcely was he aware that these parasites were quite inconsequential when compared to the monsters that slowly coiled and writhed inside his body.) He did realise that to scratch one bite would be to trigger a war of irritation on many fronts, and that would surely wake Agnes, a lump-like form swathed, Robert noted with some irritation, in some of their warmest bits of hide and soiled cloth. Poor Agnes, one by one she had watched most of her children die – but had never ceased to search the hedgerows for better cures and to struggle keep the home of mud, straw and sticks clean. She had attacked the earth floor with her besom so many times that now it was scooped-out like a woodcock's nest and anyone sleeping along a wall foot would roll slowly towards the hearth. Then the last ember dimmed and she was invisible.

It was a suffocating sort of darkness. With the coming of dusk, the ground had chilled rapidly under clear skies with needlepoint stars. Then the mists had come sliding down the slopes to blur the slender moon and hold in the sounds of the valley. It was quiet in a numb sort of way; the owls did not care for the mist and the crippled warrener stumbling along the ditch-side was keeping the timid rabbits in their coneygarth. There would be no dagger-sharp squeals when the stoats and weasels struck tonight. Wolves had been silent here for quite some time. There were still a few in the Holderness marshes to the south-east and some away in the Dales to the distant west, but their yaps and yowling were much too distant to be heard. There were some sounds – the nervous conversations of uneasy sheep; nobody had told them that the wolves were no more.

The dubious notion that counting imaginary sheep would summon sleep had yet to be invented, but the topic of sheep had stolen into Robert's head with the bleating and now it would have to run its course. Sheep were not new. Several of the village households kept a ewe for milk. You could water it down and spread it over your salted oatmeal or turn it into hard cheese. Sometimes, out on the highway, one might meet a great flock moved along by rascally dogs and a lay-brother from one of the great abbeys, or maybe shepherded by a tenant of the monks. As neighbours, however, flocks were new. Robert remembered the day last summer when he was high on the 'bank' or hillside with his hoe, one tiny skirmish in the communal campaign against charlock and thistles. 'Chink, chink', the shuffling blade rattled against the flints which littered the chalky soil of the hillside. This time it was not just a natural fragment from a flint nodule that it struck, but a polished axe of the New Stone Age, already well over 4,000 years old. Robert turned the lustrous axe around in his stumpy fingers: a fairy stone, there was no doubt about that. They were always turning up and so there must be a great many fairies around. He put it on a boundary stone at the edge of the grass balk so that the fairies would be sure to find it again.

Having reached the balk, his legs began to sag, so that whether he had intended to or not, he was now sinking down to rest. By some mysterious means, this news was beamed to the homestead, and soon a speck-like child bearing hard bread and thin ale could be seen ascending the sticky chalk paths and balks that led to Robert's perch. It was a clear morning and while he waited he noticed that the features on a distant, swelling bank had changed. What seemed like a grey-green fallowing field had gained a homestead and some of the hedgerows that bounded the furlongs had vanished. Not only was the presumed fallowing field too green, but so too were the other fields where the community living two townships away should have been growing their barley, wheat and beans. Instead of hoers or mowers there was now a great flock of sheep, frayed at the edges and moving so very slowly over the sward. It reminded him of a mass of maggots, remorselessly consuming their way across a rotting joint.

In the spring that followed, it was the next township that suffered, with the summary eviction of the people from its three hamlets being followed by the installation of a shepherd, his servant, four crouching, darting dogs of varying sounds and sizes and a large flock of jittery sheep. Just two seasons later, whenever Robert went up to hoe his strips he would hear bleating pressing in on him from several directions. The Wolds chalk country that had, for thousands of years, marked the changing of the seasons by turning from a mud-streaked white to seedling green, and then through ripening stages of green to harvest gold, was now locked in a pasture hue. You did not see the dancers with their fronds and ribbons skipping in to the harvest fields any more. There were no far-off voices calling for whetstones or water. At Mass, the donging of single bells from eight or more directions had become a monophonic toll. The landscape had almost surrendered to bleating and yapping, while the creatures of the grainfield, ploughsoil and meadow were moving on.

For those villagers who remained, there was no mistake. The landlords, whose forbears had been so accommodating and so welcoming after the great mortality, now sang a different song. There were no more whispered promises to forget about feudal 'boonworks', to drop rents or to enlarge holdings with land from the tenancies of the dead. Now, the lords' agents sneered that nobody wanted their miserable rents or toil. Sheep would pay more and the tenants had better move on.

★   ★   ★   ★

The village did not amount to much. In some other places, tenants were building walls – or at least wall-footings – of stone. Here, there was just the 'clunch' from the tougher chalk beds to work with. Sometimes, they used a bed of chalk rubble to raise a beam above the wet earth, but really, the houses were just mops of thatch raised aloft on a framework of cheap posts and sticks, with the gaps filled with a woven wattle from the coppice that was caked in a plaster of mud strengthened with cow dung and chopped cow hair. However, each thatched heap was a home and in each home there was a heavy stench of foreboding that would not go away. When they returned, bright-eyed and thyme-scented from the common, the stench reminded them that their games there would end. When they awoke and the skies were clear and the swifts flashed like salvoes of screaming arrows, the stench reminded them they would die beneath a different sky. And in the evening, when the white-bibbed dipper bobbed in the chalk-stream and the valley seemed to be all slumped down and at ease with itself; then they smelled it.

Living in a world where, for generations, little had been subject to debate or change, the villagers were now confused. That lords should be inhumane was not considered unusual. Anybody might be run down by a hunting party or arbitrarily whacked with the flat of a sword – that was accepted. The problem was that since time immemorial, communal life had been guided by the custom of the manor: a body of local and country-wide traditions concerning the relationship between a feudal community and their overlord. Villagers were far more concerned about upholding the ancient customs of their manor than they were with any ethical or judicial concepts. But there was nothing within the custom of the manor about evicting tenants and thus ending the ancient tryst. Tenants were there to be exploited, so how could the manor function if they were cast out? Its main instrument, the manor court, existed to enforce the exploitation. And so the villagers were not affronted by the fact that their lord was likely to cast them out on the road, for lords did terrible things – that was what being a lord was all about. They were deeply affronted by the sundering of the custom of the manor, the custom that accorded them the right to endure, in servitude, exploitation and periodic famine, in their village and under the laws of the manor court.

This lord made sure that his harvest and rents were safely in before turning the forebodings into reality. His steward barged straight into the reeve's house and announced that everybody had to leave the village after the morning Mass that Sunday coming. By dusk they were to be out of the township, even outside the parish, too. Some gave the last Mass in the cramped church their very best efforts and left, dipping their heads as they departed to the priest, who had also lost a living. Others seized the exceptional opportunity to dodge the services without fear of fines or strictures. And then the evictors arrived at the spot where the converging lanes formed a 'Y' at the head of the small village: the steward, a shepherd, a burly hired farmhand in the lord's pay, and a quartet of roughs hired for pence from neighbouring manors. Nothing was said. The villagers melted into the dappled shade of the lane and the only work left for the cudgels was that of battering down the houses. One was saved and by dusk the shepherd was installed in it along with his dogs, which sniffed in the corners and scratched beside the hearth. As they slavered on their loaves of the grey bread and were tormented by odours of an illicit rabbit stewing, the world of the departed husbandmen might never have existed.

The evicted ones could not smell the rabbit, but they could see the smoke seeping out of the thatch, like steam from a leaky pie-crust. It was the last that most would see of the place where they had been so sure that they would die. Those of us who ply the motorways and hop around the airports, those stepping stones of lifeless life, cannot imagine the strength of bonding between a Medieval community and its little bit of ground. We are ill-prepared to understand the life of a bondsman who spends most of his waking life toiling on the clutch of land ribbons that comprise his holdings. He might have around thirty of these 'lands' or 'selions', averaging around 200m (around 219yds) in length by about 5-10m (around 16-33ft) in width. In his memory, our villager needs to store images of around 12,000m (39,370ft) of selion boundary – clods, stones, balks and puddles – for if he does not, his neighbours in the great fields may steal a few inches here or shave the edges of a boundary there. Then, too, he must remember the position of each boundary stone that defines his shares or 'doles' in the common meadow, lest another villager might roll a 'mere stone' a few inches on to his ground.

He is completely sensitised to the coming and going of birds, the way that the repeated frosts crumble the soil, the likely movements of local storms during the mowing and drying of the hay, and to countless other events that bear upon yields and survival. An invisible umbilical cord binds him to the ground and through it moves a traffic of information, lore and identity. Nobody can see this cord, but if it is cut, the pain can be unbearable. He is where he is. His very body is built of atoms from the village fields and one day they will return to village ground. His standing comes from what he tenants there and from how he is regarded by those who toil alongside him. They will judge his skill with the scythe, his bearing with officials, his courage when injured and his dignity in adversity. And they are bound by their invisible cords to the village, the township and its land.

Meanwhile, at home, our bondsman's wife defies the low fertility and lassitude caused by malnutrition, moving through successions of birth and bereavement in a struggle to bring just a couple children through to adulthood. On them, they pin their hopes of sustenance in old age. This is her goal: to pass on the holding and receive a contract that will bind her son to tend them when their arthritic bodies can bend and scour no more. Her head is packed with information about the locality, some of it useful and some of it nonsense. She knows where to find comfrey, fleabane and a host of other cures, herbs and poisons. She also shares the community's irrational fear of shrews, and knows how to entomb them in cavities in trees. And she knows exactly which oaks have shrews in them, as well as which aspens have nail clippings from fever sufferers inserted in their trunks. The facts that this had never seemed to do the patients any good and occasionally killed the trees does not register. Lore is stronger than fact. She will pass the location of the wolfbane clump on to her nieces, even though there are no wolfs left to poison. She, too, sways to the tunes of the locality and her senses house a calendar linked to the arrival of cuckoos, the departure of house martins, the gathering of sloes and the rendering to the lord of a pair of hens (always the ones due to go broody) at Martinmas.

The band of villagers remained together till they reached the lane at the foot of their track. Neighbours, who had shared each year's struggle to subsist, would soon be neighbours no more. Households drifted away like thistledown. The village did not die when the homesteads were battered down, rather it died on the road to Malton. Some young men left their families and ganged together under the premise that nobody needed to starve in a land overrun by sheep. They darted among a panicking roadside flock, slit the throat of a ewe, chased the shepherd and stoned his dogs. The law was not enforced, for there were no real enforcers. So while their families shivered and starved among the hedgerows, the young men stole and rustled and ransacked their way around the countryside, terrorising petty officials and beating and maiming any shepherds who crossed their path. The freeholders and petty gentry wished they had wider moats around their houses and armed retainers on their payrolls. They knew that the rates of arrest were so low as to make the apprehension of the outlaws quite unlikely and they dreaded the bands roaming openly across the countryside. Eviction had filled the fields with sheep but the lanes with homeless, landless desperadoes.

However, the greater landowners and nobility did have moats, and drawbridges too. They had liveried men at arms as well. Of course, they deplored the desperate state of lawlessness afflicting the land and acknowledged the need that something be done. And then they set about distancing themselves from the last episode of sheep evictions and preparing their plans for the next.

The village toughs moved around the locality ransacking farmsteads, disrupting markets and intimidating manorial officials and shepherds until the community at large ran out of patience and they were hounded into the plains, woods and marshes of the Vale of York. They linked with other outlaws in the Forest of Galtres and led wretched lives being flushed from spinney to grove and coppice to hurst by the king's foresters, regarders and bow-bearers. Sometimes, they would glimpse the towers of York Minster rearing up from the woodland embrace. To men of their notoriety the city was out of reach, but to a few of their former neighbours it was a symbol of hope.

York was a baited trap. Like some grotesque fish from the deeps, it dangled a lure: freedom from bondage. Behind this lure was a great, insatiable maw that devoured victims as quickly as they might be enticed. Like other Medieval cities, York was such an unsanitary place and so permeated by disease that it could not maintain, let alone increase, its population by natural means. To fill the space within its walls or to expand beyond them it had to continually suck in new occupants from the surrounding countrysides. It needed potential plague victims to replace those whose potential had been realised. The city had some potent attractions. It was the seat of an archbishopric, it had a circuit of walls and mural towers that amounted to a resounding proclamation of urban status, while above all, it conferred the gift of freedom on all escaped bondsmen who resided within its bounds for a year. And so it was to York that many of the dispossessed villagers came. There they would be shunned by the powerful crafts guilds and would gravitate, like immigrants to towns throughout the ages, to the most menial, arduous and disease ridden of occupations. The shortest track to the graveyard must have been trodden by the outsiders who had no resistance in their bloodstreams to the city's particular cocktail of diseases. Some however might acquire a degree resistance to the foulness of the city. Their descendents would eventually become part of the more permanent community, looking rather different from newcomers and exemplifying the process of inbreeding that gave the indigenous population of Medieval York those rather asymmetrical faces.

Those still on the roads faced unenviable futures. Any with skills, like smithing or wood-turning, had a slight advantage and all the able-bodied men had the possibility of finding work as hired labourers, though the evictions had created a great excess of such workers. Women, especially those with children to tend, faced harsher prospects. The demand for female servants and wet nurses was not high and even if a spouse found employment, few would want to hire the partner as well. Unlike the situation facing the victims of the Georgian and Victorian evictions, there were no emigrant ships waiting at the quays and no factories baying for recruits. One place was no better than the last and the further one left the old village behind, the more one became a foreigner pleading in a strange dialect. You were the land and when you left it, you were nobody. The pillories and gallows claimed their share of the victims, others ended in the urban plague pits. Most children froze in ditches, sweated through fever in hedge-bottoms or starved in the lanes and rick-yards. 'Progress' can be very hard on those who get in its way.

How did it happen?

Sheep are the forgotten villains in the story of lost villages, even though the events in Tudor England would be repeated across the landscapes of Georgian Scotland in near-modern times. Clearances for sheep destroyed many, many times as many settlements as were extinguished by the Black Death. Such, however, were the horrors of plague that even today, the country folk who know of a deserted settlement in their locality will parrot the (probable) myth that it fell to the plague. With only its slit-like pupils to tarnish its fluffy, dim and dithering image, the sheep seems such an unlikely culprit. During a prolonged recuperation I worked part-time on a Dales sheep farm. I never learned much affection for the creatures, only a certain pity. Their existences seemed to be one long courtship with cruel fate. They could scarcely walk across a damp field without incurring foot rot; they had to be pumped full of drugs to prevent their coughing; were immersed in a toxic dip to kill surface parasites, and their lives were punctuated by humiliating up-endings to have the rot hacked out of their hoofs or a 'dagging-out' of their matted back ends. Perhaps the most endearing quality of the sheep is its readiness to forgive those who impose these humiliations upon it. As one old shepherd said: there never was a creature so ready to meet its Maker. Of course, the sheep themselves did not conspire, the conspiracy involved landowners and the economy, often a lethal alliance for country folk.

Sheep had led innocent existences in Britain for thousands of years. Not native, they were introduced by the agricultural innovators of the New

Stone Age as part of the 'cultural package' of farming. The original sheep were small, wiry, troublesome to control and with coats that were hairy rather than fleecy. (Archaeologists usually find it impossible to differentiate their bones from those of goats, but the latter, being environmentally very destructive in their habits, will always have been kept under close control.) Coming from a lineage of creatures evolved and adapted for life on dry rock slopes and screes, sheep were never really suited to vales and plateaux, particularly the sodden clay lands and waterlogged uplands of Britain. The first sheep to be brought to Britain resembled the Moufflon breed and will have been kept mainly for their meat, their hairy coats being suitable for felt rather than for spinning and weaving into cloth. The strong flocking habit and the development of wool suitable for yarn were attractions that developed later. The sheep of the Bronze Age, resembling the Soay breed, were still horned, rather goat-like and still frustratingly athletic. Their fleece had become woolly, but it was naturally shed and was plucked rather than being sheared around the start of summer. Gradually, the animals became meatier, woollier and also more easily controlled as their tendency to flock together intensified. Shearing was adopted and the different provinces of Britain developed regional breeds that were adapted to the particular resources, hardships and terrain. During the Iron Age the availability of yarns and the development of a range of natural dyes ensured that flocks had a significant place in the countryside and they will probably then have become valued more for their fleeces than their mutton.

On the chalk downlands, shepherding must have been a widespread activity in Anglo-Saxon times as the numerous 'ship' (sheep) placenames show. In the northern glens and on the fells and moors, things must have been more challenging, for the wolf packs were still numerous, the last of the lynxes still roamed the Yorkshire Dales and bears may still have been found in some fastnesses. In the North, the practice of moor-burning or 'swaling', which encouraged the heather to produce young growth – a 'soft bite' for the flocks – was developed. The sheep was well-established as a versatile animal, as useful to the cottage economy as to that of the manor. It gave meat and milk but could neither draw the plough like an ox nor tolerate wet ground quite as well as cattle. Nevertheless, it produced one of only two cloth yarn fibres in widespread circulation (the other was linen), the fat from the fleece was made into lanolin, a soothing ointment, while the skin of lambs provided the clerk with his parchment. In the decades leading up to and beyond the Norman Conquest of England, fulling mills (where the woven cloth was pounded in urine and fullers earth and cleaned and felted to mat together) were established in scores of places. The simplest were the 'walk mills' where the miller trampled on the wet cloth, though fulling was among the first of industrial activities to move into water-powered mills. Indeed, the sheep had complementary roles in the village economy, with flocks being folded on the fallowing grain fields to enrich their exhausted soils.

During the early Medieval centuries, wool was a modest industry involving small producers and cottage manufacturing for local markets. English cloth must have gained some reputation abroad, for in 1056, ten years before the Norman Conquest, the Count of Cleves was awarded lordship over Nijmegen in return for a nominal rent to the Holy Roman Emperor of three pieces of English woollen cloth that were dyed scarlet. Gradually, an organised export industry developed. Little entrepreneurs discovered lucrative roles as middlemen, gathering together the wool production of their localities, moving the bales by strings of pack ponies and selling-on at the rising wool markets to bigger merchants. These merchants would trade in turn with still bigger markets – markets that were increasingly patronised by the traders of France, Italy and the rising cloth-making towns of Flanders. Meanwhile, the Cistercians of the great northern abbeys were demonstrating how an international industry could be organised. They had great advantages over the demesne farmers, free peasants and bondsmen. By endowments, moral blackmail and coercion, the white monks had acquired huge agricultural empires that included continuous tracts of countryside. This allowed them to shift their flocks about and avoid the prolonged occupations that would encourage disease to build up in a piece of ground and its water sources. In addition, the monastic life favoured the research that explored the medicinal aspects of shepherding.

It so happened that the century that experienced the horrors of the Black Death was also the one in which English wool production rose to the fore of national life. Edward III (1327-77) underlined the symbolic role that shepherding had achieved when the Woolsack, a cushion stuffed with English wool, was made the seat of the Lord Chancellor in the House of Lords – an emblem of the new prominence of wool in national prosperity.

At this time, there were few hints that sheep would soon become the downfall of villages. For countless country people, the first sound that they heard on entering the world was the bleating of a ewe which shared the village homestead and helped to nourish its human occupants. As they grew older, they might wander amongst the flock on the fallowing field, its surface made into a pincushion by the scores of hooves that stabbed in the goodness. Certainly, some villagers had been displaced around the northern abbeys as the monks increased their flocks and expanded their estates, but the people there, precariously co-existing with the monks, were almost as likely to be evicted in the creation of monastic cattle farms or even horse-studs. Popular culture gave the cloven-hoofed goat a somewhat satanic ethos, but the sheep was almost dove-like in its imagery. Parables in the gospels of Luke and John likened Christ to a shepherd, the role of the good shepherd and carer of the flock being expropriated from the pagan god, Mercury. The lamb was the meek victim of sacrifices in both pagan ritual and the Old Testament, while Christ became the sacrificial lamb for the salvation of mankind. The lamb was the attribute of John the Baptist and of St Clement, and was seen to symbolise innocence, passivity and patience. Everyone knew the symbolism associated with the sheep and images of the animal appeared in ecclesiastical wall paintings, glass and wood carvings.

When the plague struck in the middle of the fourteenth century, the sheep seemed to offer nothing but good. Had the plague not struck, it is hard to see how the flocks could have wrought their devastation. Before 1348, the country was seething with rural over-population. Communities of bondsmen were everywhere and could scarcely have been got rid of, for there were no empty places to send them to. This over-population assisted the spread of disease and the occurrences of famine, but it did have advantages to the landowner. A crowded market of workers, wherever it is found, means low wages, cheap labour and a subservient population of servants and tenants. The most miserable tenancy on the meanest and most reactionary feudal estate was better than the brief life of an outcast in a country with no empty holdings. When tenants were many and holdings were scarce, people took what they could and did not challenge the terms of their exploitation.

Almost overnight, this situation was turned on its head. The Black Death had pierced gaping holes in the landscape of settlement. As people, stunned, groped to rebuild their lives, it was realised that many of those holdings that marched from horizon to horizon had become untenanted. Widows, whose minds had been set on rest and time to gossip on the verge outside the houses, now wrestled with a bucking plough, grasping handles polished to a sheen by the coarse palms of a lost husband and son. Tenants who had survived took over fragments from abandoned holdings and then saw the nettles springing on the other untenanted strips that bordered their own. With the plantain, feverfew, docks and chickweed surviving to seed freely, there were fewer hoes, but far more work for those that remained in use. Those lords who could read might roll out their rentals on the very table where rents aid were paid and calculate how much the onslaught of the plague had cost them. This cost might be composed of money rents, of produce and services, or of all. The bond tenants had their rents to pay and their work services to perform, while the scrawny cottagers, working tiny holdings, could be rounded up to set up new hedges or fences, thatch a barn or do whatever else was needed. Now the manor was short of rent and short of labour. Typically, the manor would have a 'home farm' or demesne. It might consist of holdings that were scattered, like those of the villagers, or else these lands might have been dragged together to form a consolidated holding more suitable for specialised roles, such as horse breeding. The demesne was worked by the feudal tenants, who notionally performed these 'boonworks' for the love of their lord. Soon, the lords would discover how very notional this love really was.

The situation in a countryside starved of people was unpredictable. Any coming to terms with the trauma of mass mortality could be, and periodically was, destabilised by new eruptions of the Black Death. Each locality had its own characteristics, and while some lords led the modest life of the backwater squire (albeit a very autocratic one), there were many others who owned strings of manors, and on each manor there were shortages of tenants, of labour for hire and of drudges to tend the demesne. One issue, the defiance of the erstwhile chattels, was decisive. Throughout England, Wales and the feudal south and east of Scotland, there were communities of people who had never defied their masters. Their parents, grandparents and a good ten preceding generations of forebears had not done so either. Certainly, they had grumbled and muttered, particularly when obliged to work on the demesne when a building storm was threatening to flatten their own hay crop or harvest. For these and other complaints, they expected to be fined by the manor court, and, as the records show, they were quite relentlessly. However, openly and unabashedly to stand up and defy the lord or lady was almost unthinkable and unprecedented. Just to look at them in the eye with a level head juddered on the grain of upbringing and tradition. Defiance was something that had to be learned.

Learn it, the villagers did. Gradually, those bred for bondage realised that they actually had worth. This was confirmed when lords, tired of gazing across estates run down to thistles, charlock and the seedlings of ash, thorns and oak, attempted to poach tenants from their neighbours. Now, cottagers were being addressed as though they were villeins, villeins treated like stewards, and stewards like squires. The world of the manor might not be on its head, but it was very much out of kilter. The bond tenant was, according to feudal custom, bound to his or her manor and denied any freedom to move. Desperation was a great lubricant. Households that had been struggling for generations to subsist on 'half-virgate' holdings of about fifteen acres (6.1 hectares) were bribed to move with tenancies of a full virgate or more. Cottages were emptied as families slipped away at evening to take a better existence somewhere beyond the estate boundaries. The slippings away might be furtive or blatant, depending on the desperation of the lords concerned. Landsmen who had worked, shirked and grumbled their ways back and forth across the demesne since childhood were offered relief from boonworks and moderate rents in cash if they would just stay in the very places that feudal law and custom formerly compelled them to stay.

Having discovered their true value, the survivors then began to test their economic strength. If tenants preferred paying cash rents to the diversions to work on the demesne, this meant a greater dependence on hired, wage-earning workers. But the general shortage of labour caused by the plague meant higher wages and rising inflation. Before looking at the consequences of all this, it will be useful to look at the prevailing wage rates. Of course, they do not tell us about the real worth of people, just the value placed on them by the social power system. Also, attempts to translate the wages into modern rates are largely ridiculous. What we do discover is the high value that a society that was still largely feudal and dominated by a martial aristocracy placed on the profession of arms. A mercenary knight could expect to earn 2*s* (10p) per day, with a man at arms being paid at half this rate, while an archer earned one-eighth as much, about 3*d* (1.25p) per day. If the archer's wage seems modest, it was equal to that of a master carpenter and comparable to the income of a chantry priest. Amongst the craftsmen, meanwhile, armourers were an élite, with a master armourer earning 1*s* 3*d* (6.25p) per day. An accomplished armourer therefore earned as much as five archers, but he earned far more than a whole host of grooms, carters, maids, kitchen staff or other servants, who received their upkeep but were paid next to nothing. Thus the scales of pay were very much skewed in the direction of men who furthered the practice of war. Otherwise, craftsmen associated with the various trade guilds might earn as much as 5*d* (around 2.1p) in the case of a skilled weaver, with the norm around 3*d*, while ordinary foot-soldiers were earning at least twice as much as the skilled tradesmen. However, wages do not tell the whole tale, for servants enjoyed free accommodation and men hired as parkers, stewards and constables or in other responsible positions could enjoy attractive perks, including useful baubles like liveries and even the incomes from farms.

The rising wage rates caused by the shortages of labour scandalised the ruling classes; the idea that lords should compete for the services of scoundrels was considered outrageous. The changes must have come very swiftly, for in 1351, just three years after the appearance of the plague in England, the landed gentry took their grievances to the government and Edward III issued the *Statute of Labourers*, a largely unsuccessful attempt to peg wages at pre-plague levels and return to the more agreeable days when the lord of the manor had the first claim on the services of his tenants, while farm workers under contract could not leave their masters or be employed by others until their contracts had run their full terms. There was also an attempt to appease the masses with price controls, but these were stillborn. There were strictures against any employers who offered to pay more wages or provide more liveries or other rewards but there was no mistaking the targets for this legislation:

> If any reaper, hay mower, or other workman or servants, of what estate or
> condition that he be, retained in any man's service, do depart from the said

service without reasonable cause or license, before the term agreed, he shall have pain of imprisonment; and no one, under the same penalty, shall presume to receive or retain such a one in his service…

Landlords could see the advantages that would accrue if incomes were pegged at low levels. However, when it came to the specific challenges of finding tenants for a clutch of empty, weed-infested holdings, getting someone to repair the rails around the horse paddock or patrol the deer park then they would bid against each other, thus undermining the laws that were enacted to protect their privileges.

Village England stirs

The sprawling country lay fractured and ill at ease with itself, but as yet there seemed to be no threat to the village. A swollen population had begun to experience successions of famines as un-ripened grain rotted on the sodden stalks, storms beat down the hay and murrain spread among the herds. Nature solved some of these problems with the plague and the mortality among the consumers made for cheap food prices. Then, among the cottage huddles, the once-unthinkable thoughts crept into heads, festered there a while and escaped from village mouths. For centuries, feudalism had held each village in its vice. It accorded a role and a daunting set of personal obligations to every villager. It was built on infallibility and inevitability, and nobody could recall a time before feudalism or an incident where it had not prevailed. It was not negotiable: born into bondage, one was little more than a chattel. Escape was too unlikely and too perilous to merit much consideration. Now, all that had changed and tenants and artisans who had bowed before their manor courts were now, effectively, going on strike.

The lord who rode home to his favourite manor to see a mass of jobs undone and glowering tenants sprawling on the green or leering from their doors might then gain the manor house, only to hear his one literate official listing the decline in the estate's income. Meanwhile, the taxes that he was required to pay were rising. Some of the lords and the sons of the lords who had argued for the pegging of prices a decade earlier thought they had discovered a less painful means of raising revenue when, in 1377, Parliament proposed a Poll Tax under which every person over the age of fourteen would pay the same amount. For the rich, the tax was a trifle, but for those at the foot of the economic ladder, a charge representing the income from four days of work could buckle at the household economy. In recognition of the rumpus that the 1377 Poll Tax had caused, a more equitable one

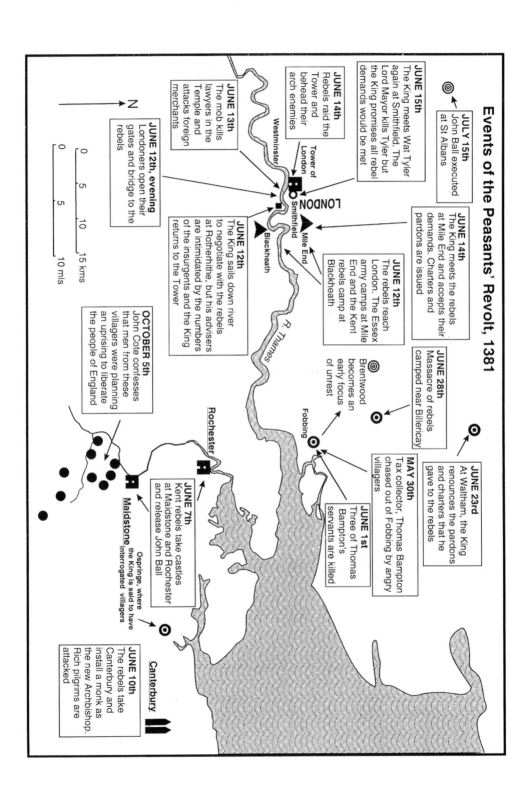

Events of the Peasants' Revolt, 1381

JULY 15th
John Ball executed at St Albans

JUNE 15th
The King meets Wat Tyler again at Smithfield. The Lord Mayor kills Tyler but the King promises all rebel demands would be met

JUNE 14th
Rebels raid the Tower and behead their arch enemies

JUNE 13th
The mob kills lawyers in the Temple and attacks foreign merchants

JUNE 12th, evening
Londoners open their gates and bridge to the rebels

JUNE 12th
The King sails down river to negotiate with the rebels at Rotherhithe, but his advisers are intimidated by the numbers of the insurgents and the King returns to the Tower

JUNE 14th
The King meets the rebels at Mile End and accepts their demands. Charters and pardons are issued

JUNE 12th
The rebels reach London. The Essex army camps at Mile End and the Kent rebels camp at Blackheath

JUNE 28th
Massacre of rebels camped near Billericay

JUNE 23rd
At Waltham, the King renounces the pardons and charters that he gave to the rebels

Brentwood becomes an early focus of unrest

Fobbing

MAY 30th
Tax collector, Thomas Bampton chased out of Fobbing by angry villagers

JUNE 1st
Three of Thomas Bampton's servants are killed

OCTOBER 5th
John Cote confesses that men from these villagers were planning an uprising to liberate the people of England

JUNE 7th
Kent rebels take castles at Maidstone and Rochester and release John Ball

Ospringe, where the King is said to have interrogated villagers

JUNE 10th
The rebels take Canterbury and install a monk as the new Archbishop. Rich pilgrims are attacked

Westminster

Tower of London

LONDON

Smithfield

Mile End

Blackheath

R. Thames

Rochester

Maidstone

Canterbury

N

0   5   10   15 kms
0   5   10 mils

was levied in 1379. However, the boy king, Richard II (1377-99), who had been continually under threat from his ambitious uncles, had developed to become an extravagant autocrat with a household of 10,000. He was self-indulgent though not warlike, yet the seemingly interminable French wars were an unending drain on English resources. It was against this background of financial stress at many levels that a third and a fourth Poll Tax were levied in 1380 and 1381. They returned to the inequitable and widely unpopular models of the first Poll Tax, though in 1381 all those above the age of fifteen were required to pay 1s (5p), a three-fold increase on the level of the first tax. Now, a carpenter might work for a week to earn enough to pay his tax, though a leading lawyer could earn the same amount in half an hour and the leading aristocratic landowners would do so in minutes.

The consequences were at first not so very different from those of the British Poll Tax of 1990, when the slogan 'Can't pay, won't pay' encapsulated a widespread mood of defiance for a tax that was regarded as unjust because it did not recognise the wide differences in the ability to pay. Tax collectors had been particularly disliked since the launching of the first Poll Tax. People with histories and ancestries stretching back into the days of feudalism still resented the ways in which the collectors with their bullying retainers could arrive, unannounced, in a village and begin to interrogate people about their sources of income and abilities to pay.

It was 30 May 1381 and a tax collector making his unwelcome way between the villages of Essex arrived at Fobbing. There was nothing to set the place apart as a special hotbed of anger and defiance. The village then was much smaller than the Fobbing of today, which is an enlarged but ancient settlement that lies a couple of miles north of the Thames estuary. Now, it is virtually lassoed by the housing estates of Corringham which have spread across Fobbing's Medieval fields, themselves almost lassoed by London's eastward advance.

In the late fourteenth century, Fobbing was a modest, straggling village seemingly aligned along a track leading, via tidal creeks, across a former salt marsh to the great river. The core of the village seems to have lain at the river end, with the settlement growing in a strung-out fashion along the track leading north by north-west towards Chelmsford. And so, along this lane came Thomas Bampton. He must have been a fairly thick-skinned and resilient character, even by Medieval standards. Collectors in London had recognised that to enforce the collection of the tax would be to provoke unrest, but the king's council had opted for a hard line. Thomas had already witnessed the contempt of country people in East Anglia, some had even spat on his back when his head was turned. Even so, he was no vilified but innocent public servant, but a man of some position and substance with his own retinue of servants.

1 A reconstruction of the pagan Saxon village at West Stow in Suffolk, from virtually the last of countless generations of ephemeral villages. From around AD 800–AD 900, villages tended to be permanent.

2 The ancient minster at Stonegrave on the southern edge of the North York Moors. The earthwork and nettles in the foreground mark former dwellings and tell of a village that has shrunk.

Above: 3 Furness Abbey was second only to Fountains in wealth at the time of the Dissolution.

Opposite: 4 Bolton Priory, by the River Wharfe, was deserted for a few years when the dangers of Scottish raiding were added to the problems of a farming estate deteriorating in the grip of a worsening climate.

Above: 5 The threats of a climate in turmoil return; unseasonal storm surges are again becoming part of the British climate, as here at St Monans, Fife.

Opposite above: 6 Cottages by the green at Old Byland.

Opposite below: 7 The village that accompanied the famous Saxon church at Breamore in Hampshire was destroyed by emparking.

Above: 8 The remains of a medieval village farmstead at Hound Tor on Dartmoor.

Opposite above: 9 The site of the deserted Norfolk village of Egmere.

Opposite below: 10 Dunvegan Castle, the seat of the MacLeod chieftains, was an early centre for experimentation with the 'improvements' that produced the clearances.

11 The deserted shores of Loch Scavaig on Skye, which was once a heavily populated island.

12 Wharram Percy in the Yorkshire Wolds, painstakingly excavated by M.W. Beresford and J.G. Hurst and a band of enthusiastic helpers over many seasons.

As he approached Fobbing, he will have seen the young grain crops standing green in the great fields that clasped the village, he will have smelled the salt air wafting from the Thames, and so he cannot help but have wondered how much farming and trade and the harvest of the shore contributed to the villagers' ability to meet the tax?

So violent was his reception in Fobbing that he would never find out. Whatever may have happened when Bampton began to make is survey, he was soon hounded out of the village. There must then have been some renewal of the confrontation, for armed men attempted to enforce the law on 1 June and three of Bampton's servants were murdered. The incident had become an uprising. There were many villages that might just as easily have played the role assumed by Fobbing. The fact that the insurgency erupted in Essex and Kent can hardly have been accidental, for in these regions there were disproportionately high numbers of small, free households. They were composed of people who may have been no more affluent than those in bondage but who cherished every ounce of independence, every tiny privilege that raised them above the un-free. What was now the Peasants' Revolt raged across Essex; people in Brentwood revolted and the insurgency spread across the Thames to Kent. There, the priest, John Ball, was an unlikely supporter of a campaign against the exaction of unpaid peasant labour by the church. The insurgency gained strength and castles at Maidstone and Rochester surrendered in the first week of June, while Hertfordshire and Suffolk men joined the rebel forces to the north of the Thames.

If the Poll Tax had sparked the uprising, a host of other grievances were seething in the undercurrents of the revolt. Wat Tyler, from Kent, perhaps an ex-soldier, became the leader of the dissidents, but without being able to discipline the mass or focus their demands. On 12 June, the armies from Essex and from Kent converged on London. After the king was prevented from negotiating with the rebels, his advisers being intimidated by the sight of combined forces numbering up to 100,000, the rebels were admitted to the city by sympathetic townspeople, who opened their gates and bridge. The revolt seems to have signalled the breaking point of feudalism's victims in the South East and also the release of loutish forces that even feudalism and the manor courts had barely managed to suppress. Brutal suppression and mindless thuggery had lived side by side in most villages for ages; perhaps they were related? Much of what the insurgents did was well-advised. Though their destruction of the rolls of their manors has deprived historians of invaluable information, it did erase the details of their bondage. Similarly, they were careful to burn records wherever they could gain access to government buildings. The slaughter of lawyers in the Temple on 13 June was, at least, understandable, though the drunkenness, which alienated support, and the attacks on foreigners in London or those on rich pilgrims in Canterbury after the capture of the city on 10 June, seem mindless.

On 14 June, the fourteen-year-old king met Wat Tyler at Mile End. What followed is well-known, if poorly understood. The demands from Village England were that the peasants be given charters setting out their rights; that the current Poll Tax should be abolished; that rents for land-holdings be set at just levels, and that the traitors, whoever these might have been, be put to death. The king apparently accepted these demands apart from reserving the right to determine treason. Steps were then taken to organise clerks to provide copies of the charters for the dispersing rebels to take home. Meanwhile, however, a party of insurgents had raided cells of the Tower of London and had beheaded three of the rebellion's most powerful opponents, the Archbishop of Canterbury, the Treasurer and John Legge, the inventor of the Poll Tax. Assuming victory, the rebels began to depart, but Tyler, with additional demands to raise, arranged to meet again with the King, at Smithfield, outside the city walls. Whether according to a pre-arranged plan or in response to some disrespectful behaviour, the Lord Mayor of London, William Walworth, and a squire in his party killed Tyler. With admirable opportunism, the King then claimed leadership of the rebellion and led the rebels from the city.

In hundreds of south-eastern villages during the second half of June, small groups of rebels could be seen returning to their homes, flour-ishing charters that they could not read and boasting of their triumph. The King mustered an army and headed for Essex on the heels of his subjects. At Waltham, he paused to issue a statement repudiating all the privileges he had given at Mile End. It was at Waltham that he is sup-posed to have mouthed his famous curse, 'Serfs you are, and serfs you shall remain'. At Billericay, then still a village (and no more than a good walk to the north of Fobbing, where it had all begun), the King's soldiers found a large party of men left over from the uprising. The campers at first held up their charters, but battle was joined and 500 of them were hacked them down by the troops led by Thomas of Woodstock, the younger brother of John o' Gaunt. The Earl of Buckingham's troops car-ried out hundreds of summary executions in Essex and Herefordshire, gallows were set up around the City of London, while in Kent around 1,500 rebels were hanged. John Ball, whose egalitarian ideas had inspired so many of them, was captured in Coventry on 15 July, and taken to St Albans, where he was hung, drawn and quartered. A leading rebel, Thomas Harding, met a similar fate, living to see his bowels set on fire before his head was fixed to the gate of the King's palace at Westminster.

In a final revolt – one as naïve as it was foolhardy – villagers living in the region of Kent at the junction of the rivers Medway and Breult, in places like Yalding and its neighbours, attempted to launch a new uprising that would compel the King to honour his promises and charters. It seems that a mason living at Loose, just south of Maidstone, learned of a scheme to capture the town and he revealed it to the Sheriff of Kent. When the chief plotters assembled at Boughton Heath, near Loose, on 30 September, the troops were waiting. In the following year, the nine of them suffered hanging, drawing and quartering, a fate normally reserved for the very worst of criminals. Reading between the lines of events such as these, one does seem faintly to glimpse clandestine networks underpinning village society. Once ignited, uprisings did appear to spread surprisingly swiftly from village to village – at a pace far more rapid than mere gossip-mongering might have allowed. Perhaps the conspiracies that much later directed vengeance against rogue landowners or organised the sabotage of labour-saving machines at the time of the Agricultural Revolution had roots that burrowed much deeper into history? Certainly, the clandestine resistance to alien landlords in Ireland was channelled through pervasive and far-reaching networks, while the less literate a society, the less likely it was to leave evidence of its schemes and organisation.

A sinister phase followed, in which the King's men would descend upon a village and terrify the community into division and betrayal. Writing just around fourteen years after the events, Jean Froissart recorded that the King himself had descended on the village of Ospringe (to the south-west of Faversham) in Kent:

> He called all the men together. The King said that he knew they were not all guilty of the recent uprising… so they must say who was responsible. When the villagers heard this and realised that only the guilty ones would be punished they looked at each other and said at last: 'This is the one who first encouraged the villagers to join the rebels.' He was immediately taken and hanged, and so were seven others… And more than 1,500 people were hanged or beheaded.

Many rebels lost their lives and the pardons and charters became sentences of death to those who flaunted them. And yet the defeat was permeated by victory. The state of mind that regarded tenants as helpless chattels could never be restored, the Poll Tax was quietly forgotten and the futility of attempts to peg wages was recognised. Meanwhile, the organised church suffered a further fall in popularity, since ordinary people felt that it should have sided with, rather than against, the poor and oppressed. However, the old system had been rocked so badly that nothing could be taken for granted. It came to be realised that villages did not have to exist because it seemed that they always had done so. Landlords became aware that a lord or lady did not have

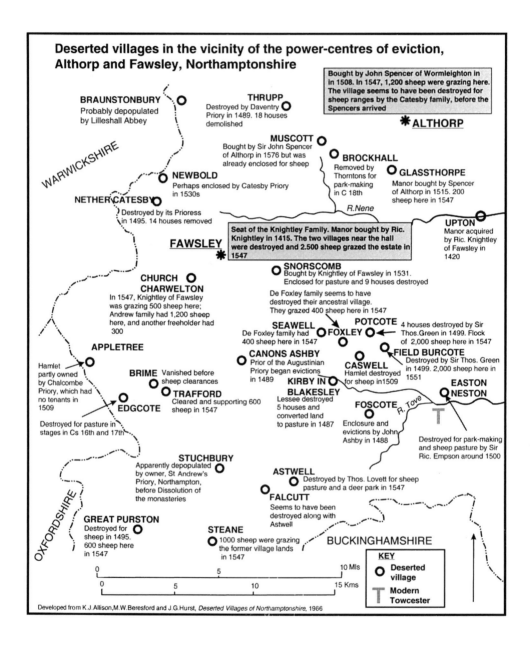

Deserted villages in the vicinity of the power-centres of eviction, Althorp and Fawsley, Northamptonshire

Bought by John Spencer of Wormleighton in in 1508. In 1547, 1,200 sheep were grazing here. The village seems to have been destroyed for sheep ranges by the Catesby family, before the Spencers arrived

＊ALTHORP

BRAUNSTONBURY ○
Probably depopulated by Lilleshall Abbey

THRUPP ○
Destroyed by Daventry Priory in 1489. 18 houses demolished

WARWICKSHIRE

MUSCOTT ○
Bought by Sir John Spencer of Althorp in 1576 but was already enclosed for sheep

BROCKHALL ○
Removed by Thorntons for park-making in C 18th

GLASSTHORPE ○
Manor bought by Spencer of Althorp in 1515. 200 sheep here in 1547

NEWBOLD ○
Perhaps enclosed by Catesby Priory in 1530s

NETHER CATESBY ○
Destroyed by its Prioress in 1495. 14 houses removed

R.Nene

UPTON ○
Manor acquired by Ric. Knightley of Fawsley in 1420

Seat of the Knightley Family. Manor bought by Ric. Knightley in 1415. The two villages near the hall were destroyed and 2.500 sheep grazed the estate in 1547

FAWSLEY ＊

SNORSCOMB ○
Bought by Knightley of Fawsley in 1531. Enclosed for pasture and 9 houses destroyed

CHURCH CHARWELTON ○
In 1547, Knightley of Fawsley was grazing 500 sheep here; Andrew family had 1,200 sheep here, and another freeholder had 300

De Foxley family seems to have destroyed their ancestral village. They grazed 400 sheep here in 1547

SEAWELL ○
De Foxley family had 400 sheep here in 1547

FOXLEY ○

POTCOTE ○
4 houses destroyed by Sir Thos.Green in 1499. Flock of 2,000 sheep here in 1547

APPLETREE ○

Hamlet partly owned by Chalcombe Priory, which had no tenants in 1509

BRIME ○
Vanished before sheep clearances

TRAFFORD ○
Cleared and supporting 600 sheep in 1547

EDGCOTE ○

Destroyed for pasture in stages in Cs 16th and 17th

CANONS ASHBY ○
Prior of the Augustinian Priory began evictions in 1489

CASWELL ○
Hamlet destroyed for sheep in1509

KIRBY IN BLAKESLEY ○
Lessee destroyed 5 houses and converted land to pasture in 1487

FIELD BURCOTE ○
Destroyed by Sir Thos. Green in 1499. 2,000 sheep here in 1551

EASTON NESTON ○

FOSCOTE ○
Enclosure and evictions by John Ashby in 1488

R. Tove

T

Destroyed for park-making and sheep pasture by Sir Ric. Empson around 1500

STUCHBURY ○
Apparently depopulated by owner, St Andrew's Priory, Northampton, before Dissolution of the monasteries

ASTWELL ○
Destroyed by Thos. Lovett for sheep pasture and a deer park in 1547

FALCUTT ○
Seems to have been destroyed along with Astwell

GREAT PURSTON ○
Destroyed for sheep in 1495. 600 sheep here in 1547

STEANE ○
1000 sheep were grazing the former village lands in 1547

BUCKINGHAMSHIRE

OXFORDSHIRE

| 0 | | 5 | | 10 Mls |

| 0 | 5 | | 10 | 15 Kms |

KEY
○ Deserted village
T Modern Towcester

Developed from K.J.Allison,M.W.Beresford and J.G.Hurst, *Deserted Villages of Northamptonshire*, 1966 to accommodate a community on their manors, even though they all had done so for centuries. Villages were there to house the creators of wealth, and if more wealth could be gained in other ways then villages must, literally, be wastes of space. A national community that had entered the second half of the fourteenth century in a state of shock, division and instability emerged from it in much the same way, though the reasons for this had changed.

Scenes of change

The conditions and the states of mind that perpetuated villages had gone. We may never know which village was the first to surrender to a flock, but we do know that by Tudor times, empty swathes of countryside spanning several parishes or townships had been created and the evictions were fuelling fears of a new uprising. While the emptying of localities by the Black Death and the turmoil that followed created the conditions in which eviction could take root, in some localities the keeping of sheep had already become a most rewarding venture a full generation before the arrival of the plague. In places like Derbyshire's Upper Dove Valley, where there was good pasture and abundant springs, specialised sheep farms or 'bercaries' were established under the stimulus of an expanding wool trade. Information collected by local researchers shows that the Earl of Lancaster's feudal Honour of Tutbury on the Staffordshire side of the River Dove was administered from Tutbury Castle and contained hunting grounds, places where tenants farmed in the traditional manner and also specialised sheep farms. From the accounts of 1313-14 it is seen that the Earl had at least fourteen sheep farms around Hartington, as well as others further afield at places like Ashbourne, Belper and Matlock. Almost 5,000 sheep were shorn in the Honour, producing twenty great sacks of wool, each one worth £7 3s 6d (around £7.18p). Sheep farming was already big business. Some of the bercaries were on open, scarcely-peopled uplands, like the fells of Northumberland, where the Umfravilles ran a flock of 1,140 sheep beside their herds of cattle and stud mares, but others were ominously close to the England of villages and peasant tillage.

With the viability of commercial sheep farming demonstrated by dynasties like the Umfravilles, it was no great leap for the masters of the countryside to elbow village communities aside to make space for more flocks. Some lords were content to remove just the one village, but a few families built great fortunes upon the corpses of settlements. The Knightleys of Fawsley, in Northamptonshire, were prime examples. Fawsley was not one village but two; one lying around the church and the other to the south of the hall. The settlements flourished, and when the Poll Tax of 1377

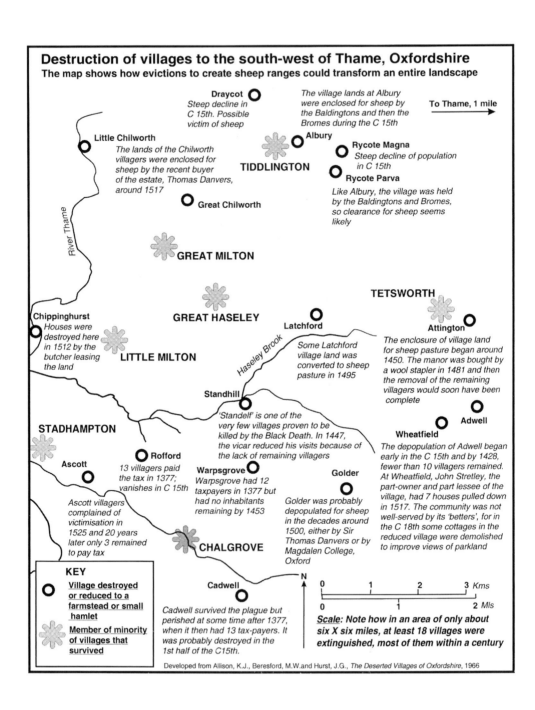

Destruction of villages to the south-west of Thame, Oxfordshire
The map shows how evictions to create sheep ranges could transform an entire landscape

Draycot
Steep decline in C 15th. Possible victim of sheep

The village lands at Albury were enclosed for sheep by the Baldingtons and then the Bromes during the C 15th

To Thame, 1 mile ➡

Little Chilworth
The lands of the Chilworth villagers were enclosed for sheep by the recent buyer of the estate, Thomas Danvers, around 1517

TIDDLINGTON

Albury

Rycote Magna
Steep decline of population in C 15th

Rycote Parva
Like Albury, the village was held by the Baldingtons and Bromes, so clearance for sheep seems likely

Great Chilworth

River Thame

GREAT MILTON

GREAT HASELEY

TETSWORTH

Chippinghurst
Houses were destroyed here in 1512 by the butcher leasing the land

LITTLE MILTON

Latchford
Some Latchford village land was converted to sheep pasture in 1495

Haseley Brook

Attington
The enclosure of village land for sheep pasture began around 1450. The manor was bought by a wool stapler in 1481 and then the removal of the remaining villagers would soon have been complete

Standhill
'Standelf' is one of the very few villages proven to be killed by the Black Death. In 1447, the vicar reduced his visits because of the lack of remaining villagers

Adwell

Wheatfield
The depopulation of Adwell began early in the C 15th and by 1428, fewer than 10 villagers remained. At Wheatfield, John Stretley, the part-owner and part lessee of the village, had 7 houses pulled down in 1517. The community was not well-served by its 'betters', for in the C 18th some cottages in the reduced village were demolished to improve views of parkland

STADHAMPTON

Rofford
13 villagers paid the tax in 1377; vanishes in C 15th

Ascott
Ascott villagers complained of victimisation in 1525 and 20 years later only 3 remained to pay tax

Warpsgrove
Warpsgrove had 12 taxpayers in 1377 but had no inhabitants remaining by 1453

Golder
Golder was probably depopulated for sheep in the decades around 1500, either by Sir Thomas Danvers or by Magdalen College, Oxford

CHALGROVE

KEY
○ **Village destroyed or reduced to a farmstead or small hamlet**

✳ **Member of minority of villages that survived**

Cadwell
Cadwell survived the plague but perished at some time after 1377, when it then had 13 tax-payers. It was probably destroyed in the 1st half of the C15th.

N

| 0 | 1 | 2 | 3 Kms |
| 0 | 1 | 2 Mls |

Scale: Note how in an area of only about six X six miles, at least 18 villages were extinguished, most of them within a century

Developed from Allison, K.J., Beresford, M.W. and Hurst, J.G., *The Deserted Villages of Oxfordshire*, 1966 was levied, ninety people paid, however reluctantly, and there were probably several who evaded the tax. It is quite often the case that the death of a village was linked to the arrival of a successful lawyer. Such people earned very good money, but realised that land was the greatest signifier of status. In this case that man was Richard Knightley of Staffordshire, who bought the Fawsleys in 1416. At first, he seems to have experienced the same difficulties that were being encountered on so many estates where the traditional demands for free labour on the demesne were now resented. He did not tolerate them for very long, and within a few years, the villagers had gone and timid sheep grazed where the houses had stood. Then some pastures were converted to parkland and the house site, once within earshot of dozens of noisy households, stood isolated, overlooking the park and artificial lakes that engulfed old meadows. Fortunes change, and in the mid-twentieth century, the mansion was reduced to a saw mill and timber store, although the tomb effigies of the successive Knightleys still dominate the church. The economic triumph at Fawsley paved the way to a greater fortune. By the middle of the sixteenth century, a vast flock of 2,500 sheep grazed the locality and the dynasty had systematically begun acquiring an empire of depopulated sheep ranges in the East Midlands.

It was a similar mission that elevated the Spencers from the ranks of the petty gentry. In the strange way that things happen, the Spencers' seat at Althorp, in Northamptonshire, straddled the corpse of Althorp village, one of the many fifteenth-century eviction victims. Yet in this instance, the Spencers were innocent, for before their arrival at Althorp, the village of that name had been exterminated by previous owners, the Catesbys. Feudal society was not completely rigid. Occasionally, a husbandman, normally a free tenant of burning ambition alloyed with ability and cunning, would scale several steps of the social ladder. Generally, the heirs would lack these qualities, so the descent could be just as rapid. The Spencers, in contrast, advanced through generations and across centuries, eventually reaching as high as they could possibly go. Originating as free tenants, in the second half of the Middle Ages they became part of the growing class of yeomen farmers. In the latter part of the fifteenth century the family exploited the opportunities gained by leasing or purchasing land for use as sheep ranges. They were based at Wormleighton, in Warwickshire, and here, as at Althorp, they were anticipated, for a John Spicer had partially cleared the village before John Spencer arrived and completed the depopulation in the last year of the century. The family name became synonymous with the purchase and leasing of land, soon to be followed by evictions.

The Knightleys and Spencers might seem to have had a mission to convert the Midlands into a desert. In many places their depopulated estates were linked in chains, as though a monstrous device had passed across the land, leaving only the grass remaining. What was being done was technically illegal, yet just before his death in 1552, John Spencer, who had done little of note except put poor people out on the road, was knighted. An exemplification of the way in which history is written by the victors can be gained from the Althorp website, where we learn: 'John Spencer became feoffee of Wormleighton in 1469, and a tenant at Althorp in 1486. His nephew another John, through trade in livestock and commodities, then bought both properties outright, was knighted, and so lay the bedrock for the family's fortune'. Well… yes, but I think there were a few hundred homeless people involved as well as the livestock.

The church, already regarded with cynicism for the excesses of its leaders and further tarnished by its role in the revolt, joined in the land rush. The mission to render comfort to the meek was habitually subordinated to the mission to obtain money. At North Marefield in Leicestershire, lands belonging to the Knights Templar passed to the Knights Hospitallers when the Templars were suppressed in 1313, amid bizarre charges of Satanism. In the years around 1500, a number of 'messuages' or farm holdings there were granted to the nearby Augustinian abbey at Owston, whose abbot was renting pastures at North Marefield for 50s (£2.50) in 1502. The Augustinians were normally more considerate to lay folk than most other orders, sharing their churches with them and supplying priests. In this case, however, the pastures concerned had probably been created by evicting lay tenants. This may have begun in the first half of the fifteenth century for an abatement in tax of almost one-eighth was granted in 1445, suggesting that there were fewer people left there to pay. Then, in 1463, one John Hartop the Elder sued four local husbandmen for chasing his sheep. They were unlikely to have been doing this for exercise or for fun and so one has a picture of the victims of the expanding flocks releasing some of their resentments in a sheep chase. By the early sixteenth century, the evictions seem to have been complete, with Marefield now existing as a great enclosed sheep pasture. Today, the site of North Marefield displays the traces of hollowed lanes, a moated manor and of village buildings, which were built on stone footings if not being walled in stone, though which one was the chapel that was used from the twelfth to the fourteenth century is not easy to know.

In the same century that the Knightleys were evicting their tenants at Fawsley, the nearby village of Canons Ashby experienced eviction at other hands. These were not the pale, grasping hands of a cunning lawyer. Neither were they paws calloused by the jerking reins of a pitching charger. They were soft hands, hardened only at the fingertips through the turning of parchment pages. The Prior of Canons Ashby was responsible for removing the village that lay to the north of the Augustinian priory church. He will have known the face of every villager that he cast out and will have prayed with them all. He threw them out in stages. Firstly, in 1489, a trio of houses was pulled down, then there was a respite of a few years before twenty-four villagers were evicted – within a decade of the first demolitions, the village was gone completely. The vocation of the canons was not as different from that of the Knightleys as one might imagine: both were interested in building fortunes from sheep. That of the canons was rather more short-lived, for within four decades of the removal of Canons Ashby, the priory, along with many others, was dissolved by Henry VIII. Fourteen years after its dissolution, John Dryden began building an 'H'-plan mansion from stone he pillaged from the priory church. Now reduced to a quarter of its original size, the church still conveys an idea of its former grandeur. It stands in a seventy acre (around 28 hectare) park that is corrugated, ridged and dimpled with the earthworks of the old village and its fields and where two of the Medieval canons' fish ponds are pegged-out for modern rods.

The scale of eviction and desertion was almost incredible. In some of the most severely affected areas, like the Thames valley in Oxfordshire, the Tove valley in Northamptonshire or parts of the Yorkshire Wolds and Cotswolds, the corpses of villages could lie so thickly that in any randomly-chosen square mile of countryside there as a 50:50 chance of finding a deserted village. And so, one must wonder whether the people living at the time were aware of the general extent and intensity of the assault upon Village England? In seeking an answer, one must be aware that the evictions took place at a time when a situation in which only clerics were literate had begun to yield to one in which many nobles and people in commerce could read and literate officials were being employed on many estates. Much intellectual effort was being given to biblical subjects and the interpretation of scriptures while literary output was small, concerned with classical and religious themes and coloured with symbolism and allegory. By far the greatest written output concerned prosaic matters of recording production and dues: who owed rents, who had paid them, what had been spent and what had been agreed. Diaries and descriptive writing were in their infancy and nobody considered that the lives, thoughts, hardships and concerns of ordinary country people were topics suitable to be committed to paper. When such people did feature in the rolls, the entry concerned the facts that they had paid their taxes or been put at the mercy of their manor court for some sad little offence or had entered into an agreement with their lords.

There is just a little in the contemporary records to give us a glimpse or mental map of England at the time of the evictions. One of the most pertinent documents was revealed by M. W. Beresford. Almost single-handedly, he pioneered the discovery of deserted villages at a time when most

historians regarded the topic as unworthy, unproductive and largely irrel-
evant. Professor Beresford went on to supervise the remarkable excavations
at Wharram Percy deserted village. He retired as a full-time member of staff
at Leeds University in 1985 and almost twenty years later I was honoured
to give the tribute lecture when he was awarded an honorary doctorate by
the university. I learned of his death in December 2005 while I was writing this section. Beresford recognised the importance of records made by
John Rous of Warwick. Rous was a chantry priest, providing Masses for the
souls of the departed. He died in 1491, leaving behind the manuscript of a
History of England, which stayed unprinted until 1716. It was generally of no
great importance, but as Beresford wrote, it broke away from conventional
narration when the author's incredulity and indignation at depopulating
enclosures burst through. Rous wrote with a rage that was quite out of
character with other writings of his day, 'The root of this evil is greed. The
plague of avarice infects these times and blinds its men'. As a churchman,
he was aware that villagers were also the payers of the tithes that funded the
church, 'They enclose the area of a village with mounds [hedge banks?] and
surround it with ditches. In such places the King's highway is blocked and
poor people cannot pass through. Where villages decay, there also do tithes'.

The most remarkable element in Rous's work was a list of villages that
he knew to have been abandoned. It seems that he could scarcely credit
the scale of the destruction and felt that if destruction on the scale that he
had seen in Warwickshire were to be repeated in other parts, the country
would be in 'national danger'. He identified some fifty-eight depopulated
places, '… none of them more than a dozen miles from Warwick'. Scholars
who discovered the text thought that the figures were being used in a
polemical way, and one claimed that they had been inserted at a later date.
However, by applying his experience in landscape history, Beresford was
able to identify the sites of all but two (ambiguously named) villages. It was
plain that by the end of the fifteenth century, Village England had become
a battlefield, with parts of it more closely resembling a charnel house.

The consequences of the changes were rebounding around society and
could not be confined to the manors. Gangs composed of the homeless rabble were swelling and growing bolder. People travelled fearfully,
never knowing on which lane, bridge or crossroads they might meet the
husbandmen who had been driven to become desperadoes. Church revenues were plummeting and priests were deprived of work and income,
for with the villagers went the tithes and the lucrative christenings, burials, mortuaries and Masses. The hacking-up of the old communal fields
was often accompanied by a cutting of the highways that had woven
between them. Thus Rous wrote of '… Church Charwelton on the
border of Warwicks and Northants, where there used to be a well-known

and healthy stopping place for travellers from Warwick and other places to London. Now travellers are forced to leave the old road and go down to Lower Charwelton. There is much danger for all these places are now totally or partly destroyed'.

If the government was oblivious to the suffering of the homeless, it was not blind to the threat that they posed to the social order. In 1489, two years before John Rous died, an Act attempted to outlaw any enclosure of common land and conversion to pasture if it involved the extinction of any holdings larger than twenty acres (around 8.1 hectares). The preamble to the Act read:

> Great inconvenience daily doth increase by desolation and pulling down and wilfull waste of houses and Towns [villages were known as 'towns']… and laying to pasture lands which customarily have been used in tillage… for where in some Towns two hundred persons were occupied and lived by their lawful labours, now be there occupied two of three herdsmen and the residue fallen into idleness; the husbandry, which is one of the greatest commodities of this realm, is greatly decayed; churches destroyed; the service of God withdrawn; the bodies there buried not prayed for; the patron and curate wronged; the defence of this land against our enemies outward feebl'd and impaired; to the great displeasure of God, to the subversion of policy and good rule of this land.

The most widely-read eyewitness condemnation of the Tudor evictions appeared in the first book of Sir Thomas More's *Utopia* of 1515. Now he is remembered as a saintly figure who, after great mental turmoil, was unable to put his personal interests before the dictates of his conscience. The real Thomas More was rather more complex. He was a harsh, we might say bigoted, judge where cases concerning religion were involved. Yet, in contrast to the various lawyers who were initiating evictions, More took a humane view of the plight of the husbandmen and their families. The most celebrated extract ran, 'Your sheep which are usually so tame and so cheaply fed, begin now, according to report, to be so greedy and wild that they devour human beings themselves and devastate and depopulate fields, houses, and towns'. He then condemned the nobles, gentlemen and churchmen who were not satisfied with their established estate revenues and who were not simply content to live in idleness without harming their country. Instead, they did it positive harm:

> They leave no ground to be tilled; they enclose every bit for pasture; they pull down houses and destroy towns, leaving only a church to pen the sheep in. And, as if enough English land were not wasted on sheep ranges and

game preserves, those good fellows turn all human habitations and all cultivated land into a wilderness.

He wrote of the victims in terms that were enlightened for his day:

> … that one covetous and insatiable cormorant may compass about and enclose
> many thousand acres of ground together within one pale or hedge, the hus-
> bandmen be thrust out of their own, or else either by cunning and fraud, or
> by violent oppression, or another, either by hook or by crook they must needs
> depart away; men, women, husbands, wives, fatherless children, widows, moth-
> ers with their young babies, and all their household, small in substance and
> large in number, as husbandry requires many hands. Away they trudge, say I,
> out of their known and familiar houses, finding no place to rest…

Then, More wrote, they would wander till the last of their small funds
were spent, when there would be nothing left for them but to steal.
He then revealed the limits of his liberality by writing that when they
did steal, they could justly be hanged (see below). Otherwise, they could
go a-begging, though then they could be thrown into jail as vagabonds.
(A modern Christian, perhaps not one ready to suffer death for his/her
beliefs like More, might argue that starvation gave one the right to take
life-saving food or alms.)

Such uncompromising words, coming from a senior lawyer who had
served as Under Sheriff of London and as a Member of Parliament and who
occupied the high office of Master of Requests, could scarcely be ignored.

By the end of the fifteenth century, there was a widespread recognition
among the thinking classes that the evictions were seriously debilitating and
dividing the kingdom and that they had to be stopped. Wool was valuable,
but it was not worth the social, political costs or the threats that the dispossessed posed for society. As More observed, once evicted, households would
sell their goods for a trifle, and, 'After they have soon spent that trifle in wan-
dering from place to place what remains for them but to steal and be hanged
– justly, you may say – or to wander and beg. And yet even in the latter case
they are cast into prison as vagrants for going about idle when, though they
most eagerly offer their labour, there is no one to hire them'. Making laws
to end the abuses was fairly easy. Enforcing these laws was not, for the landed
gentry that moulded opinion and upheld standards was largely composed of
the very same people who were offending against the Act of 1489.

What had begun in injustice ended in fraud. It was very frequent for
those facing Commissions of Inquiry or prosecution in the Royal Courts
on charges of depopulation to argue that the evictions in question had taken
place before the legislation had been put in place and so they lay outside

its scope. At Wormleighton, a commission found that twelve houses, three cottages and 240 acres of village land had been enclosed, with the result that twelve ploughs had been put out of business and sixty villagers had been evicted. This had done the owner nothing but good, for the value of the land increased from £40 to £60 per annum. The culprit seemed to be John Spencer, but in the 1520s he claimed that, while he was the current owner of the estate, the depopulator had been a previous owner, William Cope. Rebuilding was another frequently heard plea and Spencer invoked this as well, saying that four village dwellings had been rebuilt, along with two new houses by his manor house and four other dwellings. Through this rebuilding, he claimed, forty people had been housed and the village restored to its previous size, though even on the basis of his arithmetic, a third of the population was still missing. Pointing to the rise in income that had resulted from depopulation, he also claimed that the Crown, as overlord, had gained from this. Having thus muddied the waters, he then claimed that mounting a defence was too expensive and successfully pleaded for a statuary pardon. In most places, hollow promises to make restitutions were sufficient to save the offending landowners from prosecution.

In 1526 a proclamation announced a renewed attempt to outlaw evictions and the conversion of village land, and to repopulate the enclosures. The ability of the state to enforce its own policies had not greatly increased – had it enforced them there would not have been a need to re-tread the ground covered by an Act in 1515. But now there was a glint of hope for Village England: the market price of grain was beginning to rise. The economic imbalance between cultivation and the taking of rent from cultivators on the one hand and the raising of sheep and cattle, on the other, was narrowing. It was because of this tendency, rather than in attempts at self-regulation by the landed gentry, that villagers began to sleep a mite more easily.

The greatest assault on villages that the kingdom would ever know began with the Peasants' Revolt, but thereafter, while the dispossessed might turn outlaws or ruffians, there was no concerted and widespread uprising against the injustices. There was, however, a sting at the tail of the evictions: Ket's Revolt. The clearances and enclosures could fell a village in one stroke or in two or three stages. They could also strike at different parts of the shared lands, undermining a community and reducing their home, without actually killing either. While some villages were being exterminated, communities in other places stood by helplessly as their age-old common was clipped and devalued like some precious coin. Several agricultural pillars supported the village economy. The crop lands produced calories and the grazing of the aftermath; the woods and hedgerows rendered timber, fuel, browse, fruits and honey; the meadows gave hay, and the holly groves gave leaf fodder, all needed to keep the plough-beasts alive through winter.

The common gave grazing for the village herd, stone for walling, clay for pots, bracken for bedding, gorse for fuel, turf for the hearth, and very much more. If it was a lowland common, it might have rushes and reeds for flooring and thatch, fish, wildfowl, summer pasture and peat beds. When the common was stolen, the loss reverberated around the peasant economy.

The laws passed in 1489 and 1515 should have safeguarded the village folk against these incursions, but in 1517 the Royal Commission on Enclosures under Cardinal Wolsey recognised that the laws were being flouted in seven Midland counties. Then the situation deteriorated and the Proclamation in 1526 did little to turn the tide. Struggling to survive on diminished resources, villagers were especially vulnerable to any adverse weather conditions. In the 1520s, these arrived, with successive bad harvests causing famine and the famines in turn causing riots in the over-populated countrysides of Norfolk. Being now scarce, food became greatly more expensive, the spiralling prices being aggravated by the cost of funding the continental wars of Henry VIII.

One of the most evocative of deserted village sites, though not one of the most accessible, is Bawsey in Norfolk, with its ruined Norman church. The village was destroyed by the enclosure of its lands in the early years of the sixteenth century. Though the houses had gone, the church lingered on in a partly derelict state and continued to provide services of baptism and burial for households remaining in the vicinity through most of the eighteenth century until its abandonment in the 1770s. Similarly, the church at Wharram Percy in the Yorkshire Wolds, isolated by the removal of its village, served people of the adjacent township of Thixendale. They gained their own church in 1870, but the church at Wharram, though increasingly ruinous, was used intermittently until the mid-twentieth century, around five centuries after the gradual depopulation of the village by sheep grazing interests. The fate of the community of another evocative deserted village site in Norfolk, Pudding Norton, is less well known. In 1557 the village seems to have been a going concern and in 1557 a bequest of money was left for the repair of the church. By 1602, however, a major tragedy had befallen the place, for it was recorded that the church was entirely ruined and, '... decayed long since, unknowne by whome it was pulled down.'

Having been one of the most densely populated of rural counties, Norfolk experienced the most dramatic assaults on its village populations as a result of the introduction of sheep flocks on to village lands and the enclosure of commons. The shortage of building stone, which caused churches to be built of worthless flints from the surrounding fields, meant that after the evictions the church would stand as a gradually deteriorating ruin rather than being swiftly robbed for stone by the local lord. Egmere has most of its Medieval church still standing, though its community dwindled in the later Medieval centu-

Wharram Percy in a dry chalk valley in the Yorkshire Wolds.

ries. The church was actually abandoned twice, once between 1538-89, with a subsequent restoration failing and being followed by a final abandonment late in the century. The lord of the manor, Sir Nicholas Bacon, was blamed for ruining and profaning the building, as was the incumbent, Mr Thomas Bostock. Godwick, another dramatic site, was also a village of modest proportions and suffered from enclosures in the sixteenth century. The former place of the nave roof is plainly marked on the surviving church tower.

Having been proved impotent in their attempts to regulate the land-owning classes and outlaw their larceny of the land, the authorities sought easier prey: the victims of the landlords. In 1531, it became an offence for a destitute but able-bodied person to beg, punishable by a succession of penalties that began with whipping and culminated in hanging. A thankfully short-lived Act of 1547 attempted to reintroduce slavery for all those who were convicted of the 'crime' of being unemployed. Poverty, starvation, burning resentment against the state and the land-owning classes, and the religious confusion caused the break with Rome and the Dissolution of the Monasteries created a climate of revolution in the North, the South West, Wessex, Lincolnshire and Norfolk. Fortunately for the established order, the regional cauldrons of anger were unable to spill over and unite.

People knew only too well that while authority would whip or hang those who stole a goose from the common, it would let the greater criminal loose '… who steals the common from the goose'. The new hedges

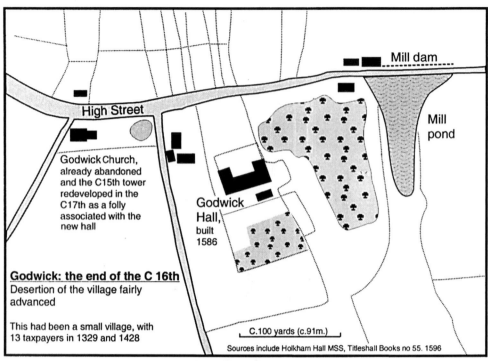

High Street

Mill dam

Mill pond

Godwick Church, already abandoned and the C15th tower redeveloped in the C17th as a folly associated with the new hall

Godwick Hall, built 1586

Godwick: the end of the C 16th
Desertion of the village fairly advanced

This had been a small village, with 13 taxpayers in 1329 and 1428

C.100 yards (c.91m.)

Sources include Holkham Hall MSS, Titleshall Books no 55. 1596

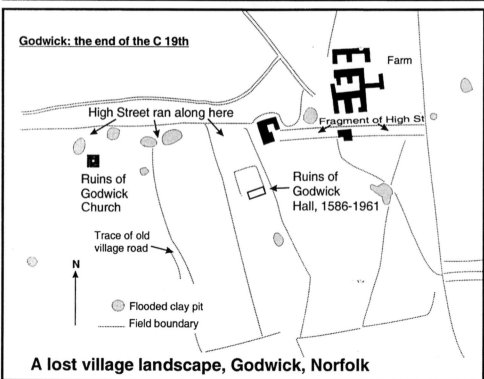

Godwick: the end of the C 19th

Farm

High Street ran along here

Fragment of High St

Ruins of Godwick Church

Ruins of Godwick Hall, 1586-1961

Trace of old village road

N

Flooded clay pit

Field boundary

A lost village landscape, Godwick, Norfolk

that guarded the encroachments were frequently uprooted and in Mid-Anglia villagers exhorted each other:

Cast hedge and ditch in the lake
Fix'd with many a stake
Though they be ne'er so fast,
Yet asunder they are wrest

It was in this situation of resentment, defiance and desperation that, in the summer of 1549, opposition began to form around an unlikely leader, Robert Ket. He was a landowner, indeed, an encloser, of relatively advanced years who discovered a compassion for Norfolk's poor. The rebellion erupted spontaneously at Attleborough, where the local squire had fenced off some common lands. The hedges and fences were torn from the ground and a frenzy of hedge-breaking began across the county as news flashed back and forth on the peasant networks of communication. On 7 July, almost three weeks after the first incident, a religious festival drew Norfolk villagers to Wymondham. This brought them close to the fences set up on Hetherset common by a Sergeant Flowerdew, with predictable consequences. Now the county was insurgent and the Ket brothers, Robert, a tanner, and William, a butcher, were likely targets for the next reprisals; Robert tenanted three manors and had enclosed common land. However, in his confrontation with the rebels his role was amazingly converted from that of target to leader. Robert Ket articulated the grievances of his, as yet, modestly-sized army of supporters and focussed them on the proposition that the goal of freedom demanded the suppression of the landlords, 'Your tyrannous masters often implead, arrest and cast you into prison, so that they may the more terrify and torture you in your minds, and wind our necks more surely under their arms'. Though campaigning against situations as unjust as any known in the feudal era, Ket's words might have been spoken by quite some modern revolutionary leader – and so provided yet another signal that the Middle Ages had run its course.

On 12 July, Ket's force skirted Norwich and encamped at Mousehold Heath, to the east of the city. In the days that followed, his army grew to become a large force of 20,000 as the news of the revolt reached out across the county. A list of grievances and demands was drawn-up and sent to the king, while a court was set up under a spreading tree, the 'Oak of Restitution' and the trial of enclosing landlords began. The precarious relations with the authorities in Norwich broke down and a mercenary army under the Marquis of Northampton was routed, while Norwich fell under the domination of the rebels. On 24 August a far larger army, with a large German mercenary contingent, appeared, under the leadership of Dudley, Earl of Warwick. By the evening, Norwich was under royal

The abbey church at Wymondham, the settlement where, in a sense, the Peasants' Revolt of 1381 both began and ended.

Castles and great houses were often funded by the fleece trade, like Stokesay in Shropshire, built in the 1270s by Lawrence of Ludlow before the great confrontations between sheep and villages.

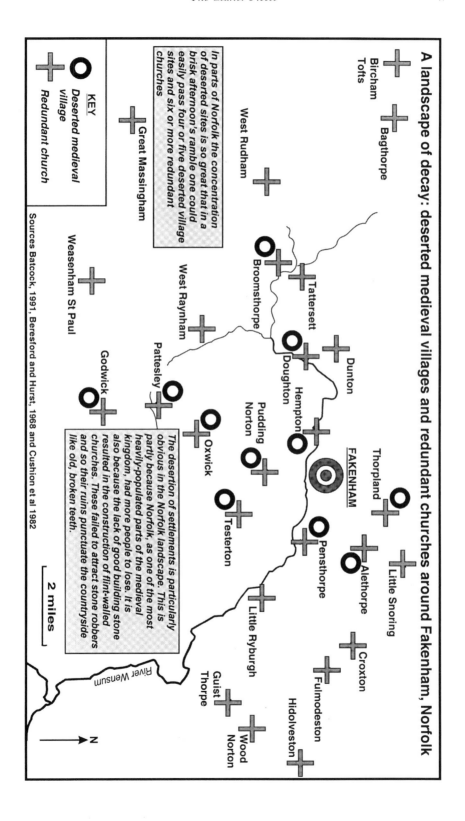

A landscape of decay: deserted medieval villages and redundant churches around Fakenham, Norfolk

KEY

○ Deserted medieval village

✝ Redundant church

In parts of Norfolk the concentration of deserted sites is so great that in a brisk afternoon's ramble one could easily pass four or five deserted village sites and six or more redundant churches

The desertion of settlements is particularly obvious in the Norfolk landscape. This is partly because Norfolk, as one of the most heavily-populated parts of the medieval kingdom, had more people to lose. It is also because the lack of good building stone resulted in the construction of flint-walled churches. These failed to attract stone robbers and so their ruins punctuate the countryside like old, broken teeth.

Sources Batcock, 1991, Beresford and Hurst, 1968 and Cushion et al 1982

Bircham Totts

Bagthorpe

West Rudham

Great Massingham

Broomsthorpe

Tattersett

Dunton

Thorpland

Little Snoring

West Raynham

Doughton

Hempton

FAKENHAM

Alethorpe

Croxton

Weasenham St Paul

Godwick

Pattesley

Oxwick

Pudding Norton

Penthorpe

Fulmodeston

Hidolveston

Testerton

Little Ryburgh

Guist Thorpe

Wood Norton

River Wensum

2 miles

N

control again and sixty rebels caught in the city were hanged and buried in mass graves. The struggle was not over, for most of Warwick's artillery train strayed out of a city gate and was seized by the rebels and there was fighting in Norwich all the next day. Then, mercenary reinforcements arrived to strengthen Warwick's contingent and the rebel force marched from its Mousehold camp to confront the royal army outside the city walls. This was a mistake, for the rebels were not trained to fight a set-piece battle, the Norfolk villagers being no match for the seasoned soldiery.

Robert Ket was captured in the evening, just eight miles to the north of Norwich. His brother was captured on the same night. Warwick executed more than 350 prisoners, many of whom must have accepted his offer of pardons in return for surrendering. On 7 December, Robert Ket was hanged in chains outside Norwich Castle and William was killed in the same manner at Wymondham. Theirs was the last great uprising of Village England. Had there been a rebellion in concert with other dissident groups in the kingdom, the king's mercenary forces would have been fragmented, and, possibly, defeated. And had this happened, the English might still be celebrating some day around the sultry side of summer as their Independence Day. Special wreaths would be laid at memorials in churchyards and on greens throughout the land. There would be a national holiday, when a procession of pilgrims with oak leaves pinned to their breasts, some having begun their march at Wymondham, would stream from Norwich Cathedral, banners flying, to the supposed site of the Oak of Reformation on Mousehold Heath. A member of the royal family – or perhaps it would be the President of Britain – would bow at the great memorial there. Then, the nations of Britain might remember the villagers of far-off times who gave their lives to lead England and then Europe out of feudalism. This vision bled away on the battleground outside the gates of Norwich, and the history written by the victors is quite different.

Unrest and persecution continued and when, after so many years, the evictions came to an end it was not because legality and compassion had triumphed. It was because the renting of land and the growing of crops could at last compete as sources of income. The uprisings and the events between them had ensured that things could not go back to the way that they had been around 1400. There were tears ripped in the fabric of community and settlement. Right across the land there were localities – scores and scores of them – that were more silent and more thinly-peopled than they had been since before the Bronze Age. Things had moved on and landlords had different ways of extracting wealth from the land than those practised by the old feudal lords. Villagers might rest a while, but slashes and gouges in their countrysides would not always heal. Places emptied in Tudor times may still be empty today.

CHAPTER NINE

THE BODY UNDER THE PARK

A country tale

Benjamin is one of the carters on the 5th Baron's estate and Hannah, his wife, is a kitchen maid there. Both are old and tired, but young Joseph is a cripple and the lack of any other surviving children to support them means that they hope to be in employment until their dying days. Ben is short and slight with legs somewhat bowed by rickets, one of the childhood hardships he experienced in the early years of the reign of George III (1760-1820). Scars from smallpox pit his face, while a lifetime of under-nourishment and vitamin deficiencies has done nothing to improve his physique. The broken bones caused when a heavy horse stepped on his foot were never properly set, and so he limps. Yet many times a week, he shoulders bags of oats and meal weighing much more than himself and bears them up and down the steps and rungs of the stables block. He sleeps in his cottage but really lives with the great horses, spending up to fifteen hours of every day feeding, grooming, harnessing and carting with his patient friends. He serves as a vet at a miniscule fraction of modern rates, dispensing the secret cures that he has inherited from his forebears. Because his wages are so niggardly, it does not matter that many hours are frittered away on plaiting horse tails, decking the wooden frames or 'hames' of the harness with tinkling bells, pointlessly washing carts due shortly for the dung trail between the midden and fields and various other uneconomical tasks.

He starts his day at 4 a.m. and at least three hours pass before the stalls are cleaned out and the horses fed, harnessed and made fit to be seen ahead of their lord's cart. The carting of goods to market, muck to the ploughlands, harvest produce to the rickyard or other such tasks continues until about 11 a.m., when Ben has his first food after seven hours of toil. There may be bread and cheese, but all that is drunk – perhaps cold tea or rough cider – must first have been boiled or fermented, for the village well is a nest of typhoid and dysentery. The cider comes with the job and he drinks five pints (around 2.8 litres) of it each working day; the cost of the estate cider is deducted from his wages. Only the beer at harvest comes free, though he may be given extra work ploughing or harrowing at any time. Lunch and elevenses are rolled into one break of half an hour, and then work resumes until 4 p.m., when the carting team return to the stables and the rituals of un-harnessing and grooming begin. Ben may allow himself a trip to his cottage for a snack of produce from his cottage garden before returning to the stables to 'supper-up' and bed-down the heavy horses. For all this, he receives 8s 6d (around 43p) per week for the six working days, nothing for the Sunday, when he is obliged to go to church, while his weekly rent of 1s 6d (75p) must be paid back to the lord.

Hannah earns much less. Before her sight softened and her fingers became stiff, she would earn a little extra by weaving straw bonnets, but the damage to her eyes from working in candlelight exceeded the value of the extra pennies. For half the year, they never see each other in daylight, except on Sundays. They live in a ratty cottage in a tatty village, and when the door is open in the summer they can look across the green to the mansion. Though the facts are long forgotten, the village is the successor of an older settlement evicted from a new deer park in the fourteenth century. Since then, the manor house has sprouted wings, ranges and chimneys and become quite grand. The village, however, has scarcely kept pace. The cottages have gained sleeping lofts in the roof space and the dormer windows thrusting through the thatch proclaim the arrival of stairs and upper-storey bedrooms. Inside however, the cottages are still strewn with extra beds, brewing equipment, cheese-making utensils and farm tools, all in jumbles that defy any attempts to designate separate chambers as lounges or workshops. Bathrooms and lavatories have not featured in the wildest fantasies of the tenants and the closest approaches to kitchens are the brew-houses in the backs of each dwelling.

Each house is built and decays as a separate entity, though the cottages are linked to form a double alignment of terraces that face each other across the track, suddenly dignified on its arrival in the village as the 'High Street'. It runs through the settlement to the green, where it forks. The terraced layout is convenient for the tenant households as their shared walls help neighbours to keep one another warm. It is also convenient to rats, which can traverse the length of the street without ever showing their noses. The animals are everywhere: when you shift a heavy sack you can see the circular mark left by dirty rat fur as the animals have circled the obstacle that pressed hard against the wall. Their tunnels weave through the crumbling daub in the wattled walls and some beams are polished by the passage of their warm coats. Occasionally, where the burrowing has worn the daub away, one can see the Roman numerals chiselled on to the timbers by the fourteenth-century house wrights, who pre-fabricated the settlement from green oak in a nearby grove. Amazingly, these cheap timber frames have held together through almost five centuries as the thatch, daub and wattle have mouldered around them.

But these times are ending. The apostles of change are meeting in the gallery of the great house beyond the green. Two strangers are there, an architect and a self-styled creator of landscapes, both extravagantly wigged and no less extravagantly perfumed. Plans have been unrolled and spread across a table and those constant companions, flattery and fashion, hang heavily in the air. The lord surveys his impending mansion and park as they gaze back blankly in aquatinted miniature. Immaculate lettering with loops and spirals, cartouches, armorial bearings and other fancy things proclaim the importance and exquisite tastefulness of that which is displayed. The sight of such attainable magnificence automatically sends the 5th Baron's thoughts hurtling towards his accounts book and rental. He need not worry: the Enclosure, by Act of Parliament, of his tenancies has met its costs for hedging the divided commons and is now sending a river of greatly jacked-up rents into his coffers. Even with the most expensive horses, the most worthless stocks and the most scandalous adventures there is still more income than can readily be spent. This, his visitors know, and they will soon solve this problem for him.

What they propose is a rebuilding that will see the comfortable old house engulfed and entombed within a monumental Palladian confection of dysfunctional architecture. It will be a great symmetrical mansion oozing good taste and packed with inconvenient rooms: a triumph of form over content. A fashionably landscaped park will provide it with a fitting context. In truth, what is proposed is just tweaking up of the old deer park landscape with its lawns, groves and pollards and the emparking of peripheral farmland. The lord is keen to exaggerate the antiquity of his lineage by displaying ancient parkland trees. Since the gout and the gluttony will soon take care of him there is no time for trees to age naturally, so hedgerow trees will be lassoed into the park; their linking hedges will be grubbed up, and a semblance of ancient parkland thus created. By raising the old mill dam a fashionably serpentine lake will result – and that is more or less it, apart for a bill as monumental in its proportions as the mansion. Oh, the village – that will have to go. A new one outside the gate can serve as a conversation piece for guests approaching the hall. Visitors can be reminded of the patronage that the 5th Baron bestows upon the dependant community of inferiors (he is a Tory and such things matter more to them than to the masterful Whigs).

Having led lives in which nothing unusual might happen for several years, the news of eviction, which came to Ben and Hannah at the same time as that of redundancy and the removal of their village, is quite a shock. The villagers were to be dispersed and then re-housed, but, with the best of their working days far behind them, the old couple would not be provided with tenancies in the new village. Those locally in authority are a little reluctant to watch the work-worn pair starve to death, and with only slightly less reluctance they install them in the workhouse. They live there in separate wings, pressing to their windows to watch their erstwhile neighbours plod to and from church each Sunday. They see each other every evening across the scrubbed and silent dining room. However, they are not allowed to cross the room to greet one another, and merely calling messages across will expose them to punishment for fraternisation and affronting the rule of silence. It is during his first few days in the work-house that Ben realises he is an alcoholic; his severance from the estate cider supply brings a difficult withdrawal. Few people in the workhouse can visualise much to live for, and soon Nature, unassisted, brings their misery to an end.

The crippled son serves a long apprenticeship as a watchmaker, marries and produces a daughter of his own. Family tales about service with the 5th Baron are passed down the family, becoming softer and more vague with each passing generation. The name 'Ben' eventually returns to fashion and the latest member of the family to bear the name becomes curious about his ancestors. He looks at the website of the hall and its owners. He learns that the hall:

> … nestles in an idyllic fold of the landscape that was created by one of the greatest geniuses of English landscaping. Standing at the park gate are the beautiful cottages designed by the same architect and reflecting the age-old concern of our noble family for its tenants. The timeless village perfectly mirrors the bonds of respectful affection between the aristocracy and the sturdy yeomen of this realm of England…

The website tells Ben nothing about the cruelty and extortion inflicted upon helpless, hapless communities of exhausted and under-nourished people. It does not tell him about the homes that were pulled down. They never do. Ben decides to visit the hall. He finds the much-lauded parkland vistas inferior to what he has seen in the working farmlands of Devon, the northern fells or the quilted slopes of the Brecon Beacons.

He visits the church that lies stranded in the park beside the hall. Inside, great dynastic tombs of limestone and marble encroach on the spaces where the side aisles used to be and the Baron's Arms are emblazoned

across the west wall of the nave. Rusting war helms hang among the cob-
webs under the rafters, family banners slowly rot as they droop from on
high and effigies of the 1st to 7th Barons jut imperiously from every wall
and plinth. 'Great heavens!' thinks Ben, 'What god do they worship in this
Godless place?'

In splendid isolation

The emparking of villages with their surroundings was widespread in
Britain and Ireland during the seventeenth, eighteenth and even nineteenth
centuries. Not all the examples have been recognised, but the number of
communities affected must run into three figures. This was not a process
that was distinct from the making of deer parks during the Middle Ages (see
Ch. 5), but rather, a continuation of it. Deer continued to be coursed in parks
until long after the close of the Medieval period and Elizabeth I and the
Stuart kings were bloodsport fanatics. In his diary for 2 May 1686, Sir John
Reresby wrote:

> I went to New Hall in Essex, the Duke of Albemarle's house, the King
> [James II, 1685-89] having promised that duke to go and stay two days there
> to hunt, which he coming the day after, performed accordingly. These two
> days his Majesty killed two stags; he was indefatigable at that sport, loving to
> ride so hard that he usually lost his company.

One cannot think of this dull, dim, bloodsporting monarch without thinking of the comment of his mistress, Catherine Sedley, who debated why
he was attracted to her: '… it cannot be for my wit for he has not enough
to know that I have any.'

Parks, primarily for hunting deer, continued to be created after the close
of the Middle Ages and poaching continued to infuriate their owners.
Whitaker, a Victorian antiquarian, had access to Skipton Castle papers that
recorded a case that had been brought before the President and Council at
York in the reigns of Henry VIII (in 1540-41) and Elizabeth (in 1559-60).
Lesser gentry, the Nortons of Rilston, contested the right of the mighty
Cliffords of Skipton Castle to hunt in their locality. The Nortons claimed
that these grounds were not a part of the 'Forest' of Skipton. Testimony
from several witnesses was provided including that of Lancelot Marton,
who said that when he was out with his father as a boy:

> … he did see keepers of Skipton Forest hunt and chase deer out of the
> grounds of Rilston; and also myne old Lady Clifford mother to my lord of

Cumberland that now is, hound her greyhound within the said grounds of Rilston, and chase deer, and have them away at her leisure, both red and fallow, till now of late that master Norton hath walled his grounds of Rilston where the Forsters [foresters] were wont to walk and to draw my lord Cumberland's deer into his ground he hath made a wall on an high rigge [ridge], beside a quagmire and at the end of the walle he hath rayled the ground so that it is a destruction to my lord's deer, so many as come.

It was generally assumed that Medieval deer parks were for hunting and harbouring the living larder of venison, while the landscape parks that followed were for the enjoyment of tastefully modified and manicured scenery. Now, we know that designed landscapes created for hunting and pleasure spanned the divide. The artificial scenery created by the supposed masters of landscaping was rooted in Medieval parkland and incorporated facets stolen from working countrysides (I have recognised 'ornamental' tree patterns that were actually derived directly from pre-existing hedgerow trees in all of the last nine park plans that I have looked at).

Perhaps the most significant difference between the periods on either side of the Reformation concerned the relationship between the country people and the landed gentry. The exclusion of villages from feudal parks was probably usually of a functional intent: hungry peasants and deer did not combine very well and neither did peasant swine and newborn fawns. Ironically, it was only after feudalism was dead and buried that landowners, recalling the attitudes of the distant Cistercians, began to regard the mere presence of ordinary people as distasteful. This underlay the urge to create depopulated and sanitised settings for their great houses in places no longer sullied by the presence of those who had created the wealth to finance such houses. The privileged classes of the eighteenth century were preoccupied by progress and what was considered the rational ordering of things. Very often, these seemingly progressive sentiments could be conveniently invoked to justify self-seeking plundering of the customary rights of ordinary people. Methods of communal farming that had been retained and improved for a full 1,000 years were ridiculed as primitive, traditional countryside was stigmatised as backward and bucolic, while poor people were deemed feckless, wanton and burdensome upon their communities. All these values made it easy to remove such people from their commons and tenancies. The institutions that controlled the lives of the poor were dominated by managers from the establishment. Official attitudes are represented in the following statement from 1833 on the administration and operation of the Poor Laws:

It may seem harsh to say that I fear great harm is done to the labourer by the public contributions from the rich. The free school, the lying-in hospital, the soup kitchen, the distribution of grain, etc., in times of scarcity, and many other similar institutions, all tend to make the labourer look to others, and feel no anxiety to save for such emergencies. These public charities *create* the necessity they relieve, but they *do not relieve* all the necessity they *create*.

Some evictions resulted from the creation of a space around a mansion that was unspoiled by the presence of ordinary people, but there were many instances where the evictions were caused by the enlargement of an existing park. Middleton Stoney in Oxfordshire was removed by the 5th Earl of Jersey in the 1820s during the conversion of a Medieval deer park into a larger landscape park. Even a village that had been shifted and replaced once could not count its future as assured. The village beside Wimpole Church in Cambridgeshire was moved and then moved again as Lancelot Brown and then Humphrey Repton had their ways with the park landscape in the last third of the eighteenth century. Eventually, the village came to rest as a row of ornate brick cottages built outside the park along what became the A603. (The former village archaeological sites were less secure, being disturbed in the creation of a display area for rare farm animals in the early 1980s.) At places like Middleton Stoney, Wimpole, Overstone in Northamptonshire, Dogmersfield in Hampshire and scores of other, the great house, the church stranded in the park and the faint traces of a lost village provide the motifs of desertion. (At least at Middleton Stoney the isolated church has a Norman castle mound to keep it company – two ancient power centres superseded by the mansion.) There is no more recurrent or emblematic trinity in the landscapes of Britain than that of hall/church/deserted village site.

The desire for majestic isolation from a peasantry that was increasingly being demonised as feckless, inebriated and demanding was not confined to the conservative heartlands of England. It spanned the British Isles, with villages being torn down and *cordons sanitaires* being looped around great houses in Ireland, Scotland and Wales, and it embraced estates controlled by absentee English landlords and indigenous Scottish lairds alike. Fochabers, in the north of Scotland, is a good example. The old village lay just to the south of the palatial castle of the Dukes of Gordon. John Wesley thought it to be a wretched, mean and dirty place, while in 1773, James Boswell, on the Speyside leg of his Highland tour with Dr Johnson, praised its orchards but denigrated the numerous ruined dwellings. However, it was not a mission to improve old Fochabers that persuaded the 4th Duke of Gordon, who was also the Earl of Norwich and self-styled 'Cock o' the North,' to

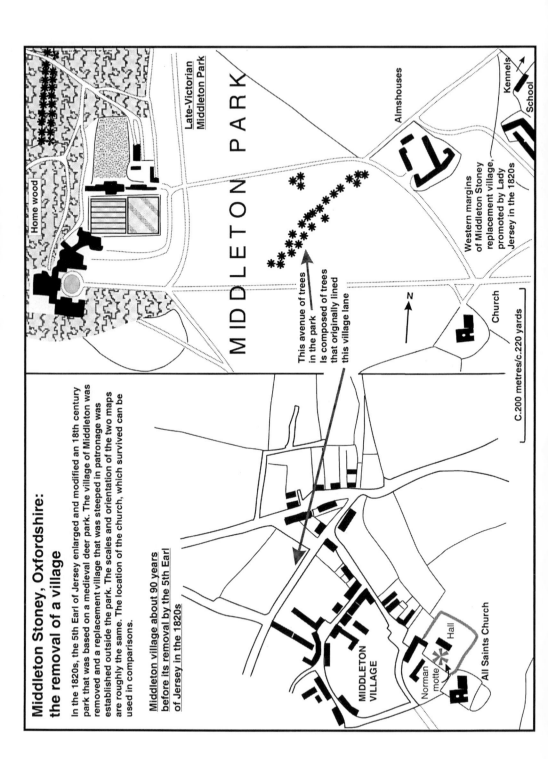

Middleton Stoney, Oxfordshire: the removal of a village

In the 1820s, the 5th Earl of Jersey enlarged and modified an 18th century park that was based on a medieval deer park. The village of Middleton was removed and a replacement village that was steeped in patronage was established outside the park. The scales and orientation of the two maps are roughly the same. The location of the church, which survived can be used in comparisons.

Middleton village about 90 years before its removal by the 5th Earl of Jersey in the 1820s

Home wood

Late-Victorian Middleton Park

MIDDLETON PARK

Almshouses

Kennels

School

Western margins of Middleton Stoney replacement village, promoted by Lady Jersey in the 1820s

Church

N

C.200 metres/c.220 yards

This avenue of trees in the park is composed of trees that originally lined this village lane

MIDDLETON VILLAGE

Norman motte

Hall

All Saints Church

have a new and highly regulated townlet built further south. He was, in his own words, '... desirous to remove the present Town or Village of Fochabers upon account of its inconvenient nearness to Gordon Castle.' Doubtless, it was not the inconvenience of the villagers that he was referring to.

Similarly, at Loughcrew in Co. Meath in the seventeenth century, a village lay just to the north of the old motte mound and Plunkett Castle. Early in the next century, however, a new dynasty arrived, the Nappers. The villagers were evicted to the uplands of the Loughcrew Hills and the setting of their former lives was taken over by a big house and its lodge, ice house, kennels, gardens and out-buildings. As the century progressed, ornamental canals were excavated in the landscaped demesne, which was extended to the north-west with the creation of a new deer park. Such transformations were common in eighteenth-century Ireland and frequently they included a reorganisation of settlements into planned estate villages with fashionably geometrical layouts and square or triangular market or fair greens, like Moy in Co. Tyrone or Kenmare in Co. Kerry. Church of Ireland churches would be provided to enforce the outlooks and interests of the Protestant landlords, though Roman Catholic churches were often excluded from the plans.

The British emparking operations were smash and grab raids. The violence concerned the forced evictions of communities that did not wish to leave their homes and that often then struggled to pay the higher rents charged for the new replacements. The theft aspect concerned the emparked land that was lost to village cultivation when parks were created or enlarged. Because the history of park-making has tended to be written by art historians and landscape architects, the emphasis in the accounts has been on the special creative talents of master landscapers like Brown and Repton. In reality what one frequently sees is a partly eviscerated and redundant working countryside. Experts infatuated by the supposed masters have proved unable to recognise the 'tree avenues' and alignments that are no more than the old hedgerow trees that were left after the grubbing out of the lines of hedge shrubs that linked them together. 'Tastefully positioned' trees have similar origins and the ready-made parkland of gnarled and pollarded peasant trees usefully hinted at a similar antiquity for the dynasty in the hall. I can see old hedgerow tree alignments in the majority of landscape parks that I look at and in North Yorkshire, the area that I know best, I can see how sweet chestnut and beech trees would be planted and pollarded to plug gaps in the parkscape where hijacked trees were lacking. The remnants of the peasant fieldscape were evident at Overstone, emparked around 1727 (see map on p. 167). At Mackershaw in Studley Royal, near Ripon, the oaks that make up an 'avenue' are demonstrably older than the park in which it stands. At Nidd, near Knaresborough, the

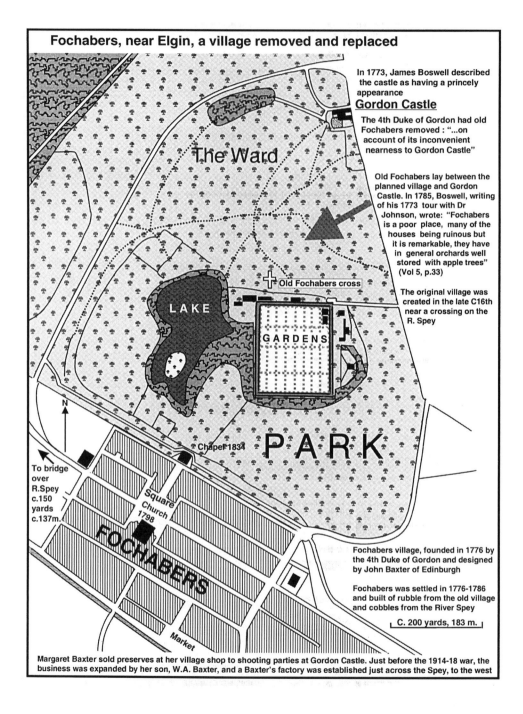

Fochabers, near Elgin, a village removed and replaced

The Ward

In 1773, James Boswell described the castle as having a princely appearance

Gordon Castle

The 4th Duke of Gordon had old Fochabers removed : "...on account of its inconvenient nearness to Gordon Castle"

Old Fochabers lay between the planned village and Gordon Castle. In 1785, Boswell, writing of his 1773 tour with Dr Johnson, wrote: "Fochabers is a poor place, many of the houses being ruinous but it is remarkable, they have in general orchards well stored with apple trees" (Vol 5, p.33)

☩ Old Fochabers cross

The original village was created in the late C16th near a crossing on the R. Spey

LAKE

GARDENS

N

Chapel 1834

PARK

To bridge over R.Spey c.150 yards c.137m.

Square
Church 1798

FOCHABERS

Market

Fochabers village, founded in 1776 by the 4th Duke of Gordon and designed by John Baxter of Edinburgh

Fochabers was settled in 1776-1786 and built of rubble from the old village and cobbles from the River Spey

C. 200 yards, 183 m.

Margaret Baxter sold preserves at her village shop to shooting parties at Gordon Castle. Just before the 1914-18 war, the business was expanded by her son, W.A. Baxter, and a Baxter's factory was established just across the Spey, to the west

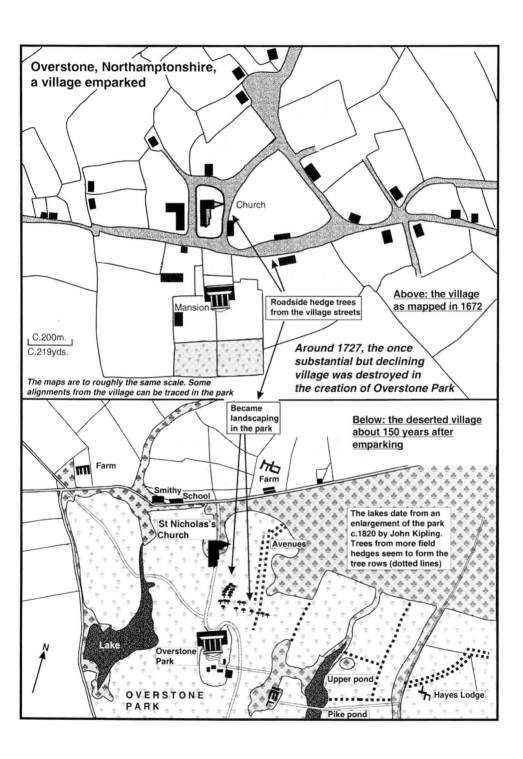

Overstone, Northamptonshire,
a village emparked

Church

Mansion

Roadside hedge trees
from the village streets

Above: the village
as mapped in 1672

C.200m.
C.219yds.

*The maps are to roughly the same scale. Some
alignments from the village can be traced in the park*

*Around 1727, the once
substantial but declining
village was destroyed in
the creation of Overstone Park*

Became
landscaping
in the park

Below: the deserted village
about 150 years after
emparking

Farm

Smithy
School

Farm

St Nicholas's
Church

Avenues

The lakes date from an
enlargement of the park
c.1820 by John Kipling.
Trees from more field
hedges seem to form the
tree rows (dotted lines)

N

Lake

Overstone
Park

Upper pond

Hayes Lodge

OVERSTONE
PARK

Pike pond

first edition of the 6in to 1 mile Ordnance Survey map, surveyed in 1847-49, actually shows the process in progress. It charts the latest extension of the park running to the new railway, the newly emparked fieldscape with both trees and hedges still in place, and the sections of the park where the shrubs had been removed from the hedges, leaving solitary trees for incorporation in the landscape park. Here, staged enlargements of the park in the nineteenth century removed the village, while the outlines of the village fieldscape was, and to some extent still is, apparent in the criss-cross tree patterns in the park. At both Nidd and Dogmersfield it appears that a section of country road was artificially deepened beneath its flanking banks to save the occupants of the halls the unpleasantness of glimpsing ordinary people going by. At Nidd, the sunken section coincides with the old Town Lane or village High Street.

Emparkers came from all manner of backgrounds: ancient gentry, hereditary clan chieftains, the ranks of old money and the ranks of the new. The only common denominator was their possession of money in the necessary amounts. Given this commodity, neither the churches, nor the monarchy, nor the government did anything to frustrate their ambitions, no matter how unjust and morally offensive their proposals might be. At first, there was no stigma attached to emparking and eviction. Indeed Sir Robert Walpole, termed the First Lord of the Treasury in his day, but generally regarded as being the first British Prime Minister, was responsible for emparking on his estate at Houghton, in Norfolk in 1722-39. Some of the emparkers were extremely unpleasant by the standards of any period in time. Joseph Damer was a Member of Parliament but this did not prevent his inundation of the little Dorset market town of Milton

Milton Abbas, replacement for the emparked townlet of Milton.

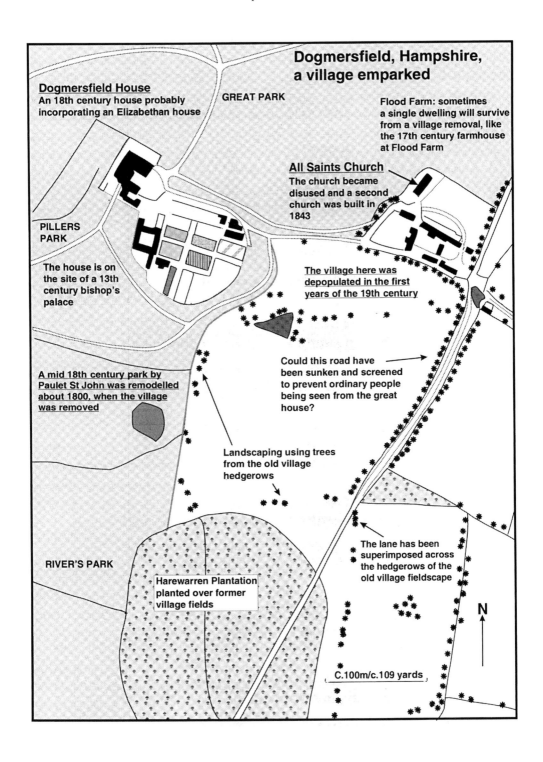

Dogmersfield, Hampshire, a village emparked

GREAT PARK

Dogmersfield House
An 18th century house probably incorporating an Elizabethan house

Flood Farm: sometimes a single dwelling will survive from a village removal, like the 17th century farmhouse at Flood Farm

All Saints Church
The church became disused and a second church was built in 1843

PILLERS PARK

The house is on the site of a 13th century bishop's palace

The village here was depopulated in the first years of the 19th century

A mid 18th century park by Paulet St John was remodelled about 1800, when the village was removed

Could this road have been sunken and screened to prevent ordinary people being seen from the great house?

Landscaping using trees from the old village hedgerows

The lane has been superimposed across the hedgerows of the old village fieldscape

RIVER'S PARK

Harewarren Plantation planted over former village fields

N

C.100m/c.109 yards

beneath a lake provided by Lancelot 'Capability' Brown and his workmen. Damer appears to have been a victim of a (clinically?) paranoid obsession that neighbours in Milton, Dorset, were laughing at him and before the protracted events were over he claimed that church bells were being rung to torment him. With remarkable single-mindedness he sat-out the determined opposition of a local solicitor, gradually accumulating the leases of Milton over a period of twenty years, until at last he was able to remove the church, break up the tombstones in the churchyard and tear down more than 100 houses. The deliberate flooding of one household was used to hasten its removal. A necessary contingent of estate and other workers was crammed into a new, purpose-built village of estate cottages, Milton Abbas. It lines a dry valley running down towards the inundated site of the old town, the work being completed in 1786. Designed as semi-detached dwellings, tenants were crammed into the cottages so that some buildings housed four families, with perhaps up to thirty children existing under the one thatched roof.

When seeking an understanding of the past, it is well to remember that history is written by the victors. A rising dynasty of Yorkshire merchants, with a fortune based on shipping, finance and iron trading, the Sykes family, acquired Sledmere in the Yorkshire Wolds and a platform towards gentrification in 1718. Thirty years later, Richard Sykes launched a campaign of aggrandisement that resulted in the construction of an imposing family seat beside Sledmere village church, the work beginning in 1748. After 1776, the church that had acquired a new neighbour lost its old one. The village that lay to its east, on the York road, was removed and transplantated to a site beyond the park wall along the diverted Malton to Driffield highway. An enlarged park was created (the sector of village to the south of the great house having already been cleared of dwellings to open-up a prospect). The park took shape with the drainage of a natural mere, the expropriation of tenants' land and the diversion around the park by circuitous routes of several local thoroughfares – all of which caused great disruption in the locality. The changes were contained in a Bill to enclose Sledmere that was presented to Parliament by Sir Christopher Sykes in 1776. The owner of the adjacent estate objected, complaining that the proposals would block the York, Malton and Driffield highways and that his tenants would be obstructed from worshipping at Sledmere Church. However, if one goes to Sledmere today, one will not find this imperious treatment of the community commemorated. Instead, the most notable monument in the small estate village is a classical rotunda inscribed: 'This edifice was erected by Sir Taton Sykes Bart. To the memory of his father Sir Christopher Sykes Bart, who by assiduity and perseverance in building and planting and inclosing on the Yorkshire Wolds in the brief space

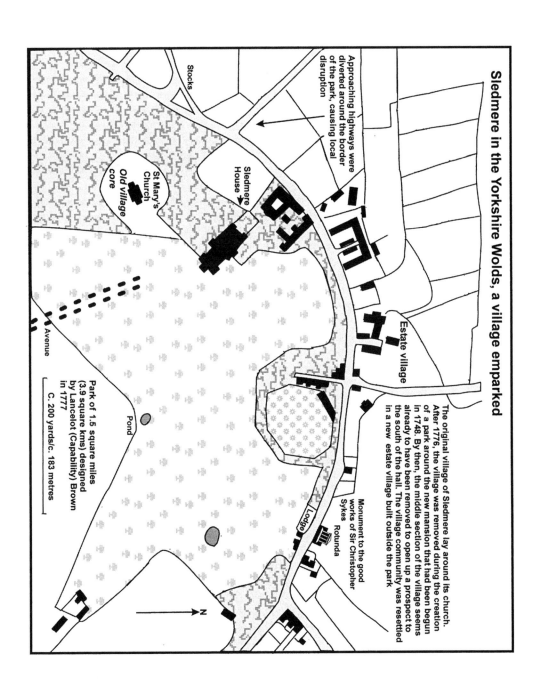

Sledmere in the Yorkshire Wolds, a village emparked

Stocks

Approaching highways were
diverted around the border
of the park, causing local
disruption

St Mary's
Church

Old village
core

Sledmere
House

Avenue

Pond

Park of 1.5 square miles
(3.9 square kms) designed
by Lancelot (Capability) Brown
in 1777

C. 200 yards/c. 183 metres

N

Estate village

Monument to the good
works of Sir Christopher
Sykes

Rotunda

Lodge

The original village of Sledmere lay around its church.
After 1776, the village was removed during the creation
of a park around the new mansion that had been begun
in 1748. By then, the middle section of the village seems
already to have been removed to open up a prospect to
the south of the hall. The village community was resettled
in a new estate village built outside the park

of thirty years set an example to other owners of land as has caused what was once a bleak and barren tract of country to become now one of the most productive and best cultivated districts in the county of York A.D. 1840'. The website of Sledmere House and gardens entices visitors with the prospect that '… an eighteenth century walled garden with roses that smell so sweet, a pond complete with fish, fountains and a lovely view across acres of open space where deer can be found grazing complete this stunning, tranquil setting'. Of the social cost of such scenery, we are not informed. History is written by the victors.

The Lascelles family at Harewood near Leeds also had new-ish money, the transformations enacted in the second half of the eighteenth century depending on slavery, molasses and sugar, the trade in ribbon and collecting

The old village church at Harewood, stranded in the park.

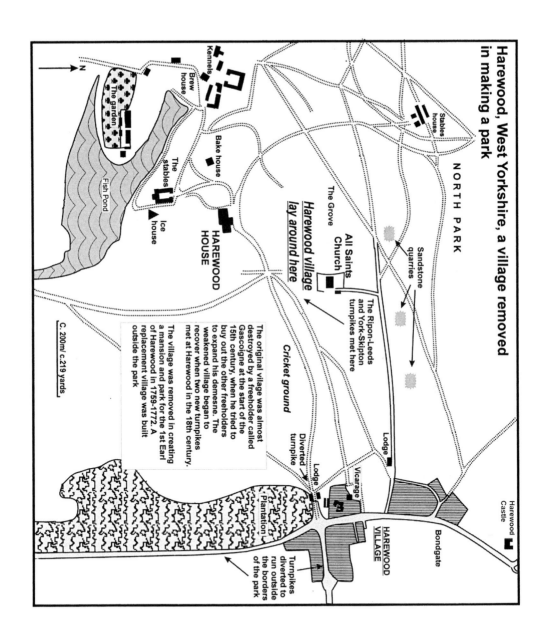

Harewood, West Yorkshire, a village removed in making a park

N

Kennels

Brew house

The garden

Fish Pond

Bake house

The stables

Ice house

HAREWOOD HOUSE

NORTH PARK

Stables house

The Grove

Harewood village *lay around here*

All Saints Church

Sandstone quarries

The Ripon-Leeds and York-Skipton turnpikes met here

Cricket ground

Diverted turnpike

Lodge

Lodge

Vicarage

Plantation

HAREWOOD VILLAGE

Turnpikes diverted to run outside the borders of the park

Bondgate

Harewood Castle

C. 200ml c.219 yards

The original village was almost destroyed by a freeholder called Gascoigne at the start of the 15th century, when he tried to buy out the other freeholders to expand his demesne. The weakened village began to recover when two new turnpikes met at Harewood in the 18th century.

The village was removed in creating a mansion and park for the 1st Earl of Harewood in 1759-1772. A replacement village was built outside the park

Harewood House, a big cuckoo in the local nest of villages.

customs dues in Barbados. After inheriting the estate in 1759, Edwin Lascelles removed one village, leaving only its church behind, depopulated other settlements and demolished the old Gawthorpe Hall. The way was now clear for the building of Harewood House, almost upon the site of the old village and within an expanse of suitably, if but recently, desolate parkland. In this case, however, the plan achieved rather more than just creating a settlement for estate workers and retainers outside the park gates. A new village was built there but it was a place of some substance, designed by John Carr, the architect for the great house. Provision was made to accommodate a doctor and a serious gesture towards improving local employment (as well as the lord's income) was made by the inclusion of a ribbon factory. (Ribbon-buyers did not play their part and this became cottages.) In all such ventures, it is difficult to disentangle the different strands of motivation. Some patrons seriously sought to improve the living conditions of their tenants, yet great kudos could be gained from being regarded as a promoter of good works (whether the villagers wanted them or not). Improved villages could advertise the enlightenment of their creators, but they could also promote a different kind of patronage, existing as conversation pieces for parties approaching the great house. At Lord Ongley's Old Warden in Bedfordshire, the denizens of the fancifully-designed village were expected to appear in pointed hats and clad in red to match the bright paintwork, while the almswomen of Milton Abbas emerged, similarly witch-like, in pointed hats.

Efforts to pass judgement are made difficult by the intertwining of patronage and good intentions, image-building and the pursuit of fashion and outright callous indifference. The question of the replacement village had different aspects. There might not be one at all and tenants could be cast out on the road; it might be of a much reduced size, resulting in a portion of tenants being evicted; it might be mean and poorly appointed; it might mimic the latest parodies of vernacular or foreign design, or it might consititute a serious attempt to improve the circumstances of life on the estate. Hinderskelfe vanished beneath the ornamental lake at Castle Howard, near York, late in the seventeenth century, and was not replaced. Even in the nineteenth century and close to the English heartlands, the villagers of Nidd, near Knaresborough, were removed without alternative homes being built. When Prime Minister Walpole emparked Houghton, the whitened cottages of New Houghton were sparsely appointed and unadorned, though Old Warden was a picturesque confection of thatched dormers, bargeboards, trellised porches and decorative window casements. Much that gladdened the eyes of the guests passing through the model village in their carriages represented nothing but extra cleaning, clipping, weeding and maintenance work to the resident villagers.

Gradually, the emparking movement was seen to be running against the social currents of enlightenment and emancipation, even though the shameful evictions of Highlanders from newly-designated 'deer forests' continued beyond the end of the nineteenth century. If any single event stimulated a questioning of the morality of evictions it was the publication of Oliver Goldsmith's poem *Deserted Village* in 1770. He wrote in the heyday of emparking and examples aplenty were to be seen by any of his contemporaries with stout shoes, a saddle or a coach fare. For years, scholars puzzled over Goldsmith's deserted 'Auburn' and wondered if it could be based on a real village. Some claimed (amazingly) that the entire notion of village eviction was a fiction. Others still believed that the poet was recalling an event that he had experienced in his native Ireland. In the 1960s, however, Mrs Mavis Batey wrote to the doyen of village desertions, Maurice Beresford, with a convincing suggestion that the village that had inspired Goldsmith was Nuneham Courtenay, near Oxford. Nuneham had been emparked by the 1st Earl Harcourt in 1760 and Goldsmith was shown to have been in the locality when the evacuations were proceeding in 1761 and villagers were removing to the new village on the turnpike outside the park gates. There must be many today who regard prose like:

Sweet AUBURN! Parent of the blissful hour,
Thy glades forlorn confess the tyrant's power

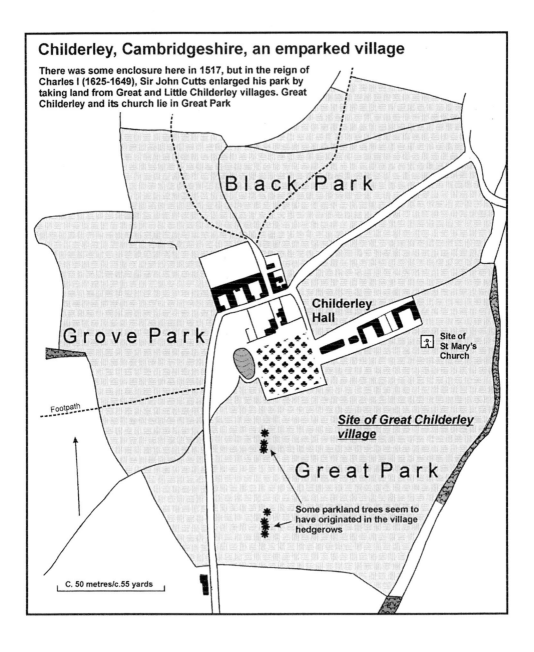

Childerley, Cambridgeshire, an emparked village

There was some enclosure here in 1517, but in the reign of
Charles I (1625-1649), Sir John Cutts enlarged his park by
taking land from Great and Little Childerley villages. Great
Childerley and its church lie in Great Park

B l a c k   P a r k

Childerley
Hall

G r o v e   P a r k

Site of
St Mary's
Church

Footpath

Site of Great Childerley
village

G r e a t   P a r k

Some parkland trees seem to
have originated in the village
hedgerows

C. 50 metres/c.55 yards

as florid and laboured, but it did make a strong impression on educated people at the time – apparently causing the Harcourts to employ the Poet Laureate, William Whitehead, to write a rival poem extolling the virtues of the eviction and relocation of villagers. Gradually, the sands of public opinion began to shift and very early in the nineteenth century that manipulator of so many landscapes, Humphrey Repton, now game-keeper-turned-poacher, was moved to condemn '… as false taste that fatal rage for destroying villages or depopulating a country, under the idea of its being necessary to the importance of a mansion…' However, nobody of influence seems to have been capable of accepting that the eviction of a community against its will was quite simply wrong. Even when Repton suggested that the appropriation of homes was wrong he felt obliged to suggest that improved cottages were desirable because they could be of advantage to the landlord and his reputation. He argued that when the habitations of the labouring poor '… can be made a subordinate part of the general scenery [they] will so far from disgracing it, add to the dignity that wealth can derive from the exercise of benevolence.'

When the evictions petered out in the course of the Victorian era, the attitudes of mind that allowed communities to be sacrificed for the grati-fication of privileged lifestyles largely came to an end. This did not signal the supremacy of community and one recent British Prime Minister felt able to proclaim that, indeed, community does not exist. It did signify that private individuals would no longer be able to shift households like pawns across the chessboard of their estate – or that if they did so, they would be exposed to ridicule. The power to level and uproot did not end. Rather, it was passed from the individual despots to the corporate institutions. Within a century, neighbourhoods would be bulldozed, communi-ties fragmented and their members installed in towers of concrete and glass – places so wretched and deprived that no household in a Georgian replacement village can ever have felt so isolated, threatened and mar-ginalized. For members of the dispossessed, Georgian or modern, it may not have mattered very much whether the orchestrator of their unease had a lineage going back to the Norman Conquest, new money, a degree in architecture or a desk in the planning department. Neither plants nor communities relish being uprooted.

CHAPTER TEN

AND THEN THERE WERE NONE

Medieval villages that stumbled

Ends that were sudden and, in many cases, violent were faced by hundreds of settlements. Lords, monks, war bands, floods and storms all took their toll. These colourful cases may lead us to overlook a great many other places and communities that perished in ways that were less direct or painful and more prolonged. Also, when thinking of lost villages, our minds tend to migrate to the Middle Ages and the ruthlessness of feudal lords and the savagery of disease. From there, our thoughts may drift to the scores of villages destroyed by the imperious park-makers of the seventeenth and eighteenth centuries. In fact, a good many villages have been removed in quite modern times, some even within living memory.

In Medieval times and the centuries that followed, a sizeable if uncertain number of villages crept gradually towards extinction. There were no tempests in the night or loutish retainers with cudgels. Rather, as the years rolled by, fewer and fewer people could be found living in the village. At last, there would be nobody at all or just the occupants of a solitary farmstead. The most frequent cause of this creeping death is known by the unexciting term 'engrossment'. It involved a landlord's steady consolidation of holdings, tenancies or leases until all, or almost all, the land was in just one pair of hands. Sometimes, the lord of the manor was responsible, with ambitions to run his estate as a single farm or sheep run, or the guiding hand might be an exceptionally able and ambitious member of the village community itself. Like a plump young cuckoo he would nudge all his neighbours and childhood playmates from the village nest until he, alone, remained. In the fifteenth century and long before being emparked by the Earl Lascelles in the 1760s–70s, Harewood in North Yorkshire had come within a whisker of decaying when the freeholders were bought out by a local yeoman called Gascoigne.

The places that perished in such ways may not be easy to detect, for the traumatic and eye-catching events that might have interested the taxation officials or have resulted in court cases did not occur. Sometimes, there are significant records. At Kilverstone, in Norfolk, it was recorded in 1737 that the once populous village, then reduced to merely eight dwellings and fifty villagers, was, 'Now wholly owned by Thomas Wright Esq. At this time there are no tenants belonging to the manor, the whole being purchased in'. By then, the village had been in a state of slow but terminal decay for about eighty years, although in 1591 there had been twelve tenant households. The lords were involved in raising sheep on ever grander scales during the seventeenth and eighteenth centuries, while towards the end of the eighteenth century, a park for Kilverstone Hall was set-out across what had by then become the deserted village site. The 'purchasing in' of Kilverstone took place against a background of disputes between the lord and villagers over sheep grazing lands and commoners' rights, a villager called John Stalham being a particularly committed protagonist and an ambitious entrepreneur. An Elizabethan enquiry in 1593 had heard that Thomas Wright's predecessors had enclosed part of the common and overstocked remaining commons with their own sheep and cattle, though conflicting testimonies were heard. This was an enduring problem and it had underlain Kett's revolt in Norfolk and the uprisings in other counties half a century earlier, in 1549. In East Anglia, the uprising came in late summer but that May, the villagers in Somerset and Lincoln had been in revolt, and in July there were riots in Buckinghamshire, Essex, Kent, Oxfordshire and Wiltshire. In Cambridgeshire a popular dirge encouraged the grubbing-up of the new hedgerows that barred entry to the enclosures from the old commons:

Cast hedge and ditch in the lake
Fixed with many a stake;
Though they be never so fast,
Yet asunder they are wrest.
Sir, I think that this work
Is as good as to build a kirk.

The contraction of the village common allowed fewer and fewer tenants to be supported and it could lead to a gradual bleeding away of the community. Certainly, the progressive souring of relations between the lords and their villagers combined with commercial ambitions led to the gradual buying-in of Kilverstone tenancies and the death of the village.

In some cases, the fates seem to have conspired against a village, which gradually surrendered leaving a legacy of doubt concerning which of the

several assailants had struck the fatal blow. Many settlements were debilitated by famine caused by over-population and climate change, while
those in the North might be simultaneously reduced by Scottish raiding.
Then the Pestilence could further undermine a once numerous community, reducing the ability of the remaining households to resist engrossment
or clearances for sheep. At the start of the fifteenth century, Papal documents show that the Church of St Margaret at Blo Norton, Norfolk, was
unable to support its own priest on account of Pestilence and mortalities,
the barren nature of the land, the decay of buildings and, in particular, the
scarcity and impoverishment of the remaining parishioners. Smaller villages could vanish and large ones could shrink. Around the close of the
Middle Ages, and for reasons that are not clear, Beachamwell in the same
county contracted from a large, sprawling village supporting three churches
to a much smaller one clustered around the only remaining Church of St
Mary's. St John's had been abandoned early in the sixteenth century and All
Saints' fell into ruin in the second half of the seveneeth century.

The story of villages is full of quirks and qualifications. It was often
possible for a village site to become desolate without any diminution
of the village community. To understand this we need to appreciate that
Medieval village dwellings were composed of sticks, stones and clay from
the common and straw, reed or turf from the surrounding fields. With the
possible exception of the manor house, the village dwellings embodied
just a few days of largely amateur toil and were almost worthless. People
were not tied to a spot by their houses. The church was quite different,
being profoundly more valuable and embodying both expensive materials and costly craftsmanship. It could, however, be left behind, for a walk
to Mass of up to a mile was nothing to a community of land-workers. In
a considerable number of cases we find that an original village site was
abandoned in favour of a move to another spot in a township or manor.
A little of the footloose character of prehistoric communities was retained,
but there always had to be a reason for a shift. Perhaps the most common
one concerned the shifting fortunes of the highways, lanes and tracks that
made up the local system of routeways. Changes in the patterns of transport and trade could cause some routes to prosper, while others fell from
favour. Villages had varying degrees of involvement in commerce and
those that supported markets depended upon the traffic of a reasonably
bustling road to bring customers and traders to their stalls and tollbooths.
Therefore, any community that was stranded by the devaluation of its
market roads was very likely to drift away to a new site beside a more
lively routeway. Of course, when the villagers departed, they left behind a
corner of the landscape that had an isolated church, earthworks and all the
other trappings of a deserted village site.

Cambridgeshire has a number of examples. As the Roman Ermine Street, later the Old North Road, linking the north and south of the kingdom rose up the transport hierarchy during the Middle Ages, it acted as a magnet to four nearby villages; Arrington, Caxton, Kneesworth and Papworth Everard. One may still see the church that was stranded as Caxton migrated about a quarter of a mile to take up a new station as a 'linear' village that was strung out along both sides of the former Roman routeway. In the same county, the villagers of Comberton seem to have slipped away from their church and homes to exploit a less prestigious local road, while at Castle Camps the move was more decisive. The Medieval church and the bailey of the castle in which it stands were forsaken by the villagers living just to the north of the great bailey earthworks of the expanded stronghold. Perhaps originally established to service the original Norman castle of the de Veres, after a few centuries the community migrated a good half mile across their fields to a new situation to the north-east, where a junction of country roads may have provided a less backwoods-like setting. The decline of the castle during the fifteenth century may have prompted the move even though the church had experienced a recent rebuilding. As usual, a classic deserted village landscape was left, although its community was alive and well, just living somewhere else. As well as the isolated church and the great castle earthworks, there are the village earthworks on land still left unploughed and Medieval pottery that is turned-up by modern ploughing of part of the village site.

Returning to Norfolk, there are various examples that suggest that the lure of common pasture in times of grassland shortages could also entice settlements to leave their moorings. Stanfield is said to have been established in Saxon times on a gravel spur beside a stream. During the Middle Ages, settlement gravitated towards a common, but the decay of rural settlement that affected the county after the Medieval period saw the disintegration of the village layout and the reduction of dwellings around the green at the west of the village. Longham had a still more eventful life. A settlement existed in Saxon times but in the twelfth century dwellings began to gravitate towards Southall Green and then towards Kirtling Common. By the end of the Middle Ages these shifts had left the old village church in a somewhat peripheral and then in a rather isolated situation, with population strung around the edges of Kirtling Common, just over half a mile to the east of the church, and Southall Green, around a quarter of a mile to its south. Kirtling Common had been particularly favoured by settlers during the decades around the close of the Middle Ages, while the dwellings around the other green declined in the two centuries that followed. In 1816, the Parliamentary Enclosure of the commons removed any of their *raisons d'être* as foci for settlement and what remains are fragments inherited from countrysides formed under completely different rules and conditions. However, the readiness of villagers to abandon their old homes in order to enjoy easier access to common grazings helps us to understand their passionate opposition to the theft of commons by Tudor landlords.

Village mortality could be quite complex – too complex in many cases, we can be sure, to have been fully recorded. If we take relatively recent demises then the information should be more comprehensive and revealing, though even a few settlements that perished in Victorian times have their fates incompletely documented. My native township of Clint in Nidderdale is an example. It was never sufficiently populous to acquire a church and the villagers attended the one(s) in Ripley, though in Medieval times it did have a tavern. It existed as a double row of dwellings flanking a lane that ran eastwards from the manor house, and in its western section, the dwellings were set back from the lane along the margins of a rectangular green. The notorious Poll Tax of 1379 was paid by some 117 Clint residents, but at some stage the village sank into a slow decline and a map of 1778 showed a settlement reduced to thirteen buildings, of which several would have been barns and byres. In 1871 a visiting antiquarian recorded a hamlet '... of about half-a-dozen old houses', while the moated stone hall had been a ruin since the late eighteenth century, its stones robbed to build a farmstead nearby. Early in the twentieth century, Clint, no longer even a hamlet, had collapsed to just two houses standing on the margins of the old green.

The reasons for its decline may partly have concerned the loss of powerful patrons in its hall, the Beckwiths in Medieval times and then the Swale family until 1733. Perhaps more important was the local economy. During the sixteenth and seventeenth centuries, numerous probate inventories were compiled to record the possessions of recently dead people and their disposition around the dwelling. It is clear that many villagers were small-holders rather than farmers, and these holdings were often too small to support a household from farming. However, scattered amongst the domestic clutter of most homes was the paraphernalia of cheese making. Cheese was being made commercially, a continuation of the tradition in neighbouring areas of paying rents in cheese to Fountains Abbey. Much more important was the equipment and products of weaving linen and broadcloth. Such weaving was a cottage industry for most households and must have supplemented the products of farming to allow them to subsist. However, when the cottage textile industry gravitated into water-powered mills a little after the dawn of the Industrial Revolution in 1760, these domestic economies must have been hit very hard, with cottage folk often migrating for employment in the mills. Another factor must have been the growth of a youthful rival, Burnt Yates, about a mile away within the same township. While the road through Clint was something of a byeway, Burnt Yates grew astride a new and busy turnpike, with one approach to the old village of Clint being gated and barred to prevent its use by toll dodgers. The upstart settlement then gained the facilities that Clint had never had; a school and a church. Burnt Yates grew steadily, having twenty-two households in 1851 and twenty-eight in 1871, the time when Clint was reduced to around six dwellings. There must have been many other old settlements that experienced this sort of crumbling as successive challenges appeared from different directions.

Villages could fall victim to environmental forces in ways that were not dramatic. The poor state of Medieval lanes and highways, which often became virtually impassable in winter, resulted in a very heavy dependence on water transport. A high proportion of the commerce of the kingdom was conducted by narrow boats plying rivers and streams as well as cuts that were little more than ditches. Bulky cargoes would invariably be transported by water wherever the directions of drainage allowed. However, inland waterways of all kinds could be affected by silting which might eventually suffocate navigation. Village river ports declined because of this, but the problem was not confined to villages, for ambitious towns, such as Hedon in Humberside, could be thrown into decline by the silting of their arteries. The Medieval town of Torksey in Lincolnshire has vanished utterly. There is a ruin on the site near the River Trent, but this is of a mock castle, an Elizabethan mansion built from stone pillaged from a nearby priory at a time when the commercial town had decayed to village proportions. Torksey began as a fortified Saxon town or *burh* and its significance lay in its position beside a Roman canal, the Foss Dyke, which ran to the Trent. It seems to have served Lincoln, but during the Middle Ages, Lincoln's wool trade was captured by Boston. This commercial decline was accompanied by the silting of the Foss Dyke, the townspeople perhaps being too disheartened to engage in the demanding work of dredging. The death of Torksey was protracted, from the first stages of decline in the twelfth century, through advanced decay in the following century, to contraction to the size of a village by the end of the Middle Ages.

The freshly dug graves

Most villages have survived from late Saxon, Norman or Plantagenet origins through to the present day. However, this transition was by no means assured and more than a 1,000 villages and large hamlets failed to complete the course. As we have seen, the hazards were numerous and varied, some resulting from the ambitions of men and some from a vengeful environment. Those villages that did endure through into the twentieth century might, metaphorically, have breathed a sigh of relief. Yet their survival in perpetuity was far from assured. Villages that have vanished in the modern era tend to fall into two broad groups. Firstly, there are those places that were specialised industrial settlements rather than more commonplace villages with agricultural economies. These places were extremely vulnerable when the resource that they worked became exhausted, was no longer wanted or could be imported more cheaply from overseas. Failing fishing villages could be reorganised as resorts to exploit the seaside holiday trade, but colliery and quarry villages found it harder to cope with failure. Deserted villages in the second group were seemingly safe and secure places that suddenly found themselves dangerously poised in time and space, the pawns of much bigger players – players like the military or water interests.

From the second half of the twentieth century, one encounters planners with visions, and in some areas of declining extractive industries their visions were of inevitable and irreversible decline. However, the visions of planners tend to be of the narrower kind, and while their predictions about the future for old-style heavy industry were sound enough, they lacked the breadth to envisage new sources of life. Co. Durham had a legacy of colliery villages that were left stranded and destitute by the closure of their associated collieries. Settlements that seemed to have the poorest prospects of recovery were classified, according to a county plan of 1951, as 'category D' settlements; discretionary supports were withdrawn and their populations were to be assimilated into centres, like new or expanded towns, which seemed to be far more viable. Some 350 villages and industrial hamlets were concerned, most of them associated with failed or failing pits. In 1969 the death row designation was changed to 'group 4' and several villages and industrial hamlets were passing out of existence. Then, during the 1960s, most of the coal mines in North East England closed and with the closure of the Sun Mine at Wallsend in 1969 there were no colliers remaining on the north bank of the River Tyne. However, the fatalistic visions had failed to recognise that lifestyles would evolve and that many of the threatened communities had powerful life forces.

Some 'doomed' villages refused to die. Haswell had a hard history. A colliery shaft was sunk there in 1833 and the mine attracted immigrants from all parts of the country. The railway came and service facilities were attracted. But the mining community was only eleven years old when it was divided by industrial strife and Haswell became a pit worked by blackleg labour in a region were 'scabs' were despised. However, it was also in 1844 that an explosion in one of the galleries burned or gassed ninety-five miners and children to death. The terrible event, killing several ten-year-olds, reunited the community in mourning and their colliery survived for a further fifty years. Thereafter, villagers had to look elsewhere for work, but in the 1960s the settlement was placed in the condemned cell of category D. However, as car-owning mobility spread down through the community, Haswell was reprieved and found a new and far easier existence as a commuter village. Binchester, the site of a Roman fort and hypocaust, is a name well known to Romanists, but Binchester was also a colliery village, developed after 1850, with five mines. In the early 1970s, however, it was classified in category D. Instead of awaiting the demise of their settlement, villagers became involved with the Durham Housing Association and the housing stock of the settlement was bought from the Coal Board for £16,000. Dwellings were refurbished, small businesses were established and although levels of unemployment remain quite high, the future of the village is assured.

Quarry villages could also defy the fates. The Industrial Revolution gave rise to a demand for granite blocks for hard-wearing kerbs, paving and for facing streets, docks and factories in places like Liverpool, Manchester and London. Granite quarries on the Lleyn peninsula in the Nant locality of North Wales were opened in 1861 on slopes overlooking the sea. A jetty was built to facilitate the export of the stone, and a string of fifteen cottages were built to house the mainly Irish workforce. As time passed, some of the quarrymen brought their wives to share their cottages and Port Nant became more a village than a navvy camp. A wooden building served as a chapel and school until a stone chapel was provided in 1878. In this year, with three quarries in full production, a further twenty-four houses were built so that Port Nant became a substantial industrial village with around 200 inhabitants. By this time, locally-born Welsh speakers formed almost two-thirds of the population, nearly all the remainder were English and the Irish element had become greatly outnumbered. The quarries were located in a rural area, so that local produce, like eggs and milk, could be bought, but as the village lacked any road connection to the outside world, the company shop, where cottage rents were collected, enjoyed a monopoly. Around the start of the First World War, the quarries entered a decline. A landslide in 1925, when some of the original cottages were carried into the sea, accelerated the demise, while as the centuries advanced, families became less tolerant of their, albeit idyllic, isolation. One quarry was reopened by a company producing roadstone, but by the start of the Second World War, production was at an end. The story was not over, for in 1970 a doctor from Manchester moved to a practice at Llanaelhaearn and resolved that his children would learn to speak Welsh. A Welsh cultural resurgence was beginning and a trust was formed. In 1978 the village, abandoned for almost twenty years, was purchased from the Amie Road Stone Company for £25,000 to become the Welsh National Language Centre. Terraced cottages were renovated and Welsh language courses began in 1982. In 1910 the Caernarfonshire authorites had recommended changing the name of the school from the Anglo-Welsh hybrid Port Nant to the Welsh, Nant Gwrtheyrn, and this Welsh name now attaches to the revived quarry village.

For people who are distrustful of unconstrained authority, the story of the removal of communities by military interests is probably the most disquieting. Towards the close of the Victorian era, the Army was faced with the decrease in available open spaces for its manoeuvres. Population was swelling and spreading, Parliamentary Enclosure had enclosed many previously open countrysides and private landowners were reluctant to sacrifice farmlands during the growing season. In 1897, the Under Secretary for War proposed the acquisition of a substantial portion of Salisbury Plain, primarily as a training ground for the cavalry, with the cavalrymen living in tented camps. Then infantry training was introduced, with a requirement for rifle ranges. A year after the initial proposal, land to the west of the River Avon was acquired as an artillery range to reduce the demands on the existing range on Dartmoor. Before the century was out, permanent barracks were built on the plain at Tidworth and Bulford, with three more barracks to follow. The undulating plain, still partly a patchwork of ploughland and pasture, was fast assuming a military character. Within five years, the military acquired almost 40,000 acres (around 16,000 hectares) of land and this holding was doubled by the outbreak of the Second World War. The character of the plain changed from the dappled patterns of cultivation to a steppe-like character of rolling grassland interrupted by saw-toothed lines of entrenchments, target butts, gun pits and cratered impact areas.

The village of Imber lay where two side-valleys joined the Imber Brook on Salisbury Plain. Medieval in origin, Imber survived the dangers of death by plague, sheep clearance and emparking but during the Second World War, it was deliberately depopulated and absorbed into the Western Range. The almost 800-year-old village Church of St Giles and the manor house were surrounded by a 10ft (3m) tall cage of chain link fence but the village homes were either destroyed or joined by other buildings of breeze-block construction and used in training. It was at the start of November 1943, that the villagers of Imber were told that they were to be removed and their evacuation took place just a few days before the Christmas of that year. It was, they were told, essential for the conduct of the war that they should make a temporary surrender of the homes, but a firm undertaking that they would be allowed to return when the war was over was given. Officialdom's promise was dishonoured and a dwindling number of Imber people remain in exile. The village remains 'out of bounds' but on fifty days

Old quarryman's houses at Nant Gwrtheyrn.

The deserted village of Nant Gwrtheyrn.

of the year the ban is lifted and on just one day of the year, a service is held in the church. There has been grumbling in the locality about the inconvenience this involves, but a Friends organisation, formed in 2001, has organised Easter services. They provide the chance to see the exceptional church with its fifteenth-century wall paintings and the remarkable bell ringing changes dated to 1292 that are also painted on its walls. It is a Grade I listed building, though sadly, communities cannot be listed and conserved.

The plight of the people of Imber was shared with those of the Purbeck village of Tyneham, near the Lulworth Cove beauty spot, which found itself at the centre of a 7,500 acre (around 3,035 hectare) firing range. In 1943, a decision to expand the Royal Armoured Corps Gunnery School ranges was made. A tank gunnery range just to the east of Lulworth Cove had been established during the First World War and after the war an extended training area was purchased by the War Office using compulsory powers. With the outbreak of the Second World War, the area was closed to the public and it was the perceived need to extend the range further in order to provide training in mobile warfare that led to the depopulation of Tyneham, the hamlets of Povington and Worbarrow and several farmsteads. As at Imber, the community was removed with an undertaking (later known as 'Churchill's pledge') that they could return when hostilities were over. A plaintive letter to the Army was left by Evelyn Bond when the villagers departed, asking that the military should take care of the church and home-place. It read:

> Please treat the Church and houses with care. We have given up our homes where many of us have lived for generations, to help with the war to keep men free. We shall return one day and thank you for treating the village kindly.

Again, the pledge was dishonoured. When the war came to an end, the military remained in possession and there was talk of the need for more extended ranges and the threat of a new war with the Soviet Union. In the face of a refusal by the military to relinquish the village, a Tyneham Action Group was formed in 1968. By this time, the issues had become blurred. Local councils had discovered pecuniary interests in maintaining an Army presence and the perennial issue of jobs was raised. Also, a release of land after several decades of military occupation could no longer result in its reversion to original 'wholesome' uses. The unrestrained pursuit of profits, whether from tourism or industrialised agriculture, could cause damage that might, in its way, be more unpleasant than the whistling by of missiles. The only certainty remaining was that an innocent community had been exploited, duped and then lost behind the agendas of others.

At the other side of England, in the poor sandy lands of the Brecklands on the Norfolk/Suffolk borders, similar schemes had been imposed. In 1940, the War Office acquired 118,000 acres (around 47,800 hectares) of agriculturally impoverished land for the practice of military manoeuvres, and in 1942, 16,000 of these acres (around 6,480 hectares) were developed as a battle area for live firing. In 1944, with the Battle for Normandy at hand, villagers in Langford hamlet and the villages of Stanford, Tottington,

Buckenham Tofts and West Tofts and the much declined settlement of Sturston were allowed a mere month to vacate their homes and depart the area, though most found accommodation within the broader region of the Brecklands. As before, the establishment provided an undertaking that the evacuations were merely temporary and would end with the armistice. Yet as before, the Cold War began to intensify before any arrangements for the return of the villagers had been considered. As at Imber, the churches (some six of them) stand devoid of any function within their mesh cages and homes have either been blown to pieces or incorporated into contexts for practising street warfare. By the end of the 1970s, some 72,000 NATO troops were training in the Stanford Battle Area and any window of opportunity that may have existed for the honouring of Churchill's pledge had by then been thoroughly slammed and bolted.

Some irreverent souls may think it a little ironic that the things that were done were said by those in authority to be essential to protect our democratic freedoms against totalitarian regimes. The time when anything could be done about the understandings concerning the lost Brecklands villages has long passed. Any ghosts haunting the lost homes can be no younger than the early 1940s. This was a time of tied estate cottages that placed tenants in bondage and restricted liberties, many of the cottages being tied to the Walsingham estate. For people in remote villages in impoverished farmlands it was a time of no electricity or domestic appliances and no gas. Those were days of candlelight and of water of dubious purity pumped from a well and clothing scrubbed clean on a washboard in a tub. (My clearest childhood recollection of such life is of cleaning carpets by dragging them across the cow pasture; some steering was required from time to time.) Very few ageing survivors could acclimatise to life in such isolated settings. While armoured vehicles have been trundling across the training area, the surrounding lands have undergone their agro-business revolution. The charming and bucolic have yielded, very often, to oilseed rape and prairie fields. If the training area was once a battlefield enclave in an idyllic setting, now it is comparatively verdant, wildlife-rich and, in its way, more tranquil than the commuter roads, commercial plantations and weekend hideaways that hem it around.

A remarkable feature of the story of village desertions through the centuries has been the general lack of organised opposition both from within the settlement concerned and from principled supporters outside. This general passivity came to an end with events in the nineteenth and twentieth centuries. An outstanding legacy of the Industrial Revolution was the emergence of several mega-cities – and as living conditions in their slums, terraces and crescents improved with the provision of piped water supplies and sewers, so the demand for water rocketed. The sprawling conurbations cast about beyond their palls of smoke and smog for new sources of supply. This took place at a time when a love of nature and wilderness had taken root among the middle class intelligentsia – with predictable consequences. With its groundwater reserves under pressure, a thirsty Liverpool promoted a Water Act that gave the city the powers to seek beyond the confines of its boundaries for surface water storage sites. About twenty miles to the north-east was the Rivington Pike locale, with a deep valley at the foot of the Rossendale Hills, overlooked by Anglezarke Moor – a pleasant and rural place in a highly industrialised county. It was here that a dam-building project began – accompanied by opposition from one of the earliest of environmental campaigns, with protests organised by a body of conservationists who were known as 'Antipikists' (after Rivington Pike). Now Rivington has a complex of eight reservoirs storing 4 billion gallons of water. Enhanced support for conservational issues and rising sophistication in the techniques of protest were apparent when, in 1876, the Manchester Corporation sought to enlarge little Lake Thirlmere and convert it into a reservoir for the industrial conurbation lying 100 miles away to the south. Eulogised by Wordsworth to become the heartland of romantic landscape ideals, the Lake District was enormously loved and even overseas support rallied to the Thirlmere Defence Association. Even so, the conservationists only managed to delay matters slightly and to temper the effects on people and landscape. The thirsty conurbation had emerged as a nigh on unstoppable force.

Thus far, the reservoir controversies largely concerned scenery rather than politics, although a flame was kindled in 1879 that would smoulder and flare before becoming an incandescent symbol of nationalism. Briefly sated by its reservoirs at Rivington, in the 1865, a year of severe drought and water rationing, Liverpool's craving for water began to grow again. With the public baths that were so essential to public health in Liverpool being closed by the drought, England's northern uplands were appraised, before Wales was seen as the best source of refreshment. In 1879, a massive dam-building programme was launched at Vyrnwy, Llanfyllin, Powys, and during the following thirteen years, a gigantic wall of stone was stretched across the valley of the River Vyrnwy. This time, a community of some size was involved, for living inside the dammed area was the village of Llanwddyn with its thirty-seven dwellings, three inns, two chapels, Post Office and ten adjacent farmsteads. The Corporation of Liverpool re-housed the community in a new settlement built further down the valley, even disinterring corpses from the old graveyard and re-burying them beside the new church. Then, the old homes were demolished and vanished beneath the rising waters – waters that would be carried away to Liverpool in cast iron underground pipes.

The thirsty eyes of Manchester turned on the Lake District again in 1935, when Haweswater was enlarged by the construction of a dam some 1,542ft (around 470m) long and 90ft (around 27.5m) tall. A partly artificial lake holding 18.6 billion gallons was created when the dam raised waters to 96ft (around 29m) above natural levels. As the rising waters extended southwards, the remote little village of Mardale was inundated. Water levels have proved variable and in 2003, they dropped to around half capacity. Not only do such drops expose unsightly areas of shoreline mud and shingle, they also reveal the otherwise submerged lanes, ruined dwellings and field walls. The old village road along the western shore of the lake was drowned and replaced by a higher one on the eastern side.

Then the focus returned to Wales, though by this time the issues had assumed a political nature, with the 'imperialist' England being cast in the role of pillager of Welsh resources and destroyer of Welsh culture. In 1957 Parliament, with a remarkable lack of foresight and discretion, and in the face of opposition by all but one of the Welsh MPs, enacted legislation permitting the compulsory purchase and inundation of 800 acres (around 324 hectares) in the Afon Tryweryn Valley, allowing water to be diverted to a once-more thirsty Liverpool and the Wirral. The area affected lay in North Wales, just north-west of Bala. Not only was it in the embattled Welsh-speaking cultural heartland, but it also contained a village, Capel Celyn, and twelve farmsteads. Even had they tried, it is hard to imagine that the English authorities could have done more to tarnish the image of national equality and promote the growth of nationalist opposition in Wales. Plaid Cymru rose to become a serious force in Welsh politics, a society for promoting the Welsh language was born and militants bombed intrusive installations and set fire to holiday homes. In 1965, the inundation of the valley was completed but forty years later, an official apology was delivered on behalf of Liverpool Corporation, 'For any insensitivity by our predecessor council at that time, we apologise and hope that the historic and sound relationship between Liverpool and Wales can be restored'. At the time of writing, an apology for the events at Llanwddyn in the 1880s is under consideration.

National sentiment is a powerful ally. Dalesfolk do not officially constitute a nation and no apologies have been proffered by the authorities of Leeds and Bradford for their transformations in the Yorkshire Dales. History has shown that the weak settlements are particularly vulnerable to new village predators that stalk into the scene. In the 1860s, Leeds, like Liverpool, faced problems of rapidly rising water consumption. To the north-west of the city lay the little Washburn valley with its failed and failing industrial villages and hamlets. Water had provided the energy for flax, hemp and cotton mills there, but now water would result in much

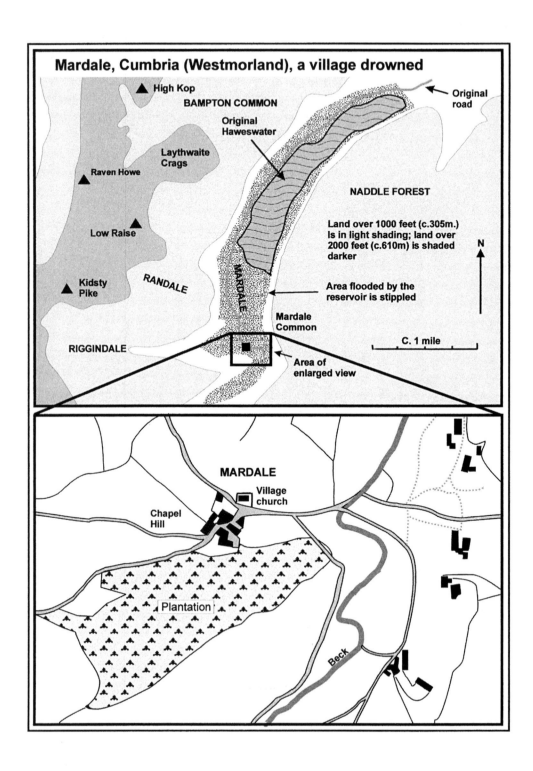

Mardale, Cumbria (Westmorland), a village drowned

High Kop

BAMPTON COMMON

Original
Haweswater

Original
road

Laythwaite
Crags

Raven Howe

NADDLE FOREST

Low Raise

Land over 1000 feet (c.305m.)
Is in light shading; land over
2000 feet (c.610m) is shaded
darker

N

Kidsty
Pike

RANDALE

MARDALE

Area flooded by the
reservoir is stippled

Mardale
Common

RIGGINDALE

C. 1 mile

Area of
enlarged view

MARDALE

Village
church

Chapel
Hill

Plantation

Beck

The remains of West End emerge from beneath the waters of Thruscross Reservoir during a drought in the late 1980s

of the valley being inundated. In 1867, the necessary Act was obtained and in the first half of the 1870s, the Lindley Wood Reservoir was built in the valley, with the Swinsty and Fewston Reservoirs following in the second half. As the Swinsty waters rose slowly across its site, Little Timble, a village reduced during that century by a typhoid epidemic and mill closures but then recovering, largely vanished. Its nine dwellings had housed sixty-three people. By 1891, only nineteen villagers remained. Then geological consequences, seemingly resulting from the saturation of the strata in adjacent slopes, resulted in the collapse of some of the dwellings in Fewston village, overlooking the same reservoir from its northern shore. A long interlude followed until the scheme was completed in the 1960s, with the building of Thruscross Reservoir. This put paid to the little village of West End, which was completely submerged by the waters that drowned its seventeenth-century chapel and inn and 142 acres (around 57 hectares) of farmland, all of which had lain in a truly beautiful setting. Though re-housed nearby, the little community lost their lovely context. Perhaps some of them would have wondered how they would have fared had the Washburn valley been in Wales?

An interesting aspect of these great reservoir-building enterprises is the fact that, while they may have destroyed settlements and communities that were centuries old, they resulted in the creation of new settlements, albeit ephemeral ones – places that were many times larger than the ones that were being inundated. Among these navvy camps for construction workers was the one at Church Gill that accommodated the workmen engaged on building the Lindley Wood Reservoir, nearby. Normally, these construction villages vanished from the landscape once the work was over, but at Norwood, quite close to the Washburn Reservoirs, there was a social hall for local residents that was constructed from two timber bungalows that had accommodated labourers engaged on building Scar House Reservoir, in Nidderdale, the neighbouring valley. Work to build a reservoir for Bradford there had begun in 1921 and it continued for fifteen years. The dam that rose to a height of 194ft (around 59m) was served by its own quarry on the hillside and an aqueduct conveyed the waters of the reservoir to Bradford, more than thirty-one miles away. Scar Village was a large settlement with ranks of hostels for the single workers and some sixty-two family bungalows, a church, community centre, shop and school. Its population included some hard-bitten navvies, but the ageing former residents recall that it was also a venue for true family life. Similarly, in the building of the Haweswater Reservoir in the late 1920s and 1930s, unemployed labourers were recruited in Manchester and industrial west Cumberland. They were provided with a virtual Rolls Royce among navvy camps, Burnbanks, with sixty-six self-contained bungalows serviced with hot and cold running water, electricity, bathrooms and kitchens. Bampton village school was subsidised to cope with expanded numbers of children, a shop was provided on site and a nurse and policeman were stationed there. Railway building and other large construction works also had their navvy camps, some ill-equipped and rowdy, but a few almost model venues for enlightened modern life. I cannot help but think that although Scar Village and Burnbank were short-lived and narrowly focussed, with their close-knit, hard-working lifestyles and low levels of personal wealth and mobility they were far truer to the village tradition than the places where 4 x 4s jostle on the pub forecourts, fat-bottomed ponies ply the lanes and Laura Ashley clothes the windows.

To add to the two categories of recently demised settlements that depended too narrowly on industrial resources and that just happened to be in the wrong place, there is a third category of environmental casualties. (It is strange that two settlements associated with other threats, Fewston and Port Nant, both experienced landslides.) Hallsands, a crabbing village on the south Devon coast is a most peculiar case. In the 1890s, in one of the numerous outbreaks of martial hysteria that regularly punctuate English history, massive works were scheduled to improve naval dockyards, including one at Keyham, near Portsmouth. The works required prodigious quantities of concrete, which in turn demanded masses of aggregate. The contractor, Sir John Jackson Ltd, was ill-advisedly given permission to dredge shingle from low on the beach between Hallsands and Beesands. Beaches, however, play a very important role in the affairs of adjacent

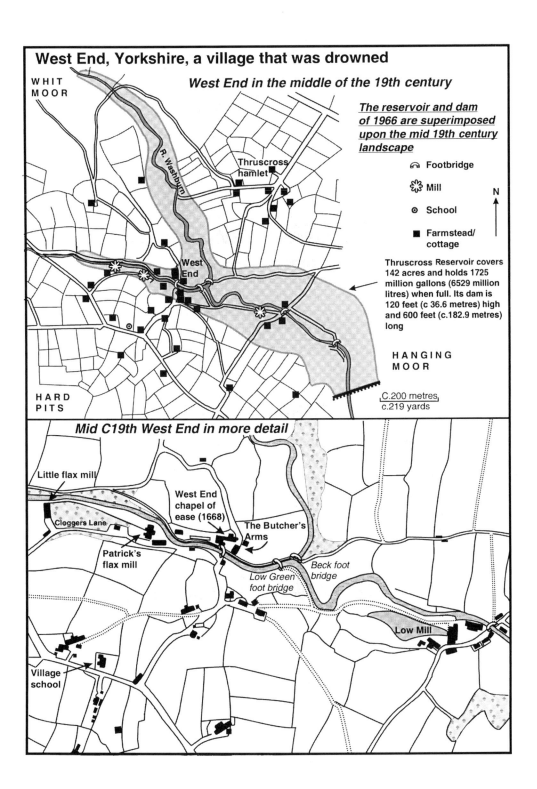

West End, Yorkshire, a village that was drowned

WHIT
MOOR

West End in the middle of the 19th century

**The reservoir and dam
of 1966 are superimposed
upon the mid 19th century
landscape**

R. Washburn

Thruscross
hamlet

🌉 Footbridge

🌸 Mill

N

⊙ School

■ Farmstead/
cottage

West
End

Thruscross Reservoir covers
142 acres and holds 1725
million gallons (6529 million
litres) when full. Its dam is
120 feet (c 36.6 metres) high
and 600 feet (c.182.9 metres)
long

HANGING
MOOR

HARD
PITS

C.200 metres
c.219 yards

Mid C19th West End in more detail

Little flax mill

West End
chapel of
ease (1668)

Cloggers Lane

The Butcher's
Arms

Patrick's
flax mill

Beck foot
bridge

Low Green
foot bridge

Low Mill

Village
school

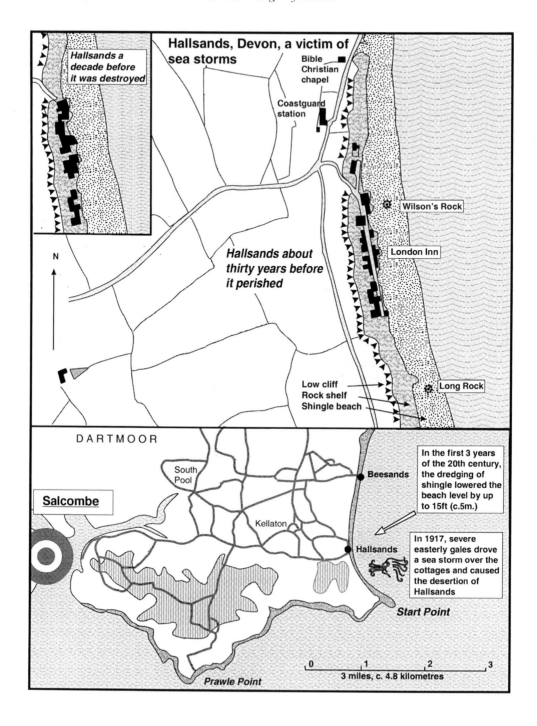

Hallsands a decade before it was destroyed

Hallsands, Devon, a victim of sea storms

Bible Christian chapel

Coastguard station

Wilson's Rock

London Inn

Hallsands about thirty years before it perished

N

Low cliff
Rock shelf
Shingle beach

Long Rock

DARTMOOR

South Pool

Beesands

Salcombe

Kellaton

In the first 3 years of the 20th century, the dredging of shingle lowered the beach level by up to 15ft (c.5m.)

Hallsands

In 1917, severe easterly gales drove a sea storm over the cottages and caused the desertion of Hallsands

Start Point

Prawle Point

0   1   2   3
3 miles, c. 4.8 kilometres

communities, for they help gradually to dissipate the energy of waves and prevent them from breaking with full force close to the shore.

The beach at Hallsands not only provided the villagers with crabbing and fishing grounds, it also protected their homes. In 1897, with fears in the seashore community mounting, an enquiry was held at which Sir John claimed that the shoreline currents would naturally replenish any shingle that was removed, though he also agreed to pay compensation. By the end of the century it was plain that the villagers' understanding of the longshore drift was better than Sir John's, for beach levels were falling and a section of sea wall was crumbling in the face of storm attacks of unprecedented violence. Damage to houses was also reported, showing that the storm waves could now span the diminished shingle barriers without breaking. At the start of 1902, therefore, the villagers decided to take charge of affairs and to prevent dredgers from landing and as a result, the dredging license was swiftly revoked. Following further damage by winter storms, the villagers accepted compensation of £3,000 provided by the Board of Trade. Six houses had gone by this time, but severe storms in 1917 reduced the settlement to just one dwelling. Finally, the community was offered £6,000 as a final settlement. Recently, Steve Melia has questioned the relationship between Sir John Jackson and the government and the extremely favourable agreement that he negotiated for the shingle that, being below the low water mark, was under the control of the Board of Trade. The suppression of the Inspector's report from the third enquiry of 1917 is also disturbing.

Some people, on considering the events outlined in this chapter, might conclude that they contain no lessons, for anybody might expect that small, often impoverished and not highly educated communities might expect to be exploited by more powerful institutions, interests and individuals. Others might decide that the story of village destruction, both past and present, contains warnings that are as relevant today as ever before about the need to defend liberties and uphold human rights – not only for the good of others, but also because one day any one of us might personally need their protection.

CHAPTER ELEVEN

DESOLATION OF THE GLENS

To Carolina via England

Alexander was leaning heavily on his stick and gazing southwards. He knew that beyond the loch and the hills there were mountains, then more mountains and still more until the land levelled out and settled down. By then one was in the more heavily farmed country of those strangers who spoke Lowland Scots and called clansmen 'teuchters'. Continuing southwards there were, as he recalled, high rounded fells and when you crossed the summits by Cheviot, you were in England. Beyond England? Well then things became uncertain. France? Spain? He was not sure, but he had been to England. He had been there five times with his father and uncles. They were driving black, Highland-bred cattle across the lonely tracks that followed the plateaus and ridge tops, sleeping in lofty inns with other drovers or curling up in their plaids beside the green stances where the cattle munched and rested before the eventual descent to the market at Malham. He was only a lad then and could not speak the language, but he understood that the English were not kin to their lords, that many of them worked slavishly, but that when they left their looms and benches they were their own masters. How odd. Strange, too, that the only folk that one saw bearing arms were uniformed soldiers or plump squires.

The last time he went to England he went as an invader. That was in 1745 and he was a youth by then. He recalled that it was as hot as summer gets when the people of his *baile* or township looked up from their work. Bright against the brae, they saw a fiery cross being ridden through the glen to muster the clan. They had the harvest on their minds and did not want to go – though there was never the faintest doubt that they would. Later, they learned that their chieftain had also rued the call to arms, but he was a loyal Jacobite and honour was more important than sound judgement. Charles Edward Stuart, son of the Jacobite pretender to the British throne, had been put ashore by a French frigate on Eriskay. Duty demanded that the chief should deliver his clan. He could not be shamed by Lochiel and his Camerons.

Despite a rather doom-laden departure and an awareness that there were many Highlanders, even clans, that would rather fight the Jacobites than join them, things went rather well at first. The Jacobite clansmen had a remarkable victory at Prestonpans, near Edinburgh, which provided opportunities for revelry and braggadocio, and then a lesser triumph at Clifton, near Penrith. The Highland army was now in England, but Alexander felt rather uneasy. He had not envisaged entering the country – his country, too, since the Union of 1707 – as an invader. He thought he would be a welcome liberator, offering his superior martial skills and courage to the popular cause of restoring the true line of kings. He expected that as they approached the vestigial industrial towns, a swarm of citizens would rush from their mills, workshops and terraces, clattering across the cobbled squares to rise to join the cause. In fact, even the Highlands was divided, with clans and regiments fighting for the Hanoverians; some McLeods were there against the wishes of their chief and some Camerons squabbled and skirmished with McLeans. In an exemplification of the old loyal code, MacLeod of Berneray honoured his obligation to deliver the specified number of clansmen to fight on the Hanoverian side for his superior, MacLeod of Dunvegan – and then he departed to fight for Charlie.

There was no rush of English people to join the host, and though it reached as far south as Derby, the prospect of concerted and overwhelming opposition and a bleeding away of manpower and supplies caused a grim retreat back to the citadel of the Highlands. Comrades in arms slipped away with their booty or returned to support their families, but Alexander stayed in the thinning ranks. He did not care too much about the succession to the throne, but he did not know how to face his kin, his neighbours or his chief's tacksmen if he should sneak back to the glen with the army still in the field. He stayed with it all the way back to the Highlands and then to Culloden Moor, near Inverness. It was now the April of 1746, with no hints of spring. Looking across the moor to the enemy lines he could see not only the red, white and yellow of the English regiments, but also the dark blue/green plaids of the Cambells and the fine uniforms of the Royal Scots and the Royal Scots Fusiliers. There, he stood waiting for an eternity in the driving rain and sleet for the order to charge that the fuddled commanders would not give. He stood gripping his broadsword, dirk and targe (a small round shield), as the grapeshot splattered him with parts of his adjacent relatives and childhood friends. At last, he charged, but before reaching the waiting

bayonets he tripped in a hollow and was almost suffocated in the bog by
the weight of corpses and wounded bodies. When the wounded were
being shot or bayoneted, he was so pale and blue that he was judged to be
already dead. Then he hid in a ditch as the dragoons slashed down fragments of the retreating host.

He was scarcely home when the assault on the martial culture of clan
loyalty began. Gaelic, the plaid, tartans, war pipes and arms were all, for a
while and to varying degrees, outlawed. Ah but all that was a long time
ago, even if the pains in his back and knees reminded Alexander of the
great retreat every time a cold dampness filled the air. There had been a
lull, a period of uncertainty as the grip of the Gaelic reprisals began to
loosen and the Highlands nation wondered what to do next. Poverty,
famine and illness were commonplace, but now there were other things
on his mind. His tacksman (petty chief) had come to the neighbouring
baile to warn the people that their lord wanted to move them on. They
could find land by the coast and seek their fortunes on the strands and
bays, or so they were told. The lord concerned was the son of the old
chief, returned a scholar and gentleman enhanced with an Oxford education. Recently, in 1784, the family estates had been restored, so now he
was back in the lands where the people had lived since their common
ancestor arrived.

Any hopes that the restoration of the clan lands and lineage would
signal a return to more wholesome and settled ways were soon dashed.
There had been murmurs about the arrival of flocks with Lowland shepherds, encouraging some sages to recount dreams of hearing a distant
bleating and younger men to think of raids and skirmishes that culminated
in a mutton stew. Yet how could loyal tenants quit their homes and not
be there to serve their chief? The rumours must be wrong. The young
laird was the son of the old chief, and he was not so long removed from
chieftains who exercised the right of pit and gallows over their subject
clansmen. For those in the glens there was nothing wrong with this, and
for all the differences in wealth, power and culture (the chiefs were often
accomplished and fluent in several languages) everyone knew that if one
went back far enough it would be found that very member of the clan was
descended from a single patriarch. They shared the same blood, the same
name and so, surely, the same fate? The chiefs demanded, and received,
unqualified loyalty. The clansmen could surely rely on the young laird to
show them no less?

Already a brig was entering the sea loch. In a few weeks the people who
had survived the crossing would see Cape Hatteras and the Carolinas, then
Cape Fear and Wilmington. They would know little of their destination,
for it was their chieftain who had chartered the ship.

A road to ruin

There are battles, like several of those in the First World War, that result in astounding levels of injury and death but yet seem to do little to deflect the course of history. There are others which, while much less voracious for life, swing the course of events in important new directions. At Culloden in April 1746 less than 2,000 clansmen died, while the Hanoverian army is recorded as having but 346 casualties. This, however, was a landmark battle. It signified the death of centuries of cultural identity, the end of an economy, of autonomy and of martial traditions and the erosion of the sense of kinship that bound clans together and, often, set them against their neighbours and the Lowlanders. During his tour of Scotland, the great Dr Johnston remarked on the transformations to his companion, Boswell, when they stayed at the MacLeod stronghold at Dunvegan on Skye in 1773:

> After breakfast, he said to me, 'A Highland chief should now endeavour to do every thing to raise his rents, by means of the industry of his people. Formerly, it was right for him to have his house full of idle fellows; they were his defenders, his servants, his dependants, his friends. Now they may be better employed. The system of things is now so much altered, that the family cannot have influence but by riches, because it has no longer the power of ancient feudal times.

The refined sensibilities of many members of the aristocracy of the Highlands stood in contrast to their existence as warlords in a world of virtual anarchy (albeit warlords charged with a special responsibility for their 'children'). The quasi-autonomy that these chieftains were able to exercise had sustained a form of lawlessness in the Highlands as a whole, where insecurity was a condition of life. Neither the Scottish kings of old or their British successors had been able to extend effective sovereignty across the Highlands. Recalling recent times, the Earl of Selkirk wrote, in 1805, of well-born life in this unruly world:

> … every person above the common rank depended for his safety and his consequences on the number and attachment of his servants and dependants: without people ready to defend him, he could not expect to sleep in safety, to preserve his house from pillage, or his family from murder; he must have submitted to the insolence of every neighbouring robber, unless he maintained a numerous train of followers to go with him into the field, and to fight his battles. To this essential object, every inferior was sacrificed; and the principal advantage, of landed property consisted in the means it afforded to the proprietor of multiplying his dependants.

Selkirk was no friend of Gaelic culture but there is truth in what he wrote. Because others of his rank tended to be as quick to take arms as himself, the typical chieftain sought to protect his dynasty by maximising the size of his body of retainers. Unlike English tenants and villagers, these men were fiery, skilled in arms and either owned their own weapons or were armed by their chief. The charge of Highlanders armed with swords and axes had overrun far more sophisticated forces and was to be dreaded within the Highlands as well as beyond. In addition, status as well as security was measured by the size of the clan army. These factors urged the chieftain to over-populate his territory and to measure his wealth in loyal soldiers rather than economic production, As Selkirk added, 'The value of property was in these times be reckoned, not by the rent it produced, but by the men whom it could send into the field. It is mentioned indeed of one of the chieftains, that being questioned by a stranger as to the rent of his estate, he answered that it could raise 500 men'.

British forces had experienced the terrifying effect of the Highlanders battlefield tactics on several disastrous occasions. They were simple but effective and involved a headlong dash for the enemy lines, the discharge of a musket, that was then discarded, and a final sprint with a raised broadsword or Lochaber axe. An opponent in the enemy line was knocked to one side by hard contact with the round shield or targe, braced by the left forearm, and a dagger or dirk was grasped inside the shield and used to slash as the shield was moved. New methods of employing the bayonet were effective at Culloden, but the Hanoverians were determined to never again have British troops facing the terror of a Highlanders' charge. It was realised that the martial nature of Highland life was part of a larger, archaic, Gaelic culture, so the whole social edifice would be dismantled. This left the holders of great Highlands estates, whether they be hereditary chieftains that escaped forfeiture or interlopers from the Scottish Lowlands or England, in the position of commanding masses of soldiers who could no longer fight. The human currency of the Highlands had become worthless on the day of Culloden. Other means of running estates and wresting income from the braes, straths and glens would have to be found. Rents seemed to some to be the answer. However, since chieftains had divided holdings and divided them again in order to maximise the number of clansmen in their territories, the tenants of these holdings struggled to survive and had little income remaining for rents.

Then an unexpected answer quietly suggested itself – unexpected because it was traditionally assumed that sheep were too fragile to survive in the Highlands. There can have been few Lowlanders that both became admirals and had reels named after them, but Sir John Lockhart was one. More significantly, in 1762, he introduced black-faced Linton

Roofless and decaying, the Church of Cill Chrioso on Skye.

sheep on his Balnagowan estate in the north of Scotland. With the care of Lowland shepherds, they defied the predictions of the Highlands cogniscenti and flourished on the exposed and rain-lashed moors. (On Skye, the MacLeod of Dunvegan had experimented with 'improvements' in 1732, three decades before Admiral Ross took his flocks to Balnagowan.) Now an alternative to renting or rack-renting was there for all to see, just as the Cistercian flocks must have exemplified an alternative to the lords of fourteenth-century England. The more that the sheep expanded, the more that new converts were attracted, particularly when the white-faced Cheviots were shown to be even better suited to the Highlands environment. However, like the Cistercians and the Tudor sheep barons before them, the Highland gentry and the interlopers alike realised that for sheep to prosper, their ranges must be cleared of communities. Few clansmen would have watched a flock taking over the grass needed by their cows and calves without whistling up their dogs and reaching for a knife. Using the characteristic language of Georgian progress, Selkirk put a businessman's gloss on the situation of evictions that would have gladdened any commercial banquet. Despite all the fuss about the depopulation of the Highlands, he claimed that the real fact was that:

> … the produce of the country, instead of being consumed by a set of intrepid but indolent military retainers, is applied to the support of peaceable and industrious manufacturers. Notwithstanding the marks of desolation which occasionally meet the eye of the traveller, impressing him with melancholy reflections on the change which is going on, it cannot be doubted, that the result is ultimately favourable to population, when we take into account

that of the whole kingdom, balancing the diminution of one district by the increase in another.

In other words, it was quite acceptable for the Highlands to suffer for the good of business and the south. However, the suggestion that the traveller in the Highlands might occasionally witness marks of melancholy desolation was quite misleading. Selkirk wrote at a time when chains of populous estates were suddenly becoming desolate. Even now, after around two centuries for possible healing, the whole of the great region of the Highlands and Islands is like a vast battlefield, with the gables of ruined homesteads studding each vista like dragons' teeth. Today's travellers in the Scottish Highlands do not usually need to be given elaborate directions to a landscape devastated by Georgian or Victorian clearances. The chances are that they are already in one.

The people who were suddenly valued so lightly had lived in settlements that contrasted with those of England and the Lowlands. *Bailes* were found in the Highland glens, and in the Gaelic-speaking farmlands there were straggling villages or formless hamlets known as *clachans*. These are referred to as 'group farms', consisting of several homesteads and households that combined to share the working of the surrounding territory. The 'run-rig' system of farming that was employed somewhat resembled the in-field/ out-field method employed on some poorer English farmlands. Fertilising manure was concentrated on a great strip field that was kept in constant production growing barley, oats, pease and rye, while bits of out-field land would be broken in, worked to exhaustion and abandoned to a long fallow. Land was ploughed in a way that corrugated the in-field with great ridges, while the less amenable land was ridged-up using spades. Beyond the in-field and out-field areas stretched the great commons of the banks and braes (peat mosses and hillsides), while the floodplain of the river or burn would grow hay. The *clachans* looked nothing like the contemporary villages to the south. They lacked structure, organised streets and lanes and, usually, churches and they might have seemed like turf-roofed shanties that had dropped randomly from the skies, some running one way and some another. Where the run-rig lands spilled over into the Lowland Scots speaking area, as in the North East, so the *clachans* became 'fermtouns' or farm-towns – or mill-touns or kirktouns if they had mills or churches. The English villages of the Napoleonic era will have little resemblance to those Christmas card places with their coaches and welcoming inns, but they will have had charm in their vernacular buildings, ponds with ducks, geese on the green, (working) stocks and a few had maypoles, too. But the *clachans* and fermtouns looked much more grim. There was no romance to these places, and if not built of mud, the dwellings were certainly surrounded by it.

These were the places that were doomed by 'progress' and sheep. Historians build reputations on discovering new perspectives (including the one that involves a return to the original thinking on a subject). One can certainly argue that life in the *baile* and the *clachan* was unsustainable. Their martial outlooks and insecurities had led the old clan chieftains to grossly overpopulate their territories. Famine and disease did their best to reel back the population numbers. Episodes of malnutrition punctuated by eruptions of starvation, which both paved the way for epidemics, were traditional characteristics of life in the Highlands. It is also true that some of the people who were actually responsible for initiating evictions had been tortured by the dilemma of maintaining communities in the glens and on the braes – and had only turned to eviction when they could discover no other viable alternative. Additionally, there is some viability in the notion that the clearances in the Highlands were part of a far broader package of agricultural reforms, producing the Improvements in the Lowlands, the Enclosures in England and other changes beyond. And yet, and yet…

People, some of a Scottish separatist persuasion, are beginning to reawaken the term 'ethnic cleansing' from the recent wars in the Balkans and to apply it to the clearances in the Scottish Highlands. It might be hard to deny that this was, indeed, a purging of indigenous culture from the Gaelic heartlands. I doubt that after the initial post-Culloden purges this was a deliberate English/British policy – but it certainly was not policy to affront business and privilege by preventing its outrages. At this time, people in positions of influence – landowners, politicians, people in positions of authority – were besotted by 'progress' to the extent that the imposition of almost any degree of hardship upon a community was granted a false aura of respectability if it could be cast in a progressive guise. Usually, the 'progress' that was invoked amounted to no more than speculative profit for a sectional business interest. However, a fashionable belief in progress deeply permeated Georgian agriculture, commerce and manufacturing. It would be wrong to suggest that the English villager who was broken by the costs of Parliamentary Enclosure was as wickedly misused as the crofter who was a victim of the clearances. Even so, were the villager standing on the quay at Liverpool with nothing but his fare to Boston, it would be hard to argue that he was better off than his penniless Scots and Irish shipmates-to-be in the stinking hold of some pitching hulk.

Communities condemned to clearance were likely to learn their fate from a tacksman, a man who served as a tenant-in-chief in times of peace and a clan officer in times of war. The tacksman would sublet his tenancy, and it was likely to be sublet again and again into holdings that offered the barest subsistence, or less. Once the bad news had been delivered and digested, the move itself might go peacefully. However, it might not, and sometimes evictions took place at the points of muskets and swords. The agents responsible could be paid workers in the lord's employ, perhaps the newly arrived Lowlander shepherds who would take over the lands. Houses would be torn down to prevent any return, though often, if the community was being relocated, the dispossessed clansmen would carry away the curving cruck beams of the 'A'-frames that had supported the house in a land where timber was scarce.

The aftermath of eviction took several forms. Many families walked to the coast, hoping to earn a living from the dry, shell-rich soils of the shoreline *machairs* and from fishing and extracting iodine from seaweed or 'kelp'. Sometimes, these shifts of tenants were a part of estate reorganisation policies, with the potential of the resettling ground depending on the goodwill of the laird. Patrick Sellar, the notorious factor (agent) on the Sutherland estates where the most controversial evictions took place, wrote that his Lord and Lady:

> ... were pleased humanely to order the new arrangement of this country. That the interior should be possessed by Cheviot shepherds, and the people brought down to the coast and placed in lots of less than three acres, sufficient for the maintenance of an industrious family, pinched enough to cause them to turn their attention to the fishing. A most benevolent action, to put these barbarous Highlanders into a position where they could better associate together, apply themselves to industry, educate their children, and advance in civilisation.

A rather more graphic and honest description of the aftermath of eviction was provided by one of the crofters on the Sutherland estate, Donald McLeod. He described the burning of homes, the cries of women and children and the roaring of frightened cattle that were hunted by the yelling dogs of the shepherds, and then:

> A dense cloud of smoke enveloped the whole country by day, and even extended far out to sea. At night and awfully grand but terrific scene presented itself – all the houses in an extensive district in flames at once. I myself ascended a height about eleven o'clock in the evening and counted two hundred and fifty blazing houses, many of the owners of which I personally knew, but whose personal condition – whether in or out of the flames – I could not tell. The conflagration lasted six days...

Though his wife was eventually hounded to madness by the agents of the Countess and he became exiled in Ontario, McLeod's accounts of the clearances did have some influence on mobilising liberal opinion, though not as much as Harriet Beecher Stowe's *Uncle Tom's Cabin* had had in opposing slavery. It was a remarkable irony that McLeod published his *Gloomy Memories* (Toronto, 1857) with its grim recollection of the Sutherland clearances to refute the *Sunny Memories,* in which Stowe (1811-96) had recorded her disappointingly favourable and partial recollections of a holiday with the Sutherlands at their Dunrobin Castle.

Even if well-intentioned, relocations of tenants to the coast could not allow for the sheer pressure of the many evicted families upon the limited resources of the sea and shoreline. When the potato blight arrived in 1846 – the same blight that caused more than 1 million people to die of starvation in Ireland – a crucial pillar of crofting life was cast down. Failed crofters then looked to the alien, industrialising lands to the south or headed for ports of embarkation. Other evictees made directly from their shattered homes for the emigration ships and a crossing as vile and dangerous as that endured by Negroes on the evil slavers. Sometimes, they walked 100 miles or so to an international seaport, but sometimes their laird, so desperate to see them go, chartered ships and had them sailed to the nearest haven or sea loch. An entire community might vanish on a single boat. If any relatives or old neighbours remained, within years or even months the letters from the New World would arrive, igniting a sequence of chain migration that could empty a district and see the old community restored and reconstructed in some North American valley or township.

Each estate, whether owned by a Gaelic aristocrat or an English or Lowland interloper, had its own story of clearance. Sometimes, the landlord would stay his or her hand until no possibilities of maintaining a population remained, while in other cases, the owner wasted no time in creating desolate sheep runs. On the Strathglass estate of the Chisholm leader the clearance began in 1801, and within a year, half the tenants were in Nova Scotia, elsewhere in Canada or on their way there. Then, with the chieftain dead and his heir studying at Cambridge, the removal of tenants was continued by his wife. She was a MacDonnell of Glengarry, a family responsible for some of the most spiteful of all evictions. The son then returned to the north and completed the clearances so thoroughly that within a decade of their commencement, about 10,000 clansfolk were removed from the strath and the only Chisholms remaining were said to be the chiefs themselves. The estates of Cameron of Locheil were forfeit after Cameron had played a prominent role in the Jacobite uprising of 1745. In 1784, the fifteen-year-old Donald was restored to his Cameron birthright, but weak and deeply in debt, he began replacing the holdings of his tenants-in-chief with sheep walks. Other tacksmen made their lands more profitable by removing their sub-tenants and introducing sheep.

There were, however, some chieftains who honoured their traditional obligations.

The clearances had a geography of difference from estate to estate and they also had a history of evolving in their impact and targets. In the first period, following the diffusion of stories about the profitability of raising sheep on Highland estates, there was a phase that ran from about 1780 to 1820 when the most notorious and brutal of clearances were enforced on the Sutherland and Glengarry estates. Yet this was also a time when Highland landlords often seemed uncertain about how their estates and dependents might best be managed. To some, it appeared that a humane kind of profitability might somehow be found as an alternative to clearances. At first, the high level of emigration from the Highlands was not universally welcomed by the establishment. Indeed, in 1803 an Act was passed that attempted to stem the flow. One labour-intensive possibility seemed to be a reorganisation of settlement into coastal crofting townships where the rod-like stems of the seaweed, *Fucus vesiculous*, could be collected, dried and burned in small kilns to produce iodine. Merchants arrived at the crofts to buy the iodine and to sell it far and wide. However, in the 1820s, the market price for kelp collapsed and the industry was destroyed when salt duties were abolished in 1825. It seemed to many that as the problems intensified, the range of opportunities contracted. Attempts to find new sources of employment abounded. In 1784, for example, a Glasgow businessman, David Dale, tried to stem the emigration of people from Argyllshire and the islands to North America by establishing a new mill town at New Lanark. Ultimately, some of the worst clearances were born of failure, and before the Countess of Sutherland, a Gordon married to an English marquess, had her factors, Patrick Sellar and James Lock, enact the despicable Sutherland clearances, they had experimented with root crops, coal mines, brickworks, fishing for herring and salt pans. Their final solution to the problem posed by their tenants culminated in eviction at the rate of 2,000 families per day.

The next great phase of clearances ran from around 1842-54. This was a time when a remarkable system of double standards or schizophrenia dominated attitudes in the lands to the south. In the eighteenth century, all people bar the most committed members of the declining band of Jacobites regarded the armed clansmen as a source of real danger. A distinct 'otherness' governed attitudes to the Highlanders, with their bizarre dress, incomprehensible language, flamboyant behaviour and peerless valour and loyalty. They may have seemed almost as alien as the natives encountered by the vessels of the dawning empire. Such attitudes may even have influenced some chiefs. Indeed, the transactions in 1739, when McLeod of Dunvegan and Macdonald of Sleet sold some of their Skye tenants, both men and women, to the Carolinas to work as indentured servants, placed the clan tenants just one notch above slaves.

By the time that Victoria came to the throne in 1837, the social climate had changed, and those to the south were becoming captivated by the courage and romance that was attached to the Highlands. The British army had not been slow to appreciate the martial qualities of the Highlander, particularly in aggressive contexts. The Black Watch had been raised in 1725 and recruited from 'loyal' clans – Campbells, Grants, Munros and Frasers – to assist the British pacification of the turbulent Highland clans. Between 1730 and the Battle of Waterloo in 1815, some eighty-six more Highland regiments were raised and the deeds of the Highlanders at Waterloo and during the succeeding era through to the Crimean War and beyond transformed the image of the Scots – Highlanders and Lowlanders alike. The threatening, alien scoundrel was being replaced by the steadfast hero. Sir Walter Scott, the historical novelist, set the seal on the rehabilitation of the Highlander when, along with General Stewart of Garth, he masterminded an elaborate pageant of tartan and whimsy to orchestrate the visit to Edinburgh by George IV in 1822. In the very years directly preceding Waterloo, when the Sutherland clearances had blackened the northern lands with anguish and hatred, a hopelessly romanticised image of life in the Highlands was being forged and fostered. After staying at Balmoral in 1848, Queen Victoria fell in love with Scotland, though perhaps more with the image and Brown, her manservant, than with the real land. Two years later, she bought the house, kitted her offspring out in kilts, and revelled in the 'Balmoralism' that she had, in part, created.

In the real world of the Highlands there had been riots accompanying evictions in Ross in 1820, and Sutherland in 1821, a cholera epidemic in 1832, a famine in 1836 and again in 1846, following the spread of potato blight, which was particularly devastating to any crofting communities that had survived the collapse of the kelp industry.

Now the focus of the evictions turned to the Hebrides, where, on Skye alone, some 1,740 writs of removal were served between 1840 and 1880. In 1882, the very same modernising year when Charles Darwin died, Louis Pasteur was honoured by the Society of Arts and Epping Forest became a public park, the evictions on Skye culminated in the despatch of a naval gunboat and a troop of fifty hard-bitten Glasgow policemen to force hapless tenants out of their homes. With their shoreline resources to diversify their economy, the islands had escaped relatively lightly as clearances scoured away populations from the mainland. Now, as the options diminished, some landlords readily resorted to clearances, while others cast about in desperation for alternatives. The Macdonalds of Sleet, controlling much of Skye, had attempted road building, peat drainage and hemp cultivation, but with mounting debts from their enterprises they turned to eviction on a particularly ferocious scale. In the years between 1855 and the riots of the 1880s, emigration had reduced the population of Skye from 23,074 to 17,680 and the plight of remaining tenants deteriorated when landlords, like the Macdonalds, had removed their customary rights to common resources. They replied to this by withholding rents, which resulted in eviction orders being served. However, on one occasion, reminiscent of the Medieval Peasants' Revolt in East Anglia, the officials of the sheriff found themselves surrounded by a gathering of women and children and were forced to burn their bundle of eviction papers. This resulted in the landing, at 6 a.m. in the dark of morning, of the Glasgow policemen. Most able-bodied men were away in the fishing boats but the people who remained brawled with the police and pelted them with stones. Then, members of one of the hardest police forces in Britain turned with unrestrained violence to dragging families from their homes. Just to locate these events in time once more, lest we seem to have strayed into some unenlightened age, in the following year, electric lighting was introduced in Surrey, *Treasure Island* was published, London's Inner Circle Line was nearing completion and, more pertinently, the Highland Land League was formed to secure tenure for crofters.

At least it might be good to suggest that the story of the clearances ended here, with impoverished Skye crofters resisting a British gunboat. Sadly, it was not so. Clearances to create deer forests provided a last manifestation of the awful injustices. Their detestation is disproportionate to their scale, and the depth of the enduring resentment for the deer forest clearances is because there are people still living who remember those who knew, or were parented by, their victims. The developments of that most innovative century, the nineteenth, had, as we have seen, transformed perceptions of the Highlands. This was no longer a mysterious misty region of the Celtic twilight zone, with intimidating mountains and still more intimidating occupants. Now, one could take the waters at Ballater, the Queen was gently mourning at Balmoral, not far away, while the steamboats and railways were opening up the country for the less energetic visitor. By the middle of the nineteenth century, some sheep ranges were being replaced by deer forests. Improvements, both in transport and in firearms, meant that, without exerting himself too much, a mill owner could leave his factories on one day, or a squire depart his estates in an English shire, and be blasting grouse or pulverising red deer on some lofty Highlands moor on the next. By the 1870s, overseas sheep producers were rendering the vast sheep runs of the Highlands much less profitable, while the grazings seemed to have deteriorated after the removal of clan cattle. Many lairds sought salvation in the creation of deer forests, with the associated baggage of Gothic mansions, bothies and shooting lodges, carriageways carved across the braes, shooting parties, flirtation, intrigue and insider dealings. By 1922, when the deer forest craze was well past its zenith, a Commission reported that the 'forests' (which were little wooded) covered 3,584,966 acres (1,440,000 hectares). Naturally, such extensive hunting reserves had not been created without dislodging substantial numbers of Highlanders, despite the fact that the Crofters Holdings Act of 1886, a reflection of public revulsion at the Skye clearances, had provided protection to families in the designated crofting areas.

On the southern and eastern fringes of the Highlands, where Lowland Scots dialects were spoken, the situation was different. Here, there were deeper and better-drained soils, often comprising sand and clay particles borne away from the Highlands by glaciers. In these places the problem was not so much the poverty of the land as the poverty of the fermtoun communities, whose semi-subsistence lifestyles left little that could be paid to a landlord as rent. And here, the almost invariable solution was found in Improvements (the Scottish equivalent of England's Agricultural Revolution). These transformations were pioneered by the large landowners like the Earl of Cawdor, Lord Gardenstone, Grant of Monymusk, Garden of Troup and Ferguson of Pitfour. The Improvements had familiar features, like the attempt to establish more remunerative employment in fishing or small textile mills, but they also involved attempts to replace a community of farming paupers with a few 'progressive', well-organised and substantial tenants who were able to deliver a decent rent. Across the Highlands fringes, and nowhere more than in places like Buchan in the north of Aberdeenshire and the adjacent coasts, one sees mile upon mile of countryside that still dances to the tune of Improvements. There are the precisely planned villages of the post-Culloden decades, with their straight roads and square greens; the 'mains' or head farms of estates; the solid little farmsteads, again all dating from the late eighteenth or nineteenth centuries; the walls or 'consumption dykes' built of stones cleared from the ploughland, and sometimes a purpose-built setlement in the hopeful form of a fishing village. As for the old fermtouns, milltouns and kirktouns, a few – usually the more important ones with a mill or a church – live on in rebuilt form. Most, however, have vanished, and vanished more completely than one might imagine given that their demise could have been an event of the Victorian era.

Though shamefully overlooked in England, the clearances remain a smouldering source of anger and resentment for many people living in the Highlands and Islands. This anger can be used as a stick to beat the English, though in truth the Gaelic chieftains and tacksmen were as deeply implicated as the Lowlanders and the English. It is not the case

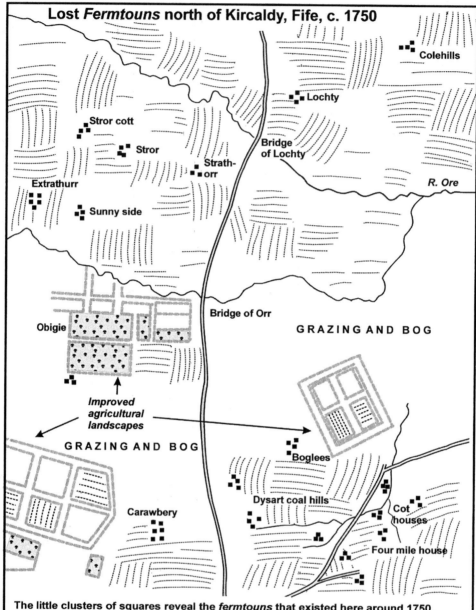

Lost *Fermtouns* north of Kircaldy, Fife, c. 1750

Colehills

Lochty

Stror cott

Bridge
of Lochty

Stror

Strath-
orr

R. Ore

Extrathurr

Sunny side

Bridge of Orr

Obigie

GRAZING AND BOG

*Improved
agricultural
landscapes*

GRAZING AND BOG

Boglees

Dysart coal hills

Carawbery

Cot
houses

Four mile house

The little clusters of squares reveal the *fermtouns* that existed here around 1750.
They have all either gone or were converted into farmsteads by improving landlords.
The geometrical hedge patterns south of the Bridge of Orr mark the beginnings of the
changes. This area is now sandwiched between Kircaldy and Glenrothes. The coal
seams suggested by the names 'Colehills' and 'Dysart Cole Hills' became worked
on an industrial basis and Dysart became a colliery village. The names of most of the
fermtouns have vanished from the map. Distance, left to right margin: about 5 miles.
The pecked lines show directions of the old plough ridges.

that the English were exceptionally tyrannical (some Irish episodes apart) and the examples of Estonia, Latvia, Belgium, Poland, Palestine, Croatia and several other cases show that life next to a more powerful neighbour can be much worse. Life for the illiterate speakers of an alien language occupying an impoverished backwater that was perched just beyond an industrial cauldron starting to ignite was never likely to be easy. History can be set aside, and should be when its ills cannot be righted, but one thing that can be corrected is the insufferable crassness that both colours modern English attitudes and infuriates those northern neighbours that encounter them. The more inane the presenters that the television media employs, the more frequently one is left to cringe at the patronising and ill-informed treatment that license-paying northern viewers are expected to endure. Hamish Brown, writing in *The Angry Corrie*, represented the views of countless Scots when he wrote:

> In the 1960s, I once took two delightful English schoolteachers on a Highland Tour. They were *history teachers* [my ital.]. They had not heard of the Clearances. Our Scottish history, languages and traditions were marginalized, forbidden, trivialised, for all too long. Now that we are potentially a people again, questions are being asked that go right to the roots of these past misdeeds.

Nothing much has changed since then. Those of us who cling to a vision of Britain as a nation of equal nations may only stand in silence when the northern door closes and the English are left to puzzle why they are suddenly diminished and alone. That door could very well close and when it does, the bafflement will be one the faces of those who are the losers.

CHAPTER TWELVE

THE NEXT CHAPTER

Lessons of history?

The story of lost villages is a story of injustice and heartless authority.
Those exploring the life and death of villages may wonder if there are any
lessons to be learned from history? I believe that there are. However, in
terms of human behaviour, the only lesson of history is that, however plain
and stark its lessons may be, they always go unheeded.

Dwellers in doomed villages were at the very forefront of issues and events
concerning the rights and freedoms of people. Conditions have changed
and mass evictions, in Britain at least, are far less frequent. The reforms that
have led towards more civilised ways of living embody both the sacrifices of
the victims of eviction and the selfless campaigning by those who found the
injustices insufferable. Over the centuries, justice has gained strength in many
ways. In the feudal world, those who had their homes and crops destroyed
by armies, the people who were the surviving remnants of communities
devastated by pestilence, or households that had stood helplessly as the tides
invaded their fields might receive modest relief from government taxation.
These were not great humanitarian gestures, for the destitute victims had
been rendered unable to pay their taxes in any event. In the Tudor era, there
was the broadest assault on English villages of all times. The villagers still had
no rights, but when the evictions filled the lanes and highways with crowds
of desperate, hopeless people, authority attempted to end the clearances. It
did not act for the victims, but to preserve the State and the status quo from
the wrath of those who had nothing left to live for. It failed to end the injustices and failed largely because the members of the privileged classes who
manned the inquisitions were very much the same sorts of people, and sometimes the very same people, as those perpetrating the clearances. In countless
issues, large and small, the members of the ruling classes showed a greater
readiness to protect the guilty members of their own class than to provide

justice for the poor. History has shown that only a vigorously democratic and egalitarian society that has its institutions and liberties protected by a strong body of laws can hope to achieve justice and freedom for its members.

By the time of the appalling clearances in the Scottish Highlands, an Age of Enlightenment had supposedly already dawned. In 1792, Thomas Paine's *The Rights of Man* galvanised the many reform societies that had appeared in Scotland, while in Ireland, the Protestant Wolfe Tone was leading a movement for Catholic emancipation. The next year, Thomas Muir was sentenced to fourteen years in Botany Bay for organising radical clubs for workers in the industries of western Scotland. In 1797, eleven people died when the British cavalry charged down a group of Scots at Tranent, local folk who were protesting against the militia draft. The cavalrymen followed the carnage by looting homes in the vicinity – yet in spite of all this, the climate was one of ultimately irresistible change. New Lanark was founded by David Dale in 1783 as a model of enlightened, socially-orientated indus-trial accommodation, while at the start of the next century, Wordsworth began to celebrate the lives and thoughts of ordinary people. The greatest landmark in reform came in 1807, with the abolition of slavery in Britain.

In the course of the nineteenth century, Britain gradually and sometimes painfully gathered the trappings of a Parliamentary democracy. Each step towards democracy made the destruction of villages less frequent and more difficult to achieve. However, during this century, particularly during its first half, wealthy and aristocratic landlords did not usually encounter any insuperable challenges to their designs to replace a village with an empty park. The evictions of Highlanders continued throughout the length of that century, a century that would be long dead before the deer forest clearances had receded into the mists of infamy.

People discovered that democracy, with its standards of decency and its associated laws, offered some protection. However, any probing of the armour of the prevailing democracy revealed many chinks. New despots had emerged with a level of authority much greater those of the lords and dukes of old: the State and the great urban/industrial conglomer-ates. If the State sought to commandeer land for a military training area, it could and would do so. If a great conurbation sought to drown a valley and its settlements, the Parliamentary instruments were there to allow this to happen. One might argue that acts such as these are compatible with democratic ideals concerning the greatest good for the greatest number (if 'democratic' and 'ideals' these be). The State and its agencies adopted the garments and language of democracy so effectively that any success-ful communal opposition to a State-sponsored development was virtually miraculous. Our liberties are much lauded, but it is the gaps in freedom that should be at the forefront of thinking in a healthy democracy rather than the rights paraded in popular slogans. As a schoolboy, a part of my parish was taken over to become a US spy base. Decades have passed and it has remained so. When constructions and developments are planned at this base, the plans are held up in silence at the parish meeting; residents are not allowed to comment and their elected councillors may not speak a word. One may wonder how this furthers the cause of the Free World?

More worrying, I think, is the fact that laws, rights and liberties that were won at the cost of so much blood, sacrifice and courage can now seen to be bleeding away. Politicians now tell us that such freedoms may have to be surrendered because of current political situations. However, the time-honoured message of democracy is that rights and freedoms are indivisible and not conditional upon political expediency, spin or whatever terrorists may, or may not, be doing. No date for the restoration of the forfeited liberties has been given. It is a strange and sinister sort of democracy that compels us to surrender our democratic freedoms in order to protect it. From the point of view of villages, the resounding lesson is that all settlements that exist without the rights and liberties of their inhabitants being enshrined in law face uncertain futures. The ogre at the gate is no longer a Tudor landlord or crafty monk; he may stand there in the guise of the road builder, the developer or the airport authority. He does not need a special knowledge of the weaknesses in the law and the plasticity of local democracy; he pays minions by the score to know such things. He is infinitely more cunning and in many respects more

A village, like Barrington in Cambridgeshire, can present a beguiling face – but the prospects for village life can prove uncertain. In modern times the calculated demolition of villages has been relatively rare, but there are more insidious threats to village character and community as towns burst into their green belts and planners and developers scour the uneasy countryside for building sites.

powerful than the ogres of old, and so, one might argue, communal rights and safeguards are more important now than they ever were.

The road ahead

So what of the future? Resonating through this text is the fact that the makers of the 'chocolate-box village' myths have done their subject a great disservice. Villages have become embedded in national perception as timeless, resolute and unchanging places, where the 'old-fashioned values' (whatever they were) still prevail. All the evidence summarised in this book shows that instead of being rigid fixtures in the rural landscape, villages were very responsive to pressures. If the pressures were sufficiently hostile, then villages could die, sometimes in droves. Rather than preserving time-less forms, villages adapted to fickle circumstances and were transformed, so that they might even migrate across their fields to exploit better sites. In the light of experience, more fitting adjectives to attach to villages are 'fragile', 'responsive' and 'unstable'.

I have said that to exist, villages had to have roles and that if the prevailing role were removed, the village would swiftly need to discover a new one, or perish. The feudal village was, almost invariably, a dormitory for a servile agricultural population. This role certainly persisted in most places until the latter part of the nineteenth century, though it does not fit any of today's villages. One might argue that the millennium of the village at last came to an end during the Victorian era. It died after the Parliamentary Enclosure of common lands; the mechanisation of farming; agricultural depression, and the importation of overseas produce, had devastated the land armies that had formerly toiled in the crowded fields. Never again, would one see the men-folk of a village ranged with their scythes in a long line across some great meadow or see the swarm of village women and children gleaning after har-vest in some vast field like scores of maggots crawling on a cheese. Everyone knows that Islington, Finsbury and Paddington are no longer villages. I have defined a village as a dormitory for servile agricultural tenants/workers. With this in mind, could any settlement which had gained more employees in the blossoming service industries – like postmen, roadmen and shopkeep-ers – than it retained land workers, smallholders and farmers still be regarded as a village? It might be said that real villages died when they lacked that commonality of interest, experience and skill associated with a community working together, in harmony, on the surrounding lands and enduring the same discomforts and injustices. Once the village community changed, so did the conversations in the churchyard, tavern and doorways. The dialogue was different and so were the intensity and meaningfulness of the communication between people. The whole community was no longer conversant with the vagaries of growing rye, the uses for nettles, the cures for foot rot and the spirits inhabiting old thorn trees, and a thousand other rural topics.

If the village did not die for the reasons described, it staggered on with the possibility of demise casting a dark shadow. It had, in Victorian times, gradually ceased to be a homogenous community of oppressed land workers and had become a little service centre for local farms, cottages, mansions and estates. It might have a shop, a Post Office and perhaps a few other tradesmen, like undertakers, wheelwrights, joiners, stonemasons, tailors and innkeepers. However, this new function could not fill the boots of the old. As farm employment crumbled, so gaps appeared in the village landscape and without a major social transformation, scores of villages would have limped into oblivion. The innovation that heralded salvation came, of course, in the form of commuting, firstly in the South East and in association with places linked by short rail journeys to London. Soon, however, the tentacles reached out and within less than a century people could be found commuting to the capital from the Isle of Wight, Bristol and South Yorkshire. Meanwhile, the effect of the rise in personal mobility brought by the motorcar had been to convert virtually every village in England, most of those in Wales and in central and southern Scotland, into commuter villages. Any village within around twenty miles of a town was likely to be converted in this way – and in a place as small and as heavily populated as Britain, most villages did lie within such a distance of a town. If villages did, indeed, survive the Victorian era it was the fortuitous emergence of commuting that allowed the survival of the village as a settlement, though no longer as a harmonious community of like-thinking people. The sole remaining farm worker lingering on in his council house, the stockbroker in his period residence beside the church, the potter in her converted barn and the weekend cottage that was locked and empty throughout the week scarcely amounted to a community of interest.

This emergence of a new function saved the village heart, if not its soul. Had it not happened, the landscape of Britain would be strewn with dead and shrunken villages. During recent years, various factors – such as a fear of rising urban crime rates and a belief, widespread but often inaccurate, concerning the superiority of rural schools – has accelerated the flight of higher earners to the countryside. Some could argue that villages are more desirable and their accommodation more sought-after than ever before. So what of the future? The desertion of villages has been a phenomenon that has run throughout recorded British history. The rate of desertions is currently about as low as it has ever been and yet there are no reasons to suppose that the death of villages has come to an end. In a way, the present situation is more, rather than less, unstable. In the past, confrontations, like those concerning how much land should be worked by lay brethren rather than villagers or how much should be devoted to sheep rather than mixed farming, caused evictions. But there was always an unspoken underlying certainty that humble tenant farmers based in villages and growing crops in the fields around would dominate most countrysides. Now, however, tillage is powered by subsidies and machines; villages are not needed to accommodate land armies and so there is no agricultural safety net and no lower limit for village viability.

It is possible to imagine ways that would reverse the trends of village expansion caused by commuting and urban overspill programmes. The most obvious of these is the increase in fuel prices, which, with depleting reserves, must rise ever more steeply upwards. This would have the least immediate effect on the purchasers of village retirement homes, though weekend home-owners and commuters will be increasingly affected as oil resources diminish and prices rise. One does not need special talents to imagine a likely scenario, for, as the costs of travel rise, so other negative factors will increasingly influence the choices concerning places in which to live. The more unattractive the village environment becomes, the less ready commuters will be to meet remorselessly escalating fuel bills. A minority may be able to set up schemes for working partly from home, but as the first households opt for urban dwellings and migrate, the fall in rural house prices can be expected to trigger a tide of panic selling.

A quite long-standing disincentive concerns the fact that in many villages there is a community that is not polarised so much as torn in several different directions. The middle-class commuter may not share much sympathy for the infatuation with bloodsports that permeates most of the old-established squirearchy. The dwindling community of indigenous villagers resents the fact that the 'in-comer' or 'off-comer' elements have driven the prices of village housing out of reach and far out of sight of their children. They blame the closure of the village shop on the mobile immigrants who shop at supermarkets on their way back from work and the failure of the village school on the in-comers who send their offspring to public schools. They also resent the ways in which the erudite and assertive newcomers have taken over all the old village institutions, from the church to the fête, and have displaced the old committee members to the margins. Similarly, they claim that the parish council is being used to ring-fence the interests of the owners of expensive village properties. Then there is the village pub, often more a social centre on television than in reality. (On a recent photographic project in the Yorkshire Wolds I went to five villages, one after the other, and still failed to find a lunch snack in a pub that had not been turned into a pricey restaurant, open only in the evening or at weekends.) In short, the village has become a place where conflicting interests collide and where great chasms of culture, self-interest and understanding divide the different parties.

Commuters living under the threat of rising fuel bills may also look at the countryside around their adopted settlement. Let us look too at a not atypical example. It no longer resembles those Constable images on the backs of the place mats. The hedges went in the 1960s and '70s, as did the ponds and most of the woods. There is a surviving copse, where rather worrying people fire paint balls at each other, a prairie-like expanse of oilseed rape, smelling of bad cabbage and making one sneeze, as well as an estate of 'affordable houses'. These were supposedly built for the offspring of those grumbling old villagers, though no local actually managed to secure a home there (still, the farmer who owned the land did rather well. He stopped shouting at villagers to get off his land for the whole duration of the planning enquiry.) Perhaps the most obvious feature of this countryside, apart from the mobile phone mast, is the income now deriving from recreation. The birdsong has gone and the air is filled with the perpetual cracking and popping from the clay pigeon shooting area. Then there is the golf driving range (where the orchid meadow used to be), the ponds where captive fish are hauled out by sportsmen within moments of being put in, and the executive off-road driving area, where fun can be had tearing apart the slopes and hollows of a deserted Medieval village site. There is still a footpath in the locality, complete with a huge signpost that disclaims every mishap that could conceivably occur in a field. Just as a reminder that the setting is rural, one quango or another has set up a colourful board allowing visitors to identify hedgerow birds and butterflies, most of which have actually perished owing to the failure of the movement to prevent the spraying of pesticides and herbicides on field margins. Searching for the majority would be an indefinite process, but it is nice to be reminded of what they looked like. This is now a countryside that stands to Constable Country as Passchendaele did to paradise.

Faced with such concentrated joylessness, the commuters, whose kind breathed life into a withered village carcass, may decide, one by one, that living in such divided and ecologically destitute places no long exerts an attraction strong enough to compensate for the rising costs of dwindling fuel. If these things happen – and all of them are currently happening – then the future for the village can seem uncertain.

1,000 years as a dormitory for land-workers, a century and a half as a service centre, five to ten decades as a commuter and weekend cottage settlement, and then…?

Perhaps there may be a place for any settlement in a country that is conspicuously overcrowded? Still, with no obvious new function to vitalise and perpetuate the old settlements in sight, it is not easy to envisage what villages will become or what will become of them.

This is not a summary of the story of lost villages. It is just a summary of the story thus far.

CHAPTER THIRTEEN

FINDING THE BODIES

The finding feeling

It is a clear and sunny day in spring. The grass has not grown very much and so conditions for recognising the shallow earthworks that signal old farming and building sites are still quite good. I have always enjoyed fieldwork, but this time it is particularly welcome as it helps me to escape from a bureaucracy that is becoming ever more leaden and idiotic. And today I am lucky, for a sponsor has provided a little cash so that I can employ Lisa to help with the mapping of archaeological features. Up to this day, we have been mainly involved in work on the ancient trees in the deer park at Ripley, but on this occasion we are exploring the park's outer limits. And so we set off, the sun warming the left sides of our faces and our backs pleasantly, towards the distant source of life's frustrations. There is nothing more therapeutic than spring sunshine and serious fieldwork: combined they can cure almost anything. We pause to measure the girth of the stump of a once-massive ash tree and continue westwards. Underfoot, the ground is rippled by grassed-over ridge and furrow ploughland. Some of it curves and measures about 4.5m between furrows, typical of the Medieval plough ridges of the area, but some of it is straight and narrower – the result of Victorian or Edwardian ploughing that employed steam engines to haul a plough to and fro. Just a few trees are dotted around in the fieldscape and they must have been hedgerow trees, for they stand on the slight ridges that mark the lines of former hedgerows.

Then I spot it: a level shelf. Horizontal platforms are seldom part of nature's design and one's eyes can be trained to recognise these unnaturally level features. Lisa cannot see it, but she is an environmental scientist and they have other things to bother about. Getting close to the place concerned, we see a little slope, like an abandoned river bank, with the flat shelf above it and with an old pollarded oak growing on the slope. I mention that the shelf suggests the site of a Medieval farmstead. Rabbits have

This is pottery brought to the surface by moles and rabbits from the vicinity of the lost village of Owlcotes. Most is crude, unglazed and belongs to the twelfth and thirteenth centuries, but there is some later medieval glazed ware, upper left, and the odd bit of fine china from the eighteenth and nineteenth centuries, probably from broken pots discarded on a muck heap and later spread on the land with the muck. Also, there is a fragment from the stem of a clay pipe, some slag from a forge and a few bits of coal scraped from the bedrock in ploughing. Pottery can be dated by experts and so it may help to date a deserted village.

been digging away between the roots of the oak, and as they have dug, they have kicked-out old shards of pottery. Most of it is rather coarse, unglazed and resembles worn bits of plant pot that have been charred on one side and gained a white encrustation on the other. This was the typical crude pottery of the area in the twelfth and thirteenth centuries. There are also a few fragments of more sophisticated glazed pottery from later Medieval centuries, but mainly the pottery is of the twelfth and thirteenth centuries. A few steps further on, beneath the trees lining the park wall, fragments of stone can be seen – and now I am sure that we are dealing with a lost settlement site. Some archive work identifies the place as 'Owlcotes' and when English Heritage kindly flies the site under ideal conditions, the pictures that result show the remains of a substantial, elongated village far more clearly than the view from the ground seemed to allow.

It was about this time that Lee, a York University post-graduate student who had helped with my work on the ancient trees, invited me to look at the Medieval lordly site that he was working on in the West Riding. He pointed out what were officially classed as garden terraces – but what was there seemed to be nothing of the kind. Slabs emerging from the turf formed right-angled patterns and some gently prodding with a ranging pole revealed the other stones just beneath the sward and showed that they marked out rectangular features. They were the footings of Medieval houses – and so another lost settlement came to light. Not long afterwards, I was back in Ripley following the road that had led to the township's common. On the left, just beyond the roadside ditch, were platform-like features with sunken centres: the traces of a row of fairly substantial Medieval houses. This proved to be the remains of Birthwaite village, deserted in the seventeenth to eighteenth centuries – and I had just recognised a roadside hamlet of the fifteenth to seventeenth century on the way up. Discovering deserted settlements seems to be easiest when one's mind is tuned-in to the phenomena like some sort of radio receiver. When everything behind the eyes is set up properly, the outlines of cot-

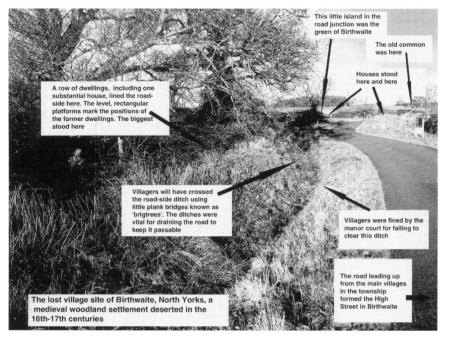

The photograph shows the site of the little village of Birthwaite in Nidderdale. The labels and arrows pick out some features.

The stars mark the corners of a dwelling in a nameless roadside hamlet. It was probably occupied from the 15th-century to the late 17th-century. 'House platforms' such as this are frequently found and reveal the sites of former farmsteads, hamlets and villages

There can have been no roadside hamlet until this road was created, some time after AD 1400

Pottery of the 17th-century was found on the floor of the former dwelling

This is a house platform from a hamlet on the lane up to Birthwaite. The eye can be trained to pick up these roadside shelves marking former house sites.

tages, farmsteads and village streets can emerge quite clearly, even though one may have passed that way twenty times and noticed nothing.

Three deserted villages and various deserted hamlets and farmsteads discovered within a year may exaggerate the ease with which such things can be found, but it does show that there is still a great deal remaining to be discovered and recorded. There must still be sufficient unknown deserted Medieval settlements to give any dedicated sleuth the prospect of discoveries. The best opportunities now are presented by what were the smaller villages and the hamlets of the upland margins. The first step towards success comes from realising that there is an explanation for everything and every tiny slope, kinking hedgerow, curving track and eroded bank has its own story. Then, one must scour the scene with a penetrating gaze to discover the clues embedded in the landscape. But before the local stories could be told, people had to realise that there was a story – and that it was worth telling.

The founding finders

Anyone that has enjoyed a close engagement with the countrysides of Britain will, like me, find it hard to imagine that until the second half of the twentieth century deserted settlements were considered to be very unusual and landscape history and landscape archaeology were thought, by members of the academic establishment, to be rather third-rate pursuits. Medieval archaeology/history stood just above local history and oral history in the hierarchy of scholarly scorn. Quite a few prominent historians regarded the outdoors as a suspect place, full of discomforts but devoid of suitable materials for study. Of course, the widespread ignorance about the nature of the countryside was partly a consequence of such prejudices. Today, it is easy to hold different views, but we depend very much upon the advances made by pioneers who were undeterred by judgements made by the self-appointed arbiters of things worthy of study.

There were some early inklings of an understanding, notably in 1908, when Adrian Allcroft published his *Earthwork of England*. He showed that earthworks were the key to many a historical riddle and that some of them were produced by deserted settlements, but the interest generated was modest. The most celebrated, though not the first, of the pioneers was William Hoskins (1908-92), and by far the most important was Maurice Beresford (1920-2005). In 1969, in a letter to the archaeologist and deserted village specialist, John Hurst, Hoskins described his first encounter with a deserted village some thirty-one years earlier. He told how he and his wife

Evidence comes in all manner of forms. This church at Wensley in Wensleydale is far too large for the present congregation and so it suggests that the village is greatly shrunken. It was an outbreak of the Black Death that closed down the village market, causing a loss of trade to neighbouring centres.

had cycled to Knaptoft in Leicestershire to save a little money by feasting on blackberries and:

> While roaming round the remains of Knaptoft Hall, I spotted a largish field to the north of the lane-end, heavily marked with what seemed to be a regular pattern of low earthworks. It was clearly a man-made site, but though I had a good working knowledge of English archaeology (even lecturing on the subject) I could not identify this type.

The problem seems to have been that at that time virtually nobody knew what a deserted Medieval village site was supposed to look like. In due course, the plan of earthworks at another lost village site lying in Nottinghamshire was unearthed, and it was then that Hoskins was able to identify what he had seen at Knaptoft.

It was in 1946 or 1947 that Beresford and Hoskins met at a deserted village site that the former was studying at Bittersby in Leicestershire. In the years that would follow, Hoskins gained celebrity as the author of the renowned *Making of the English Landscape*, while Beresford would inspire hundreds of enthusiasts who assisted with the excavation of the deserted village of Wharram Percy in the Yorkshire Wolds. When they met at Bittersby, the various technological and conceptual steppingstones forming the pathway to the scholarly investigation of deserted villages had been put in place and were waiting.

One of the most important of these was aerial photography. Those pilots and observers who had been so very fortunate as to survive the First World War had recognised the remarkable attributes of the aerial view, and discovered how to interpret many of the terrestrial features that they discovered, and learned how to locate and record the evidence on maps. The leading name amongst these pioneers was that of Osbert Guy Stanhope Crawford (1886-1957) and even today the initials O.G.S. are remembered and revered by field archaeologists. He was among the earliest intakes of geographers at Oxford University and during the First World War he was part of the courageous many who transferred from their regiments to become observers in the Royal Flying Corps. His background in geography, his pre-war excavation of a long barrow on Wexcombe Down in Wiltshire, his service with the Survey Division of the Third Army and his aerial observations defined the course of his career. Crawford was shot down and imprisoned in 1918 and, following a period of uncertainty after the war, he became an Archaeology Officer with the Ordnance Survey.

Military service had sensitised him to the potential of aerial photography and in 1928, he produced *Wessex from the Air*, a remarkably mature exposition of the archaeological significance of the aerial view. He did this in collaboration with Alexander Keiller, who enjoyed a fortune based on marmalade and who had served as a pilot in the Royal Naval Air Service. This was not a mere association of innovation and patronage, for Keiller had also recognised the value of aerial observations and photography. Remarkable results were achieved using large and highly wind-resistant handheld plate cameras from open cockpits. Crawford was blessed with a defiant measure of independence, storing the original Ordnance Survey maps in his garage during the Second World War (and thus saving them) when higher authority refused to arrange for their protection. On this occasion, and in other such encounters, he had a habit of hurling the cap that he always carried to the ground to express his anger and frustration.

Crawford was aware of deserted villages but his broad enquiries were spread across Britain and far beyond, with an emphasis on prehistoric and Roman subjects. In his greatest work, *Archaeology in the Field* (1953), deserted villages were not awarded a chapter of their own, an indicator that the organised study of lost villages was still in its infancy. By this time, a crucial new repository of evidence had arisen, for in 1949 Cambridge University had constituted a committee to promote the development of air photography and in the following year, a curatorship was established. Wartime reconnaissance had produced a wealth of images while in 1962 the Cambridge Committee obtained the use of an Auster aircraft, allowing the special selection of subjects to be photographed. In 1965, a Cessna 'Skymaster', with a longer range of operations extending throughout Britain, was obtained. Supervising the developments was J.K.S. St Joseph, highly secretive about his wartime intelligence work, but gifted both in the detection of archaeological sites and (though he might not have cared to have admitted it) in pictorial composition. As the reputation of the unit grew, it became less narrowly the servant of the university and undertook many commissioned programmes of aerial survey.

With the establishment of this capability in air photography, the gaining of an awareness of the multitude of unrecorded deserted settlements was inevitable, but great tenacity and historical expertise were still needed to relate the undulations revealed by the camera to British social history. The photographical evidence was arriving in a variety of forms. In the case of lost villages, the most common was that of 'shadow marks' produced when a low sun shone across the slight irregularities of a former village site, so that the little swells cast shadows and the slight dips were shaded. The preservation of these sites varies greatly, while the nature of the living village has an effect, too. There may be a ruined church still upstanding and rubble footings and stone wall bases may still rise above the pasture to produce clear and sharp images of former dwellings. However, a house of timber, wattle and mud daub will soon slump and subside into a mass of ephemeral thatch and sticks engulfed in mud, so that such remains will have a more 'smeared' and indistinct appearance.

Any village that has surrendered to permanent pasture can be expected to leave reasonably pronounced traces. However, once a plough has been over a site a few times, the picture is very different. Even so, a village can be levelled by the plough and yet still be detected. Under cultivation, it can be betrayed by 'crop marks'. These are visible from ground level as slight variations in the height of the growing crop, though one can never make much sense of the patterns. From the air, however, they are resolved into dwellings, ditches, pits and ponds. The crops growing over ditches and other depressions will be able to send their roots deeply into the infilling silts, and will stand above the adjacent crop, while plants rooted in the stone litter of buried walls will be disadvantaged and become over-topped by neighbours. These differences in growth patterns result in shadows being cast: shade patterns in a darker shade of green that can outline buried features surprisingly well. Then, in drought years, there are the 'park marks' that form as vegetation on stony ground parches out and browns first, while that growing in ditches and hollows parches out more slowly and stays green longer than the rest. Shadow marks and crop marks are evident every year, but parch marks are unpredictable – though serious drought produces a flurry of activity in air photography as infrequently observed features come, briefly, into view.

While air photographs – in conjunction with the host of rescue excavations associated with the rapid expansion of motorways and housing estates – would establish the existence of a profusion of deserted village sites, other information had lain, largely unrecognised, in the archives for centuries. As a gifted historian with a fascination for landscape, Beresford was able to uncover relevant material. Since the sixteenth century, chroniclers and antiquaries had commented on lost villages that they knew or had stumbled upon, but nobody had recognised the breadth of the historical evidence or attempted to draw all the threads of evidence together. In 1979, in association with St Joseph, Beresford described a plan of Boarstall in Buckinghamshire, dating from 1444, that portrayed the subsequently deserted village, its church, gatehouse (still surviving) and fields. In 1695, a more detailed depiction of the village, seen in an oblique view, was made, with each item of topiary in the garden painstakingly represented, as well as the decayed church and other evidence of desertion. Many paintings and representations of stately homes and their settings were commissioned in the seventeenth and eighteenth centuries, while the aristocratic enthusiasm for emparking the environs of the great house resulted in a good number of villages or, more usually, their relics, being 'accidentally' included on the canvas. As Beresford noted, 'In virtually all cases the painting shows a situation where the village had been deserted and in a significant number the country house with its raw, newly-planted garden and avenues has a village church standing with them'.

Far more profuse than the evidence of paintings was the Medieval material buried in scores of archives. One example that greatly impressed Beresford, and to which he returned several times, was contained in the *Historia Regnum Angliae*, an otherwise unremarkable history of England written by the chantry priest, John Rous, around 1491, which listed villages destroyed in the vicinity of Warwick. Beresford followed the leads suggested by the list and in 1947 he wrote an article for the *Birmingham Post* on the search for lost villages. One of his great attributes was his readiness, rather unusual at the time, to transgress disciplinary boundaries. He had always been receptive to the ideas of the geographers, but 1948 saw him excavating a deserted village site at Stretton Baskerville in Warwickshire. Meanwhile, Hoskins was digging one at Hamilton in Leicestershire, of which he wrote:

My 'excavation' at Hamilton is best forgotten. It was simply ignorant enthusiasm and produced nothing; though I have a faint recollection that someone more competent took over on another part of the site and uncovered a house-site with a good circular hearth in the middle of one room which local vandals came out and smashed before we could take any photographs.

Beresford's engagement with archaeology was more fruitful and culminated in the prolonged dissection of the deserted village of Wharram Percy in the Yorkshire Wolds – surely one of the two or three most celebrated and rewarding of all British excavations.

The components of a vitalised study of lost villages were coming into sharp focus. In the June of 1948, St Joseph obtained aerial images of a number of deserted village sites in Buckinghamshire, while in the same month Beresford, just employed as a lecturer at Leeds University, went rambling in the Wolds with a couple of companions and stumbled upon the impressive earthworks of Wharram Percy. A year later, coincidentally, they were photographed by St Joseph. Then, in 1949, Beresford launched excavations at two other deserted settlements in Yorkshire, East Lilling and Wilstrop (their choice may have reflected his state as a non-driver, for both were readily accessible from Leeds). Wharram was a more difficult proposition, but was made attractive by the opportunity to use Manchester University student labour in survey and recording work. In addition, a nearby village school was made available as a dormitory for excavators. In the summer of 1950, work began on a modest scale. Beresford's expertise was now considerable and he agreed to write *The Lost Villages of England*, announcing the birth of a new field of study for professionals and amateur enthusiasts alike.

In 1952 he was contacted by a young researcher, John Hurst, and this combination of Beresford, primarily a historian, and Hurst, an archaeologist, proved to be one of the most productive partnerships in British archaeology. Thereafter, Hurst specialised on archaeology and Beresford on administration and logistic support for work that, year-by-year, attracted more and more volunteers. The excavations continued until 1990: forty years of enquiry fuelled by the voluntary efforts of amateur enthusiasts and producing remarkable evidence that opened our eyes to the complexities of the Medieval villages. It was an excavation of a dead village, but it taught us more about the world of the living village communities of the Middle Ages than any other site.

If Maurice Beresford was a pacifist, John Hurst was a peacemaker, universally liked and dying in 2003 in circumstances so tragically at variance with his gentle nature. I last saw him and his collaborator in the late 1990s at a conference session in Leeds that celebrated the legacy of Wharram Percy. Maurice was now distinctly rotund and John's whiskers were completely white, and they beamed benignly around a room filled with those who had feasted on their legacy. While academics are not much given to praising others, I think we were all aware that we were in the presence of a special sort of scholarly greatness.

There is no doubt that the realisation of their historical potential drew scholars to the new studies of deserted villages. A number of able researchers soon joined the quest – Hoskins, K.J. Allison and others, and then J.G. Hurst. Even so, Maurice Beresford was the undisputed founding father of the drive to discover and understand deserted villages. He worked within the framework of an unfashionable and grossly under-valued field of study, Medieval history. He refused to be deflected by the negativity that coloured conventional wisdom about deserted villages, and he also showed a readiness, not shared with all his co-historians, to embrace the concepts and techniques of other subjects. In such ways, he was able to discover lost villages in the archives and to explore them in the field. Had he bowed to conventional wisdom he could never have been the founding father.

A couple of years before his death I went to interview him in his terraced house near Leeds University. Although I had known him for quite some time, I needed to obtain some information for a tribute lecture on his work that I was due to give. I had a list of questions, which he preempted, and the first thing that he wanted to establish was that he was a 'townie' rather than a country boy. Some landscape historians had rural roots and Hoskins had spent some time in the Devon countryside as a boy.

Maurice seemed to want to record that he had no claims to a rural background or familiarity with country lore to advance, but came from the industrial West Midlands. An inspirational schoolmaster was responsible for his conversion from English Literature to History, which he studied at Cambridge University. Two further points that he wished to establish came out almost in one breath: he was a socialist and a pacifist. I think his socialism was of the 'old Labour' variety, and he had a strong sense of social justice, being concerned with prison education and the democratisation of university departments.

His pacifism was remarkable, because it was shared with a surprising number of other members of his calling. Arthur Raistrick (1896-1991) was an inspirational leader of landscape studies in the Yorkshire Dales, where his followers – disciples might be more apt – can still be met. He, too, was a socialist, a founder member of the Independent Labour Party and, as Robert White recorded in 1915:

> … instead of accepting a reserved occupation, he observed the strict pacifist outlook of the ILP and refused to take part in activities which could be connected with the war effort. After spending some months attending pacifist meetings and tramping round West Yorkshire with his uncle, he was arrested, court-martialled and imprisoned, first at Wormwood Scrubs along with his uncle and other Bradford objectors, and then Durham gaol, until 1919. During this period he joined the Society of Friends, an act which was to have a profound impact on his life, both spiritually and as an inspiration for some of his research.

When Beresford and Hoskins met at Bittersby it is quite likely that their conversations included references to conflict, for Hoskins had a fierce contempt for anything that he regarded as war-mongering. Many people read his *Making of the English Landscape*, though far more of them claim to have done so. Strangely, the bucolic evocations are remembered while searing passages like the following have not entered the establishment consciousness:

> What else has happened in the immemorial landscape of the English countryside? Airfields have flayed it bare wherever there are level, well-drained stretches of land, above all in eastern England. Poor devastated Lincolnshire and Suffolk! And those long gentle lines of the dip-slope of the Cotswolds, those misty uplands of the sheep-grey oolite, how they have lent themselves to the villainous requirements of the new age! Over them drones, day after day, the obscene shape of the atom-bomber, laying a trail like a filthy slug upon Constable's and Gainsborough's sky.

The dawning of lost village discoveries was in an age tortured by fears of nuclear barbarism. Thoughts of impending destruction were always at one's side. Crawford was, despite the periodic hurling of the cap, accustomed to both military and civil service. Even so, in 1953, two years before Hoskins' tirade, he wrote, 'Future archaeologists will perhaps excavate the ruined factories of the nineteenth and twentieth centuries when the radiation effects of the Atom bombs have died away'. At the time when Beresford was exploring his Yorkshire sites and Hoskins was penning his great work, the greatest popular communicator of historic landscape was the archaeologist, Jacquetta Hawkes, whose brilliantly-written *A Land* inspired a mass of (educated) people to discover the land, the struggle for the salvation of which had worn them out. She was not only roughly aligned with Beresford's sentiment, but placed her career in some danger by being a founding member of the Campaign for Nuclear Disarmament and heading some of its marches.

With all this in mind, the association between a passion for historic landscape and pacifist, often leftist, outlooks can hardly be accidental. But how can it be explained? As one who also shares the passion and despises the masters of war, I can only guess that immersion in the craft of deciphering landscapes gives one a huge respect for the many generations that created our countrysides – combined with a contempt for those (their numbers ever grow) who would rip them apart for profit. Landscape is a delicate artefact, the crafting of which has been passed down through scores of hands and many generations. Thus, the passion is a passion for the anonymous multitudes who shaped the setting and for the amazingly intricate, scenic legacy that they left. The more one values this, the more is life itself respected and genocide detested.

Self seeking

By the close of the twentieth century, nearly 3,000 deserted Medieval village sites had been discovered and there are undoubtedly many still to be discovered. During the last quarter of that century, I found five unrecorded village sites all within a small area of about ten square miles, as well as several hamlets. Other places will have been more thoroughly investigated, but even in them, there may be unrecognised hamlet and farmstead sites. Anybody with a readiness to learn the relevant techniques, an ability to probe the countryside with an enquiring eye and plenty of patience might easily discover unrecorded sites – particularly in the north and upland margins, where the settlements were smaller and the existing level of investigation lower. No single technique will reveal all sites, the sleuth relies on a range of methods and concepts, of which the most productive do not demand expensive, hi-tech equipment. Here are some pointers.

Maps

Maps of British places have been drawn since Tudor times, though until the establishment of systematic national coverage in the nineteenth century, the availability of a range of maps depended on historical accidents and location. Coverage tended to be much more varied and comprehensive in the southern half of Britain, where many estates could boast a large-scale Elizabethan map. In the more peripheral areas of England the earliest approach to coverage at a reasonable scale might take the form of a map at a scale of 1 inch to 1 mile accomplished by an eighteenth-century freelance cartographer as part of a county-wide survey. In the northern half of Scotland meanwhile, the earliest map might have resulted from a military survey accomplished as part of a programme for the British pacification of the clan lands. Thus, each locality has its own particular portfolio of historic maps. In England and Wales, Enclosure and pre-Enclosure maps of the eighteenth and nineteenth centuries, nineteenth century Tithe maps, specially commissioned estate maps of any possible vintage from the late sixteenth century onwards and commercial 'one-inch' surveys predated the arrival of Ordnance Survey maps. The maps of the official survey appeared in the decades bracketing the middle of the nineteeth century and for any study location, all, some, or none of the earlier types of maps may be present. Of the Ordnance Survey maps, the first edition 6 inches to 1 mile maps are magnificent sources of historical information, showing the countryside before the Industrial Revolution had reached full speed and with each field or hedgerow tree plotted in. Such maps may contain placenames, tracks and other hints to the former existence of a settlement, clues that have vanished during the last 150 years.

Any reader is likely to have access to a selection of old maps of any selected locality. They may be lodged in the County Record Office or Scottish Record Office, housed in original or facsimile form in a local library or available on the Internet (enter 'Old Maps' on a search engine and see what results). The essence of using old maps as aids to discovery lies in comparing the landscapes depicted on an old map with the one depicted on a modern map (preferably one of a scale of 1:25,000 or larger). If a village or hamlet, or the decaying remains of one, are evident on the old map, but no longer evident on the new one, the conclusions are plain. A technique such as this might seem too glaringly obvious to produce any results, but there remains many lost places that can be discovered by such methods. The key is to scour the map carefully and systematically, aligning the old and new field and road networks and paying particular attention to creations, like parks, that could have profound effects on the local countryside and its settlements.

Roads and tracks

Villages and most hamlets had to have connections. The typical village lay astride a through-road that, when running through the village, served as the village High Street. Other roads were likely to converge upon a village, often uniting at the part where its market was held. Villages were strung together along routeways like beads on strings and so it is always helpful in any historic landscape survey to reconstruct the former route network. This will possibly not be easy, for different branches will have different ages and monastic rights of way, ancient salt-trading routes and Medieval market roads could all be components of the local road system. Often, the passage of feet, hoofs and wheels over many centuries would result in a road being ground down into the land surface to form a trough or holloway. This was not always the case, and the incision of a road into its setting was most likely to occur as it ascended/descended the brow of a hill. On the level, and contrary to popular beliefs, there might be little wearing down. Any holloways discovered are very likely to point towards villages, either living ones or ones that are lost – while, of course, they continue and run on into the old village sites, where they are commonly the most distinct of the earthworks. In some cases, the last of the roadside hedges may be marked by old, contorted, pollarded trees.

An old village road might be discovered as a holloway in a pasture, and one may even find sods that have been displaced to reveal a roughly cobbled road surface beneath. Equally, the market roads or lanes that served a village might, after its demise, degenerate into tracks and footpaths. The dedicated village sleuth could study a local map (old or modern) very carefully looking for footpaths and tracks that, for no apparent reason, converge on some uninhabited spot. The paths could be the last vestiges of the lanes and field tracks serving a former settlement. It would then be necessary to look at that spot for any corroborating evidence of a former settlement.

Earthworks

These are the traces, taking the form of slight mounds, ridges, dips and troughs, of former features of the cultural landscape, like dwellings, barns, walls, hedgerows, lanes, and so on. In landscape detection they are immensely helpful, though they do not come with convenient labels attached. The detective must decide whether, say, a right-angled feature is a junction of former field walls or the corner of a lost building. They do not have dates attached either, though sometimes one can see a feature that must be younger than another feature that it has cut – as when a building has cut across ridge and furrow ploughland. All manner of activities leave earthworks and the most puzzling example I ever found was caused by the inept back-filling of a ditch just a few decades earlier. The result was a chain of small mounds with no apparent function. Confused by a tantalising array of bumps and pits, the first thing to decide is whether the assemblage it is natural or made by humans? Regular ridges, horizontal platforms and seemingly integrated patterns of hollows, troughs and hogsback patterns are normally the work of humans. Perhaps the most confusing patterns, and the most common, are produced by ancient quarrying operations, which have left the ground carpeted in hummocky dross. They seemingly display no order or regularity.

Work with earthworks does require careful thought, a measure of experience and an ability to recognise the traces of features like low Medieval fishpond retaining banks, the little mounds that carried windmills, the 'pillow mounds' that were artificial rabbit warrens, and so on. Well-preserved deserted village sites display complexes of earthworks that include house platforms, holloways, property boundary ditches, as well as possible manorial features, like moats and fishponds. However, these are not the only sites that display assemblages of features – so too do the sites of former gardens, which are also surprisingly common and likely to confuse. Matters are eased enormously if the features concerned are mapped and then seen in plan view; it is not so easy to form a picture of the layout of a lost settlement from ground level. Mapping may be too great a challenge for many, but air photographs may provide elevated oblique or vertical views. It is worth discovering what items of aerial photography the main libraries and the County Planning/Archaeological Unit may have, as well as resources on the Internet. Depending on the conditions prevailing at the time when the photographs were taken and the nature of the remains concerned, the photographic evidence may be amazingly revealing, or simply rather disappointing.

House platforms

These are a form of earthwork formed by the remains of a dwelling. They can take the form of shelves that once supported dwellings that were terraced into a hillside, levelled house-sized pieces of ground, or rectangular level areas outlined by ridges composed of slumped mud daub or rubble from wall footings. In these cases, one can often recognise the notch(es) in the walling that marks the place of the door or front and back doors. Medieval dwellings tended to be long, rectangular and narrow, and also small – sometimes not much larger than the hall/entrance passage of a modern house.

Well-preserved house platforms can reveal a good deal about the former dwellings. The most frequent design for earlier Medieval houses was that of a 'long-house', in which the dwelling, sited with its long axis parallel to the village street, would be divided into an all-purpose family room and a byre for a milk cow or ewes by a 'cross passage' that ran from the front door to the back. Sometimes, this passage is still marked by the front and back door notches. Then the animal quarters can generally be located on the down-slope side of the passage (for sanitary reasons). Some Medieval village dwellings had stone walls, while many more had stone footings, which raised the horizontal beam supporting the upright wall posts or 'studs' above the level of damp and decay. Such footings may surface in places, or be revealed by probing with a skewer or blade. In stony places, floors were sometimes covered in a layer of shale/rubble. While house platforms are often seen as earthworks, house sites can sometimes be discovered from the nettle patches that form dense clumps in an otherwise grassy pasture. Not all nettle clumps stand on old dwellings by any means, but it seems that the scraps of food and bone that were stamped into earthen floors provide the nettles with the enriched soil that they prefer. Some clumps growing in this way can be seen to be distinctly rectangular, mirroring room plans, and I have even noted clumps covering just half the house plan, perhaps indicating the byre component?

The indications of former buildings can reveal a variety of settlement forms, not all of them villages. In some places, there are arrangements forming a hollow square, with several buildings, one of which was the farmhouse and the rest being farm buildings, arranged around a farmyard. These 'courtyard farms' were common, being favoured by the more substantial Medieval tenants and yeomen. One may sometimes recognise the gap between buildings where the wain entered the farmyard. In my own stamping ground of North Yorkshire, and probably in many other places, a common form of settlement was the roadside hamlet composed of about three to seven dwellings. These were aligned down one side of a track or in groups facing each other across the track, all with their long axes parallel to the road. In some cases, the roadside ditch would kink around the back of the dwellings, while in others, residents must have crossed the ditch on little plank bridges to step on the road. Some of these hamlets, at least, dated from the closing phase of the Middle Ages and they seem frequently to have been deserted by the eighteenth century. Some little abandoned dwelling clusters were not villages or hamlets, but small farmsteads. Their remains can often be encountered while following the course of a holloway. There may have been a farmstead on one side of the track and its out-buildings just a few feet away on the other side: the gaps between these buildings may show just how narrow many Medieval roads were.

Alternatively, the farmstead could stand in a little, formerly hedged compound, with its buildings terraced into the slope just behind it.

Documents and air photographs

Lost settlements can be found by a study of documents lodged in archives, though one might have to search hard and long before turning up anything of relevance. Also, the translation and interpretation of Medieval documents draws on specialist skills. A little knowledge can be a dangerous thing. For example many people believe that the places mentioned in *Domesday Book* are villages, so it might be thought that checking these named places against a modern map should reveal many village casualties. In reality, *Domesday Book* records estates, and these estates might contain no villages or several of them. Some of the estates shared their names with villages and hamlets and some of these did perish, but on the whole, amateur enthusiasts will find it easier to move from discoveries in the field to the documents rather than vice versa.

Countless people have developed skills in the use of archives through the pursuit of family history, and with determination much may be achieved. If fieldwork has uncovered a deserted village site then the discoverer will almost certainly want to find information about its life and death. Sometimes, the cause of the demise has been recorded, but where this is not the case, the death of the settlement will coincide with the time that it vanishes from the record. A number of checkpoints punctuated the lives of most communities. Feudal villages were listed in the *Hundred Rolls*, a great survey of local government in the late thirteenth century, and in the *Nomina Villarum* of 1316, which was concerned with the responsibilities of each township to furnish a foot soldier, while in the early fourteenth century, a series of taxes known as the Lay Subsidies was levied and left lists of taxpayers and the vills where they lived. Then there are the records of the Poll Tax of 1377, 1379 and 1381 and of the taxes on hearths running from 1662-85. Thus, for example, any community that was recorded from 1291 through to 1379, but then vanished from the records, might well have been an early victim of the sheep clearances. Moreover, any decline in population between, say, the Lay Subsidy of 1332 and the Poll Tax of 1377 could reflect an onslaught by the Black Death that left such a community diminished and vulnerable to a sheep baron.

Taking an example almost at random, Little Newton in Northamptonshire had resources sufficient for four and a half ploughs in 1220 and was recorded in the *Nomina Villarum* in 1316; eighteen villagers paid the Poll Tax in 1377, but in 1499, when the Court of Star Chamber was reviewing village depopulations, only four families remained and around 1600 depopulations in the locality by the Tresham family resulted in unrest. Early in the eighteenth century, some earthworks by the church were all that remained of the village. When one discovers specific details about the number of households living in a place, the amount of taxes that they paid and their status, the associated level of accuracy can be over-stated. Firstly, one may not be dealing with a single village, for the people concerned might have been divided between a village and a number of satellite hamlets, the 'greens' and 'ends' so common in many regions. Also smaller settlements or declining villages were sometimes paired with other villages in their parish/locality for the purposes of tax assessment. In addition, the records compiled by the officials could have been incomplete and inaccurate. The 1379 Poll Tax was heavily evaded and most other taxes inspired people to vanish from officialdom. The inadequacy of the records is shown when one compares records from two closely-spaced accounts of taxpayers or of houses: the differences can be so immense that only defective recording can be to blame. Even so, the taxation records can reveal the gradual decline and decay of settlements. It was certainly the case that the villages that had already experienced hardships and shrinkage were far more likely to perish than other members of the village flock.

Air photographs can be obtained online and on disks, while the local library may have some examples and the County Planning Department/ Archaeological Unit should have a respectable collection. What is actually held is hard to predict, for the times when vertical surveys and oblique shoots were made will vary and the sample available for public scrutiny is uncertain. If a potential deserted village site is revealed by fieldwork, the air photographs may help to establish the extent and layout of any remains. Books will understandably display those photographs that have proved particularly revealing and successful, so one can gain a false impression of the potency of the aerial image. The fact that a potential site does not seem to register on air photographs, particularly the high-level verticals, does not prove that there is nothing there. The conditions for photography could have been very unfavourable during the flight concerned.

At the time when Hoskins and Beresford were exploring and broadcasting the story of the deserted villages, amateur enthusiasts had a large part to play in the discovery and celebration of a great heritage of historic landscape. Both men wrote readable and authoritative guides to the interpretation of local history, and at the same time others, such as Raistrick, were employed as extra-mural university lecturers and as WEA tutors. Countless enthusiasms were ignited and devotees of the pioneers can still be met at historical and environmental gatherings, still eager to talk about those who inspired them. One who has maintained his enthusiasm for historic landscape wrote to me while I was writing this chapter:

On Arthur Raistrick; I didn't know him well. He was simply a tutor from another dept (geology), who took our bolshie group of ex-servicemen on some eye-opening and mind blowing field trips c.1950. We took to him because he was on our side of the cultural divide in spite of the fact that (we believed!) he'd been a 'conshie', which really takes long-term guts. What we found so admirable was his transparently high-principled nature, committed to the cause of the underdog etc. plus his enthusiasm, and great teaching ability.

Sadly, the times that gave such inspiration and encouragement to enthusiastic amateurs have passed. Scholars have turned from communication to publication and any who do seek to re-kindle the fires of amateur involvement are likely to encounter the sneers of those trapped in the bureaucratic academic treadmills. There is not much time left for education after all the meetings and networking and monitoring and delivering of the curriculum have taken place. Vacuous computer techniques have been widely adopted in the agencies and institutions of government. They offer no historical insights of any worth, but alienate all those from outside the bureaucratic systems who seek a meaningful and profound understanding of landscape. Meanwhile, these techniques have spawned a generation of bureaucrats who possess very little expertise outside the worlds of their software and who increasingly act as the gatekeepers in the realm of heritage management. Once, the education and democratic systems inspired, dispensed and cultivated curiosity and learning. Now, they kill them stone dead. A great revolution in outlook is desperately needed; a revolution that would allow the committed and gifted enthusiasts and former graduates to reclaim the centre of the stage in the world of landscape heritage. Hoskins, Beresford, Raistrick and Hawkes did not work to create a world bossed by the inflated egos of television presenters or dominated by bureaucrats whose only mission is to further the cause of their institution or quango. Like priests from a minster, they left their universities or places of study to celebrate education and local scholarship – and they did not return to be hounded by mindless managers and driven ever deeper into the realms of intellectual obscurity, trivialised publication and politically-driven mass graduation.

Yet for so long as people are touched by a curiosity about the places they love, the dream of a return to the Wharram Percy tradition, the field club and the village hall workshop can still be realised. It is time that the amateur enthusiasts reclaimed the ground that they have lost.

References

Chapter One

Bradley, R., 1978, *The Prehistoric Settlement of Britain*, RKP, London.
Clarke, H., 1984, *The Archaeology of Medieval England*, Colonnade, London.
Fryde, E.B., 1996, *Peasants and Landlords*, Alan Sutton, Stroud.
Hooke, D.,1998, *Anglo-Saxon England*, Leicester University Press, London.
Lennard, R., 1997, *Rural England, 1086-1135*, Oxford University Press, Oxford.
Lewis, C., Mitchell-Fox, P. and Dyer, C., 1997, *Village, Hamlet and Field*, Manchester University Press, Manchester.
Muir, R., 1992, *The Villages of England*, Thames and Hudson, London.
Roberts, B.K., 1987, *The Making of the English Village*, Longman, Harlow.
Roberts, B.K., 1996, *Landscapes of Settlement*, Routledge, London.
Taylor, C.C., 1983, *Village and Farmstead*, George Philip, London.

Chapter Two

Coulton, G.G., 1926, *The Medieval Village*, Cambridge University Press.
Lewis, C., Mitchell-Fox, P. and Dyer, C., 1997, *Village, Hamlet and Field*, Manchester University Press.
William Harrison, 1577, *Description of England*, F.J. Furnival (Ed.), The New Shakespeare Society, I.
Homans, G.C.,1941, *English Villagers of the Thirteenth Century*, Harvard University Press.

Chapter Three

Hey, D, 1986, *Yorkshire From AD 1000*, Longman, London.
Muir, R. 1997, *The Yorkshire Countryside, a Landscape History*, Edinburgh University Press, Edinburgh.
Palliser, D.M., 1993, 'Domesday Book and the harrying of the north', *Northern History*, vol 29, pp.1-23.

Palmer, J.J.N., 1998, 'War and Domesday waste', in M. Strickland (Ed.), *Armies, Chivalry and Warfare in Medieval Britain and France*, pp.156-278.

Rowley, T., 1998, 'All change after the Norman conquest', *British Archaeology*, no.35, June 1998.

Chapter Four

Alison, K.J., Beresford, M.W. and Hurst, J.G., 1966, 'The Deserted Villages of Northamptonshire', Leicester University Department of English Local History Occasional Papers, no. 18, Leicester University Press.

Alison, K. G., Beresford, M.W. and Hurst, J.G., 1966, 'The Deserted Villages of Oxfordshire', *Leicester University Department of English Local History Occasional Papers*, no. 17, Leicester University Press.

Beresford, M.W., 1954, *The Lost Villages of England*, Lutterworth Press, London.

Beresford, M.W. and St Joseph, J.K.S., 1979, *Medieval England, an aerial survey*, Cambridge University Press, Cambridge.

Donkin, R.A., 1978, Pontifical Institute of Medieval Studies, Studies and Texts.

Gerald of Wales, *The Journey Through Wales*, translated by L. Thorpe, Penguin, Harmondsworth, 1978.

Menuge, N.J., 2000, 'The foundation myth: some Yorkshire monasteries and the landscape agenda', *LANDSCAPES*, 1.1 , pp.22-37.

Chapter Five

Baring, 1901, 'The making of the New Forest', *English History Review*, xvi, pp.427-38.

Barringer, C., 1984, *The Lake District*, R. Muir (Ed.), Collins, London.

Cantor, L., 1982, 'Forests, chases, parks and warrens' in L. Cantor (Ed.), *The English Medieval Landscape*, Croom Helm, London.

Edlin, H.L., (Ed.), *The New Forest, Forestry Commission Guide*, HMSO, London, 1969.

Hughes, M.F., 1982, 'Emparking and the desertion of settlements in Hampshire', Medieval Village Research Group *Annual Report,* no. 30, p.37.

Liddiard, R., 2003, 'The deer parks of Domesday Book, *Landscapes*, 4, no. 1, pp.4-23.

Muir, R., 2005, *Ancient Trees, Living Landscapes*, Tempus, Stroud.

Chapter Six

Baillie, M.G.L, 1997, 'Tree-ring evidence for environmental disasters during the Bronze Age: causes and effects', The archaeology of Bronze Age Cosmic Catastrophes, paper given to the *Natural Catastrophes and Bronze Age Civilisations: Archaeological, Geological and Astronomical Perspectives Conference*, Cambridge.

Defoe, D., 1724-6, *A tour through the whole island of Great Britain*, Penguin edn., Harmondsworth, 1978.

Dugmore, A.J., Cook, G.T. Shore, J.S., Newton, A.J., Edwards, K.J. and Guðrún Larsen, 1995, 'Radiocarbon dating tephra layers in Britain and Iceland', *Radiocarbon*, 37, 2, pp.379 ff.

Fiennes, C., *Through England on a Side Saddle in the Time of William and Mary*, first published 1888.

Hughes, M.K. and Diaz, H.F., 1994, 'Was there a 'Medieval Warm Period'?', *Climatic Change*, 26, pp.109-142.

Langdon, P.G. and Barber, K.E., 2004, 'Snapshots in time: precise correlations of peat-based proxy climate records in Scotland using mid-Holocene tephras', *The Holocene*, 14, 1, pp.21-33.

LaMoreaux, P.E.,(1995), 'Worldwide environmental impacts from the eruption of Thera', *Environmental Geology*, 26, 3, pp.172-181.

Masse, W.B, 1997, 'Earth, Air, Fire and Water: The archaeology of Bronze Age Cosmic Catastrophes', paper given to the *Natural Catastrophes and Bronze Age Civilisations: Archaeological, Geological and Astronomical Perspectives Conference*, Cambridge.

Millward, R. and Robinson, A., 1978, *Landscapes of North Wales*, David and Charles, Newton Abbot.

Nelson, L.H., 1992, 'The Aurora of 1192: its causes and effects', *http://history. eserver.org/aurora-of-1192.txt*

Peiser, B.J., 1997, 'Comets and disaster in the Bronze Age', *British Archaeology*, 30, pp.6-7.

Pestall, T., 1993, 'Archaeological Investigations into the 'lost' village of Eccles-Next-The-Sea, Norfolk', *M.S.R.G. Annual Report*, 8, pp.17-21.

Sanders, J., 2003,'Ancient Farmsteads in the Central Basin of Dartmoor', notes of an illustrated talk to the Yelverton Local History Society, 18 March, 2003.

Ravensdale, J. and Muir, R., 1984, *East Anglian Landscapes*, Michael Joseph, London.

Chapter Seven

Allison, K.J., Beresford, M.W. and Hurst, J.G., 1966, 'The deserted villages of Oxfordshire', Department of English Local History *Occasional Papers*, 17, Leicester University Press.

Batcock, N., 1991, 'The Ruined and Disused Churches of Norfolk', East Anglian Archaeology *Report, no. 51*, Norfolk Archaeology Unit, Dereham.

Defoe, D, 1722, *Journal of the Plague Year*.

Messer, Andrea Elyse, 2002, 'Medieval black death not bubonic plague', Penn State University research paper 12.4.2002.

Muir, R., 2001, *Landscape Detective*, Macclesfield.

Plat, C., 1996, *King Death: the Black Death and its Aftermath in Late Medieval England*, UCL Press, London.

Scott, S. and Duncan,C., 2005, *The Return of the Black Death*, Wiley.

Wallis, P., 2006, 'A dreadful heritage: interpreting epidemic disease at Eyam, 1666-2000' *History Workshop Journal*, 61 (1), pp.31-56.

Chapter Eight

Alison, K.J., Beresford, M.W. and Hurst, J.G., 1966, 'The Deserted Villages of Northamptonshire', *Leicester University Department of English Local History Occasional Papers*, no. 18, Leicester University Press.

Alison, K. G., Beresford, M.W. and Hurst, J.G., 1966, 'The Deserted Villages of Oxfordshire', *Leicester University Department of English Local History Occasional Papers*, no. 17, Leicester University Press.

Batcock, N., 1991, 'The ruined and disused churches of Norfolk, *East Anglian Archaeology Report*, no. 51, Norfolk Archaeological Unit, Dereham.

Beresford, M.W., 1954, *The Lost Villages of England*, Lutterworth Press, London.

Beresford, M.W. and Hurst, J.G., 1990, *Wharram Percy*, Batsford, London.

Everson, P., 1994, 'The deserted village remains of North Marefield, Leicestershire, *MSRG Annual Report*, 9, pp.22-27.

Walford, W., 2005, 'Medieval deer parks and sheep farms', *Society for Landscape Studies Newsletter*, Autumn/Winter 2005, pp.4-7.

Chapter Nine

Aalen, F.H.A., Whelan, K. and Stout, M., (Eds.), 1997, *Atlas of the Irish Rural Landscape*, University of Toronto Press, Toronto.

Beresford, M.W. and Hurst, J.G., 1971, *Deserted Medieval Villages*, Lutterworth, London.

Beresford, M.W. and St Joseph, J.K.S., 1979, *Medieval England, An Aerial Survey*, 2nd edn., Cambridge University Press, Cambridge.

Cartwright, J.J., (Ed.), 1875, *The Memoirs of Sir John Reresby*, Longmans, Green & Co., London.

Darley, G., 1978, *Villages of Vision*, Paladin Granada, St Albans.

Muir, R. and Amos, J., 1998, 'Nidd, the death of a village', *The Local Historian*, 28, 4, pp.208-216.

Whitaker, T.D., 1878, *History and Antiquities of Craven*, Joseph Dodgson, Leeds.

Chapter Ten

Alred, D., 1997, *Washburn Valley Yesterday*, Smith Settle, Otley.

Barber, C., 2001. *The Story of Hallsands*, Obelisk Publications, Exeter.

Davison, A, 1988, 'Six deserted villages in Norfolk', East Anglian Archaeology Report, no. 44.

Legg, R., 1998, *Tyneham: Ghost Village,* Dorset Publishing Company, Wincanton.

Lewis Jones, Prof. Bedwyr & Rhys, Elen, 'Cymraeg I Oedilion', *www.acen.co.uk.*

McComish, D., Field, D. and Brown, G., 2002, *The Field Archaeology of the Salisbury Plain Training Area*, English Heritage, Swindon.

Melia, S., 2002, *Hallsands: A Village Betrayed*, Forest Publishing, Newton Abbot.

Muir, R., 1998, 'The villages of Nidderdale' *Landscape History*, 20, 65-82.

Ritvo, H., 2003, 'Fighting for Thirlmere – the roots of environmentalism',
    Science, 6 June 2003, no. 5625, pp.1510-1511.
Taylor, C., 1973, *The Cambridgeshire Landscape*, Hodder and Stoughton, London.
Wade-Martins, P., 1980, 'Fieldwork and excavation on village sites in Launditch
    Hundred, Norfolk', *East Anglian Archaeology Report,* no. 10.
Wright, P., 1995, *The Village That Died For England: the Strange Story of Tyneham*,
    Johnathan Cape, London.

Chapter Eleven

James Boswell,2004 edn., *The Journal of a Tour to the Hebrides with Samuel
    Johnson, LL.D.* Oxford, Mississippi.
Brown, H., 'The main ridge and Wolrige: raising hackles and shekels',
    The Angry Corrie, 47, Oct-Nov 2000.
Millman, R.N., 1975, *The Making of the Scottish Landscape*, Batsford, London.
Prebble, J., 1963, *The Highland Clearances*, Martin, Secker and Warburg, London.
Richards, E., 2000, *The Highland Clearances: People, Landlords and Rural Turmoil*,
    Birlinn.
Smith, J.S. and Stevenson, D., 1989, *Fermfolk and Fisherfolk*, Aberdeen University
    Press, Aberdeen.
Smith, R.,1997, *Land of the Lost*, John Donald, Edinburgh.
Smout, T.C., 1969, *History of the Scottish People, 1560-1830*, Collins, London.
Turnoch, D., 1970, *Patterns of Highland Development*, Macmillan, Basingstoke.
Woodham-Smith, C., 1964, *The Great Hunger*, Hamish Hamilton, London.

Chapter Thirteen

Bereseford, M.W., 1954, *The Lost Villages of England*, Lutterworth Press, London.
Beresford, M.W., 1986, 'A draft chronology of deserted village studies',
    Medieval Village Research Group, *Annual Report* I, pp.18-23.
Beresford, M.W., (1957), *History on the Ground*, Lutterworth Press, London.
Beresford, M.W. and St.Joseph, J.K.S., 1979, *Medieval England: an Aerial Survey*,
    2nd edn, C.U.P., Cambridge
Crawford, O.G.S., 1928, *Wessex from the Air.*
Crawford, O.G.S., 1953, *Archaeology in the Field*, Dent, London.
Hawkes, J., 1951, *A Land*, Cresset Press, London.
Hoskins, W.G., 1955, *The Making of the English Landscape*, Hodder and
    Stoughton, London.
Muir, R., 1998, 'Reading the landscape, rejecting the present' *Landscape
    Research*, vol 23, no. 1, pp.71-82.
White, R., 2003, 'Arthur Raistrick', *LANDSCAPES*, vol 4, no. 2, pp.111-123.

INDEX

Illustrations are shown in italics.